The

WICCAN

MYSTIC

Exploring A Magickal Spiritual Path

by

Ben Gruagach

ISBN 978-0-6151-4311-8

FIRST EDITION
Published March 2007 by WitchGrotto Press
Eden Prairie MN USA
http://www.witchgrotto.com

Cover art, book design & layout by Ben Gruagach.

Print on demand services provided by Lulu.com.

Table of Contents

Dedication

This book is dedicated to my loving spouse Daryll who encouraged me, supported me in myriad ways, and pushed me to publish. He believed in me when I wasn't sure of my own talents and ability to persevere. It's also dedicated to our two sons, my parents and in-laws and extended family who have said and done countless things to inspire me. I also owe gratitude to my dear friend Sabina for her wisdom, inspiration, and assistance as a Wiccan and as a writer as well as an all-round cheerleader. Deep gratitude to my spiritual companions in the various covens I've worked with over the years, particularly all my wonderful friends in the Desert Moonrise coven in Phoenix, Arizona and the Willow Moon coven in Eden Prairie, Minnesota (Patsy, Brion, Melissa, Nombi, Sarrah, Allie, Kristi, Sopheak, Natalie, Eric, Tiffany, Jenna, and everyone else – you know who you are!) My many online friends and acquaintances in the Northumberland Mystical Gatherings group and on the MysticWicks.com messageboard have also been invaluable to me as I wrote this book – even those who disagreed with my ideas at every turn! And finally, this book is also dedicated to my feline companion Bub. He sat with me every day as I worked at my computer, often draped over my left arm (and making typing a bit of a challenge) but a constant and loyal companion through this all.

Introduction

I grew up on a farm in eastern Ontario, Canada. It was an idyllic childhood for me. I spent many hours wandering the fields and forests, playing in the hayloft, participating in the cycle of life that is ever-present when you help care for animals. My family was nominally Presbyterian although we stopped going to church regularly except for Christmas-time when my dad would sing in the choir. My parents raised us to be curious and independent. I always felt a special connection to the natural world so Wicca was a natural fit for me when I discovered it in my early teen years.

The moon goddess with Her phases and the Lord of the green wild were presences I knew were there because I could sense Them. I used to go off into the forest by myself and worship Them in exuberant dance. Stones and trees would call out to me. The wind was my friend and seemed to come when I called. I'd sit for hours in silent communion in places I considered holy.

Years later when I went to university I started actually meeting with other Wiccans and assorted Pagans and had a chance to discuss openly what I had been reading on my own and what I had learned from my own experience. I wasn't alone in my belief that the world was suffused with the Divine presence and that we could identify with the Divine and see ourselves as very much a part of that whole.

Some of the Wiccan authors I read, and some of the Wiccans who I subsequently met and spoke with, talked about these things obliquely as sacred Mysteries, and at times insisted that the Mysteries could not be verbalized. They also told me that these Mysteries were reserved for those who had been formally initiated into established Wiccan traditions. "Only a Witch can make a Witch," I was told.

I knew this was not true.

Other Wiccans spoke in poetic ways about things that I understood instinctively even though the language used could never be anything more than a pale reflection of the reality it was trying to explain. Yet I, and others I knew, had felt these same things! The Divine touches even those without benefit of formal initiations. I knew the Moon when I stood naked in Her silver light when I was fifteen years old those many years ago growing up on the farm. The Green Man of the wildwood played with me, whispering in my ear, when I was a child climbing the trees. The Lady Brigid, a goddess of my genetic heritage, was with me when I helped bring the cows in for milking, when I fed a calf from a pail. I knew these things before I ever met other Wiccans in the flesh. Others too have felt their lives touched by the Divine and many of them are like me and have come to consider themselves Witches, Wiccans, or Pagans of some variety.

Wicca is often called a modern Mystery Religion. Yes, it most definitely can be. The reasons why that label might or might not fit may surprise some people. The key question we need to ask ourselves is what we mean by Mystery. Is it really about formal rituals of acceptance into specific groups and refusing to talk about certain things? Or is it about something else entirely: a very tangible experience of connection with the Divine?

What This Book Will And Won't Do For You

A wise person once wrote that one's spiritual path is essentially a unique journey. Through our lives we explore topics that are relevant to our own individual circumstances. We might spend large parts of that journey in the company of other seekers, perhaps playing the role of student with someone else playing the role of teacher. In the end, though, it doesn't really matter what teachers we have studied under or what titles or degrees we have attained. What matters is how we have lived our lives, how we have put the lessons into practice. If spirituality is about a personal relationship with the Divine then that relationship is what really matters and not which groups we've joined or whether we owned specific possessions in our lives. At the end of our lives we stand naked and revealed in the Divine presence and we alone will be judged. Our teachers, mentors, and companions through life will not be there with us in that final embrace; we meet the Divine alone.

This book is just one resource in your spiritual journey. Perhaps you will find something in these pages that will help you to enrich your spiritual understanding. If this book is successful it will help nurture your personal relationship with the Divine. At the very least I hope the book will suggest new questions to you and new directions to explore in your religious life.

No book can provide you with a complete education in a topic. Each author has their own bias that doesn't often become apparent until you read books on the same topic written by other authors. It is very likely that you will find you disagree with some details in every book that you read, some suggestions aren't relevant for you, or just won't work in your situation. In every book you read, though, there is something that is worth learning. One of the big lessons of becoming mature is discovering that we must take responsibility for our own learning and decide for ourselves what information is important and what information we can safely overlook.

This book is primarily about Wicca, written by a Wiccan for a Wiccan audience. It doesn't matter if you are Wiccan or not. There is something to learn in everything; it's up to you to discover what new ideas you can glean. Take what you want and use it in your own life, in your own spiritual path, to grow and love and learn. Perhaps the greatest gift that the Divine has blessed us with is the gift of choice. Celebrate that gift by exploring the choices available to you. Pray, meditate, or commune with the Divine through whatever methods you find work and seek guidance in making your choices. Rejoice in the abundance of choice the Divine has bestowed upon you.

It Will

Encourage you to think for yourself

The Wiccan Mystic was written to encourage people who have been practicing a Wiccan spiritual path for a while, as well as ambitious beginners, to think independently. When we're learning new information, particularly information about spirituality, we usually try to be open-minded. However, we must not neglect our critical faculties. When someone who presents themselves as an elder or teacher tells us things are a certain way, that way might not be right for us. Teachers and elders present what works for them but sometimes forget to point out there are alternatives. If you only learn one thing from this book I hope it's that there are always options and we must each decide which option is right for us personally.

This book tries to help put Wicca into perspective in a wider religious context. It compares and contrasts Wiccan ideas with other religions. The reader is encouraged to research topics in more depth, drawing on the valuable wealth of material available both inside and outside the Wiccan community. Spirituality is an exploration of ideas that can come from a wide range of sources. Expanding our search for knowledge beyond the boundaries of our own specific traditions helps us to better understand who we are, where we come from, what our needs are, and how those needs could potentially be fulfilled.

Suggest methods

Some of the suggested exercises and practices in this book will probably sound familiar to experienced Wiccans. Some will perhaps be new, or new twists on old methods. They are just suggestions that some have found useful. Use those that interest you, modify them as you wish, and make them your own. In Wicca we often say that the effort you put in to something will return threefold. If you attempt exercises with a solid intention and work hard to follow through on that intention you will succeed no matter what you try.

Outline alternatives

Life is full of choices. Within Wicca there is an enormous variety in theology, practice, and expression of spirituality. This book attempts to provide a selection of alternatives available to Wiccans. Contrary to what some may insist, Wicca is not a "one true way" type of religion. Each of us follows an individual spiritual path, sometimes with periods when we travel with companions, but just as often we travel our own unique ways. Wicca is a choice-filled spiritual path. We can draw inspiration for our paths from inside and outside Wicca and the realm of religious theory.

Provide context

Ecologists study a species in the context of the larger ecosystem of which it is a part. Wicca is one religious group among many in a world that is filled with wondrous creativity. It helps us to keep some perspective if we take a step back sometimes to try and get a look at the bigger picture and seeing how Wicca fits into the larger scheme. Getting a larger overview, and developing a sense of context for Wicca, also helps us to see the similarities between our spiritual path and others. It also helps us to realize that distinctions and boundaries that we might think exist are usually quite arbitrary and are ultimately artificial. Gaining a sense of context, and being willing to explore outside our self-imposed boundaries, can help us to grow and encourage Wicca as a whole to mature.

There is a lot we can learn by looking to other religions to see how they approach specific ideas or to see how they express those ideas in practice. There is no need to reinvent things that others have perfected if we are willing to observe and learn from them. We have unparalleled opportunities today for learning about other cultures. If we are respectful and genuine and willing to learn we can share in some profoundly meaningful experiences that could become part of our own spiritual repertoires.

It Won't

Present easy answers to life's mysteries

Lots of books, courses, and presenters claim to offer quick fixes to all of life's problems. In order for you to buy that claim, you have to be willing to give up your right to think for yourself. You have to give up your independence in order to turn your life over to someone else.

Many wise people tell us that the things most worth achieving are reached through hard work. Another way of thinking about it is that the process of working towards a goal is just as important, if not more important, than reaching the goal itself. If things are just handed to us without any effort on our part then we tend to not appreciate them as much. If we don't earn our rewards then what have we really learned?

The ideas in this book should not be accepted as fact merely because they are written here. They should inspire you to think, to question, to explore. Challenge each idea to see if it is valid for you. Does it fit in with what you already believe? Does it cast doubt on previously held truths? Is there a possibility that there might be more to an idea that is worth investigating?

Do the hard work for you

This book is a guide, a starting point in undertaking further exploration of your individual spirituality. It can't do the traveling for you or force you to do the follow-up research and contemplation required to enrich your life. It can suggest things to explore, paths to investigate, but it is you who must do the actual exploration. A guidebook is most useful if it helps you to actually take the trip and perhaps discover things you might have missed if you'd taken the journey unprepared.

Make you an initiate of a specific Wiccan tradition

This book was not written from the perspective of an established Wiccan tradition or sect. If you want to learn more about a specific established group, such as the Gardnerians, the Alexandrians, or other formalized Wiccan traditions, you will need to seek them out specifically. This book is eclectic in nature, drawing from a wide variety of sources, and is not representative of any one established group. It is based on general Wiccan principles but is not intended to be authoritative about the theology or practice of any specific Wiccan group.

Provide "The One True Way"

Spirituality is about living one's life with a conscious awareness of our connection to something greater than us, to some sort of Divinity. This book is presented with the understanding that we each undertake a personal journey. We each engage in a personal relationship with the Divine. There is no "one true way" that is right for all people. There is no single path that everyone should follow. It's like saying there is only one correct way of interacting with other people. We would laugh at the claim that we must relate exactly the same to our loved ones as we do to strangers. Each relationship we have with another person is unique and evolves over time. The relationship each of us has with the Divine is no different.

When it comes down to the essential matter of things all any book or other source of information can do is try to teach us, guide us, and challenge us to ask questions and seek out new information. It is up to each of us to decide for ourselves what makes sense, what works for us, and to learn how to take responsibility for our own growth. This book is not The Way, but just one of many signposts you will find along your own individual journey.

Your feet are already on your own unique path. Now, it is up to you to decide where you want to go, and how you will get there.

Wicca In Context

If you've been involved in the Wiccan community for a while you will probably find this section presents familiar concepts. It is necessary to review the basics, clear up some common misconceptions, and provide foundational definitions upon which the remaining chapters rely. This quick summary of the basics will help give us a common frame of reference to build on as we explore Wiccan spirituality together.

What Is Wicca?

Current historical research suggests that Wicca is a modern Pagan religion first promoted by Gerald Gardner around the 1950s. Wiccan beliefs are structured on the practices of witchcraft as outlined by Gardner. Modern scholars such as Ronald Hutton, in his detailed and highly influential book "The Triumph of the Moon," suggest that Wicca did not exist as an actual religion prior to Gardner, and that "uncle Gerald," as he is affectionately known, is largely responsible for its creation. There were certainly people who practiced magick and even some who called themselves Witches prior to Gardner, but the system Gardner presented as the religion of English witchcraft does not seem to have existed before Gardner appeared on the scene. Regardless whether Wicca has been around for fifty or five thousand years it is a living religion that has increasing numbers of adherents around the world. Some say it is one of the fastest-growing religions today.

It is important to remember that there are non-Wiccan witches as well; not all draw from the work of Gerald Gardner and his system. Wicca, while a very visible segment, is also just one part of the larger Pagan community.

Pagan, Witch, Wiccan: What's The Difference?

There are many debates within the modern Pagan community over the correct use of the terms *Pagan*, *Witch*, and *Wiccan*. The community is so diverse that it is unlikely there will ever be a final agreement on this matter. Despite that, there are some more or less valid generalizations within the occult community today regarding the use of these terms.

witchcraft (with a lowercase **w**): the craft or art (or to some, science) of magick. It can involve spells, divination, herbalism, brewing potions, and working to explore and use so-called psychic skills. Some who practice magick in this fashion refer to themselves as kitchen or hedge witches. This use of magick can be incorporated in a religious framework but doesn't necessarily have to be. Spells don't have to involve invoking deity although for many they do.

Witchcraft (with a capital **W**): the use of magick inextricably entwined with the worship of a deity or deities. Most Wiccans consider themselves to be religious Witches, but not all Witches are necessarily Wiccans; not all Witches base their philosophy on Gerald Gardner's system. People who consider Witchcraft to be their religion almost always capitalize the word to indicate its use as the name of a religion rather than a craft. They also often capitalize the word Witch to indicate a religious title, as the words Christian, Jew, and Muslim are capitalized out of respect for followers of those religious paths.

Wicca: a religious system very likely started but in any case promoted by Gerald Gardner, or any religious system based on or derived from the Gardnerian system. Wicca is probably the largest Witchcraft subgroup today. (Note: some Wiccans today say they are not Witches or witches — if that's the case, then perhaps they should not consider themselves to be Wiccan. Gerald Gardner was very clear that he was promoting Wicca as a religion, or "the religion," of witchcraft.)

Pagan: an umbrella term that is usually meant to include any religion that is not part of the big mainstream patriarchal monotheistic faiths. Some groups, like various aboriginal faiths, Hindus, Astatruar, Buddhists, etc. would probably say they aren't Pagan, while others would say they are. Commonly the term Pagan is used to refer to European and Western faiths like Wicca, Druidism, Greek reconstructionism, Egyptian reconstructionism, and any faith that is not Christian, Jewish, or Muslim. Pagans might or might not practice magick or consider themselves to be witches, Witches, or Wiccans.

A few examples might illustrate the distinctions more clearly.

People who practice the craft of witchcraft self-identify their religion as pretty much anything they want — Christian, Jewish, a Pagan faith, atheist, agnostic. To some witches their religion is separate from their use of magick. To make things a bit more confusing there is not really a standard about whether the word witch should be capitalized or not. Some always capitalize it whether they use it to refer to a religious Witch or a craft witch, some don't. Some capitalize it to indicate the word's use as a title but this is not always the case.

People who identify their religion as Witchcraft self-identify their magick and worship of a deity or deities as being so intertwined that they aren't separate at all. They can be Christian, Jewish, Pagan, etc. just like craft witches. That means that yes, there could be and indeed are Satanic Witches. There isn't much other Pagans or Witches can do about that whether they like it or not. No one group has exclusive ownership of the terms witch or witchcraft and therefore none are justified in trying to deny others the right to use these terms.

People who call themselves Wiccans, if they are really based on Gardnerian root-stock as I think they must be if they are to call themselves Wiccans, are Pagans. With that understanding, then, the term "Christian Wiccan" or "Satanic Wiccan" is an oxymoron; it's like saying you're a "Christian Muslim" or a "Jewish Christian." However, it's not a problem for Wiccans to choose to focus on Celtic, or Norse, or Egyptian, or even Christian or Jewish mythology so long as they are essentially polytheistic whether they believe all gods are one god or see all deities as truly distinct. It is important to keep in mind as well that while Wiccans might focus on Egyptian mythology, for example, that does not mean they are following an Egyptian religion. Similarly, Wiccans who draw on Christian myth are not Christians.

People who self-identify as Pagans might or might not practice magick, so they might or might not consider themselves witches or Witches, Wiccans, or something else. But while a Pagan might draw from Christian, Jewish, or Muslim mythology they aren't "Christian Pagans" or "Jewish Pagans" or "Muslim Pagans." The Christian, Jewish, and Muslim faiths are avowedly monotheistic and explicitly insist that you can't be Christian, Jewish, or Muslim if you hold yourself to be Pagan. Because most Pagans are polytheists, paganism tends to be more inclusive – the exclusivity is on the Christian, Jewish, and Muslim side of the equation, not the Pagan side. Being such a vague term, though, Pagan usually includes all sorts of groups including Asatruar, Celtic reconstructionists, Greek reconstructionists, Kemetic faithful, etc. Pagans can be monotheists but most are polytheists. They just have to not be Jewish, Christian, or Muslim in their base religion to be considered Pagan.

Personally, I consider myself a Witch because my magick is very much a part of my religion, and a Wiccan because I base my religion on Gardnerian ideas and structures although I'm not an initiated Gardnerian. And as a Wiccan, I'm a Pagan.

What Do Wiccans Believe?

There are a number of basic beliefs that are common to most Wiccan practitioners and groups.

a) Deity can be expressed in both female and male forms. Some Wiccans are described as "soft polytheists" and believe that the many gods and goddesses are different faces or aspects of a single unknowable deity.[1] Others believe that the different gods and goddesses are distinct and separate; this is sometimes described as "hard polytheism." Whether hard or soft polytheists, most Wiccans worship a balanced pair of a Goddess and a God.

b) The Earth should be honored and respected. Many Wiccans see the Earth as the living body of the Goddess. Gaia is one name commonly used by Wiccans for the Goddess as ultimate Earth-mother. This idea is often described in terms of the Divine being omnipresent or immanent in the physical realm.

c) Psychic powers and magick are possible and something that can be developed and used for good.[2] Psychic perceptions are encouraged, as they are believed to allow us direct awareness of nonphysical or transcendent levels of reality.

d) Sex is not something to fear or suppress. Sexual pleasure and the ability to procreate are considered holy gifts and worthy of respectful celebration. While most Wiccans consider sex to be a divine gift this does not mean that Wiccans are morally lax. Many Wiccans consider sex to be something that is expressed by committed couples in a monogamous relationship. Each Wiccan decides for themselves exactly how they will express their sexuality within the bounds of their social group and societal laws.

e) We can all have an individual and personal relationship with deity. There is no single religious path that is correct for all people — religion is largely an individual journey although we often band together in groups with people of like mind for varying periods of time. This belief results in the fact that Wicca has no central authority, no pope or Bible that is considered the final word on our religion. It also means that Wicca can be very diverse since practitioners and groups are largely autonomous.

f) We are all connected to everything else — humans are not separate from the rest of nature. This is essentially a restatement of the scientific law of cause and effect. Many Wiccans express this idea as the Threefold Law: "What you send out will come back to you threefold." This idea is also a large part of magickal theory; we believe that our actions produce results, even though on the surface the connection between a specific action and a particular consequence is not always obvious

The closest thing that Wiccans have to an overall rule is the Wiccan Rede: "An' it harm none, do what you will." This is not like a commandment in other religions, however. The word "rede" means "advice," so Wiccans tend to see the rule as a guideline and not as something that must be strictly followed. The Rede is also open to interpretation as is any concept. While many Wiccans do hold the Wiccan Rede to be central to their philosophy, there are some Wiccans who do not.

There are other beliefs that are common among many Wiccans that are not necessarily universally held. One of these is the belief in the existence of non-corporeal entities such as ghosts, angels, or faeries. Another of these beliefs is that when we die we are reborn in another physical form, that we reincarnate until we have learned enough to move on to other levels of existence, or in the case of bodhisattvas keep coming back to teach what we have learned until all are equally enlightened. Wiccans also hold a wide range of beliefs regarding what magick and psychic powers are and involve. Some practitioners are very scientific and tend to define magick in psychological terms, while others have more traditional views including the acceptance of energies that they believe science hasn't identified yet.

Wicca is a religion with great diversity among practitioners and groups. Various sects, or traditions, have arisen over the years. The Gardnerian tradition is arguably the oldest, with Alexandrian Wicca probably the second oldest. Some practitioners consider only Gardnerians and Alexandrians to be the true Wiccans but this is highly contested. Today there are many different traditions under the Wiccan label and many more who practice as solitaries without formal associations with any established tradition.

What About Spell-Work And Magick?

Wicca is a religion based on the lore of witchcraft so it is not surprising that it includes the active use of magick. Spells and rituals are often performed to achieve goals such as healing and to better one's situation in life. Many

Wiccans describe spell casting as an active form of prayer. Using spells or magick is really not that different from a Christian, Jew, or Muslim praying for healing or changes in life circumstances. Wiccan spells differ from prayers, though, in that Wiccans attempt to work more directly with unseen forces and circumstances to achieve goals.

Those who practice it define magick in many different ways. A few definitions of magick from published authors:

> "... attempting to cause the physically unusual..." or "... the art of getting results." *(Gerald Gardner, "The Meaning of Witchcraft.")*

> "The Science and Art of causing Change to occur in conformity with the Will." *(Aleister Crowley, "Magick in Theory and Practice.")*

> "The science of the control of the secret forces of nature." *(S. L. MacGregor Mathers, founder of the Golden Dawn magickal association in the late 1800s.)*

Here are some other quotes that help suggest the meaning and nature of magick:

> "White magick is poetry, black magick is anything that actually works." *(Victor Anderson, founder of the Feri tradition, quoted in Starhawk's "Spiral Dance.")*

> "Do you believe in an invisible reality behind things?" *(Dion Fortune, "Moon Magic.")*

> "Four laws of ecology:
> 1. Everything is connected to everything else,
> 2. Everything must go somewhere,
> 3. Nature knows best, and
> 4. There is no such thing as a free lunch." *(Barry Commoner, "The Closing Circle: Nature, Man, and Technology.")*

Magick is not just about apparent miracles and the supernatural. Every time a Wiccan circle is cast to establish holy space for a ritual, magick is being performed. Attempting to obtain hints about the future or clarification about present circumstances through the use of divinatory tools is magick. Meditating in order to travel in a spiritual realm and encounter non-corporeal entities is magick. Selecting and carrying a lucky amulet or religious jewelry to influence your daily life is magick. Wiccans who don't perform full-fledged rituals or spells are usually still performing magick, as magick is very much a part of the Wiccan worldview. *Living as a Wiccan is to live a purposeful and therefore magickal life.*

What Does Wiccan Practice Include?

Wiccans practice a wide range of techniques. If you identify a specific practice, chances are there is a Wiccan solitary or group out there that does include it in their practice.

One generally universal Wiccan practice is the called casting the circle, which is the basic foundation of most Wiccan magickal ritual. Casting the circle is a way of setting aside and consecrating sacred space for a specific period of time, usually the duration of the ceremony being performed. Casting the circle involves acknowledging the directions (usually east, south, west, and north but sometimes with interesting variations depending on cultural emphasis) and inviting the presence of deities and sometimes other spirits into the space. There are often additional steps taken to purify the space, often using the elements of earth, air, fire, and water in the form of salt, incense, candles, and water or wine. Casting the circle for a ritual can be a highly choreographed and elaborate portion of the ritual, or it can be very simple, depending on the practitioners' inclinations. Some Wiccans adhere to highly scripted rituals to cast the circle, while others are more spontaneous and will change their methods each time they do a ritual depending on the circumstances and moods of the participants.

Most if not all Wiccans also make regular use of meditation. During ceremonies they will often participate in guided meditations frequently described as pathworkings that are designed to facilitate personal insight and communion with divine forces. The magickal goals of meditation and pathworking are usually to encourage the mind to quiet down and allow us to perceive the Divine presence. They give us a break from the normal routine of daily life, giving us a quiet space to experience the sacred. Regular meditation also helps to build up our ability to consciously relax and encourages visualization and creative skills. And like most skills, the more you practice meditating the better you get and the more effective it becomes.

Many Wiccans also practice spellwork as a method to achieve their goals. Spellwork is not universal in Wiccan practice though. Some Wiccans focus their spiritual practice almost exclusively on worship and never engage in spellwork. Spellwork can be as simple as a prayer requesting assistance from a Divine source. It can also be complex such as a multi-session ritual sequence timed to coincide with astrological events, with special ritual clothing, handmade tools individually consecrated for the working, long memorized invocations, and choreographed ritual actions. The key to spellwork, regardless of complexity, is that there is a clearly defined goal that all the effort is directed to attain.

While there are many practices that are common among Wiccans there is no central authority that dictates any practices as mandatory for all. Individual Wiccan traditions do have their own standardized rituals and practices, and individual practitioners do tend to find their practice sticks to their own preferred tried-and-true methods. However there are no methods that are required of all Wiccans and each practitioner or tradition is free to determine their own practices.

Chapter 1:
What Is a Mystery Religion?
What Is a Mystic?

Many language scholars believe the word *religion* is based on the Latin word *religare* which means to bind or make fast. Associated with this is the concept of promises and oaths or vows. Religion, then, can be seen as a way for individuals to establish a connection with something greater than themselves that most spiritual paths consider to be the Divine. Religion in this light is about establishing a personal relationship with the Divine.

Spiritual pursuits help us to identify with the Divine and feel connected to the Divine. Many people identify religion as the center around which they base their ethical and moral behavior. The sense of connection also provides grounding so that the constant change we are confronted with in life doesn't overwhelm us. Involvement in a spiritual routine provides a solid foundation in our lives. The routine serves as an anchor upon which we can depend. Many also seek involvement in particular religious paths as a way to connect with a larger spiritual community and establish links with seekers on similar paths.

Religious scholars often talk about specific ancient cults like the cults of Eleusis, the cults of Mithras, and others as being mystery religions. Many Wiccans describe their religion as a modern mystery religion. What exactly is a mystery religion? What makes some ancient religions mystery religions while excluding others? Is Wicca truly a mystery religion? Are there other modern religions that are also mystery religions? And perhaps most important, what do mystery religions offer that might make them more attractive than any other type of religion?

Characteristics Of A Mystery Religion

The word *mystery* comes from the Greek word *myein*, which means to keep one's mouth closed. It is also cognate with the word mute that of course also means silent. The basis of this word then is to keep a secret, to have some knowledge that is not openly shared with others.

Mystery religions usually have secrecy as a main component. Only those who are formally accepted into the religious group are permitted to learn certain information about the religion, or to participate in religious practices conducted by the group.

In order to maintain some control over who is permitted to join the group and learn the holy secrets mystery religions usually include formal initiation ceremonies to welcome newcomers. Initiations are often more than just welcoming ceremonies, however, and include tests of a candidate's worthiness. Candidates who fail the tests are not considered to be initiates and are therefore barred from the group.

Another perhaps more significant characteristic of mystery religions is the emphasis on ecstatic experience as a central method of achieving communion with the Divine. For example, historians believe that candidates participating in the rites of Eleusis consumed hallucinogenic substances at the beginning stages of the initiation ceremony. Fasting, breathing fumes and heavy incense smoke, prolonged dancing, chanting and singing, even submission to pain through ritual flogging or body modifications are in evidence among all the ancient mystery cults. The goal appears to have been to transcend one's normal state of awareness and achieve, if only for a time, a sense of connection with the deities of the cult.

Mystery religions differ from other religions in their emphasis for the participants. All religions offer ways to connect the faithful to the Divine. Mystery religions, however, offer a more direct connection between worshipper and Divine. Mystery religions attempt to provide more than just an abstract or intellectual link with the Divine. They usually offer an ecstatic mystical experience so that worshippers can relate to the Divine on a primal level. Even among those without overt attempts to maintain secrecy, many mystery religions include experiences that are so individually significant that it is said to be impossible to describe them. To understand the experience, usually described as the mystery, one must experience it first-hand.

On a more superficial level mystery religions also offer special status to those who become involved. Those who undergo the rituals are deemed special, set apart from those who have not. Some mystery religions consider this special status to be a more refined spiritual state. In some instances it is believed that initiates gain special abilities. These are distractions, however, from the spiritual purpose of initiation in a mystery religion: the opening of one's awareness to connection with the Divine.

Mystery Religions Of The Past

A number of references to ancient mystery religions have survived to the present day, including hymns and invocations, partial descriptions, and even artwork suspected to have been created and used by participants in the cults. Some clues have survived in modified form within later religions or even nonreligious institutions. Some Christian churches, for example, have been built on the foundations of ancient Greek temples; Hagia Sophia, which was a Christian church, was later adopted by Islam and converted to a mosque. A lot of the material, however, has been lost through defacement by subsequent groups who wished to remove references to previous competitor faiths. Unfortunately because of the secret nature of much of these religions we do not have a complete record of them. Despite this there is a lot that is known by putting together the pieces that we do have available to us.

Eleusinian Mysteries

The Eleusinian mysteries were a cult devoted to the goddesses Demeter and her daughter Kore, centered on the town of Eleusis in Greece. It appears to have been primarily a fertility cult concerned with the cycle of life, death, and regeneration of both the crops and people.

The primary myth which it thought to have been central to the cult relates how the change in the seasons mirrors the annual cycle of Kore leaving the land of mortals to go to the underworld where she lives for part of the year, corresponding to the seasons of autumn and winter. In the spring Kore comes back from the underworld to be reunited with her mother Demeter, and the mortal world is abundant and warm again.

Archeological evidence suggests that annual mystery rituals were practiced where newcomers underwent initiation ceremonies that involved fasting, purification, and taking special hallucinogenic sacraments before witnessing and perhaps even participating in dramatic reenactments of religious myths.

These ceremonies were believed to teach spiritual truths and bestow a new status on the initiates as chosen people. One of the promises apparently involved assuring the initiates that they were now destined for a new life in some form.

One of the surviving records from the Eleusinian rites is the Homeric Hymn to Demeter that scholars believe was compiled and written down around the seventh century BCE. It is interesting to note that at least some of the basic mythological concepts, particularly the idea of being reborn either in this life or in another one after death, crop up again and again in various mystery religion philosophies including Christianity.

Dionysian and Orphic Mysteries

Information about the Greek and Roman mystery cult of Dionysus (also known as Bacchus) comes to us mostly through Euripides' play "The Bacchae," but also through frescos on the walls of a villa unearthed in Pompeii. Dionysus/Bacchus was a god of virility, wine, and apparently also the celebration of fleshly desires. The cult appears to have been very attractive to women with women playing important roles if not leading outright in the descriptions and illustrations that have survived the centuries.

Followers of Dionysus were known to participate in orgies involving excessive drinking, feasting, and very likely unrestrained sexual activity as well. The frescos at Pompeii also show ritual flagellation and nudity as a part of ritual practice.

The Orphic mysteries were a later development of the Dionysian mysteries. The philosophy is attributed to Orpheus who is said to have journeyed to the underworld to rescue his bride, Eurydice. In Orphic teachings Dionysus was killed and consumed by the Titans who were then killed and cremated for this crime. The ashes of the Titans, containing Dionysus as well, were used to create the human race. Orphics teach that humans are therefore flesh of the Titans with a Dionysian soul.

Anatolian Mysteries of Kybele and Attis

This mystery religion was based on the goddess Kybele who was often described as the Great Mother, and her consort Attis. It is frequently described as a rather bloodthirsty religion. In the myth of Kybele and Attis,

Kybele is a grain-mother, responsible for the abundance of the Earth, plants, and animals. Her consort, Attis, is a sacrificial god who gave his life by bleeding to death under a pine tree after he castrated himself.

The cult of Kybele and Attis spread to Rome where political authorities formally accepted it in 204 BCE as part of the official religion. After that, it grew so popular that Kybele became the de-facto Roman national goddess.

One of the major festivals carried out in mid-March each year involved cutting down a pine tree, decorating it, and parading it around in honor of the slain Attis. Initiates would flog themselves to the point where they bled and this blood was sprinkled on altars and generally used to purify in Attis' name. Men who would become priests of Kybele would castrate themselves during this festival in imitation of Attis.

In the latter part of this particular festival came a time known as the Hilarion when the emphasis was on feasting and making merry in celebration of the resurrection of Attis. The Great Mother's consort was first and foremost a god who dies and is reborn again.

The story of Attis was also known in Sumeria although here the dying consort of the goddess was known as Dumuzi. In Babylon he was known as Tammuz.

Egyptian Mysteries of Isis and Osiris

Isis and her husband/ brother Osiris, along with their son Horus, were probably the most popular and important deities in ancient Egypt. Their stories of death, preservation of the body through mummification and magick, and continuing life in the underworld is one of the enduring tales upon which Egyptian culture was founded.

In Egypt, the mysteries of Isis and Osiris took the form of annual reenactments of the myths. The mysteries also included magickal rites to ensure an afterlife for the royal family, and later on, for the wealthy and influential as well.

As Egyptian and European cultures interacted, Egypt became "Hellenized" (made more Greek) and in exchange saw the spread of Egyptian myths and influences outside of Africa. Temples to Isis were erected in Rome and indeed across Europe, even into Britain. This is likely when the cult of Isis adopted more of the mystery elements common in some Greek and Roman cults including formal initiations of celebrants, secret rites, and an emphasis on ecstatic identification with the deities.

One of the best descriptions of the cult of Isis that has survived to modern times was written by the second century CE author Lucius Apuleius of Madauros in his novel "The Golden Ass (Metamorphoses.)" It is interesting to note, too, that the modern Wiccan "Charge of the Goddess" derives some of its material, particularly the beginning of the Goddess' address where she recites various goddess names as being Hers, from the Isis material in "The Golden Ass."

Mithraic Mysteries

The mystery cult of Mithras was a popular warrior cult that spread across the Roman Empire all over Europe. It originated among the Indo-Iranians where Mithras was a god of light, truth, and integrity. As it developed it became a cult teaching rebirth through baptism, ideally using the blood of a sacrificial bull. The cult also included ritual meals and a system of hierarchical initiations.

As it was a martial cult only men (and mostly soldiers) were initiates of Mithras. Astute Roman politicians cultivated their associations with the cult as a way to ensure political support from the military. As the Roman influence spread across Europe through military power, shrines to Mithras were among the most frequently erected where Roman soldiers went.

Modern Mystery Religions And Related Groups

Mystery cults and groups did not disappear with the growing dominance of the Christian church across Europe. In some cases the mystery cults lived on in some form through the Christian church and in others they transformed into other types of groups working for goals not specifically spiritual in nature.

Christian Mysteries

It could be argued that Christianity itself is a mystery religion that grew to widely popular acceptance. Christianity does have some key characteristics of a mystery religion: there are initiations performed as baptisms and confirmations, there is a claim of special knowledge which is supposedly only found within Christian teachings, and at least at the start it was largely an ecstatic and very personal religion where worshippers sought direct contact with the Divine.

As Christianity has become more established some of the mystery elements have evolved or generally dropped by the wayside. For example, the Apocrypha – a collection of texts dropped from official Christian scripture over they years – provides some insight into a range of mystical ideas the churches decided to reject. Ecstatic practices have been generally phased out to the point that now it is a feature of only a minority of Christian sects or within specific orders inside the larger church hierarchy. The primary text of Christian teachings, the Bible, is widely available although its special knowledge is often taught as being inaccessible except through guided study directed by Church authorities. This is, of course, the way some sects ensure their religions stay "untainted" by inappropriate thought. Other Christian sects do encourage independent interpretation and study of scripture.

Guild Lodges

One prominent way the mystery cult structure has survived is through trade guilds and their later incarnation as charitable organizations. Originally groups like the Freemasons were an exclusive union of stonecutters and builders. They provided an organized structure for training apprentices in their trades and maintaining standards within their occupational field. They were much more than this, though, integrating a rich storehouse of mythical imagery into the organizational structure and ritual. The guilds were as much a social fellowship for their members as an occupational organization.

Entrance to a guild was often through sponsorship by an initiated member, which made it difficult for new members to join if they didn't already have some connection to the guild. This resulted in successive generations of the same family being members of a specific guild. In pre-industrial times, without a widely available general education system in place, it also makes sense that it was common for whole families to participate in the same occupation. Many family names reflect on their traditional occupations – for example Cartwright or Carter, Miller, Smith, etc.

Those sponsored candidates who were tested and found worthy were accepted into the guild through formal initiation ceremonies that sometimes served as the final test for acceptance. Initiates took oaths of secrecy in order to preserve the knowledge within the guild. The only element of the old mystery religions that wasn't necessarily evident in the guilds was the emphasis on ecstatic connection with the Divine. While usually overtly religious in their organizational culture, they were adjuncts to participation in mainstream religion rather than primary substitutes. Members were often churchgoers as well as lodge initiates.

Magickal Schools

Various overtly magickal organizations have sprung up since Christianity became dominant in western culture. These groups are pretty much universal in their use of formal initiation rites, oaths of secrecy, and the use of ritual (and often explicitly magickal ritual) as paths to communion with the Divine. One of the most popular or at least most influential of these was the Rosicrucians.

The Rosicrucians were a mythical secret society of Christian mystics who incorporated alchemical and magickal work with an active pursuit of Divine communion and revelation. The first real evidence of the group dates back to the early 1600s in Germany, when anonymous pamphlets announcing the organization began to circulate. The pamphlets and subsequent documents claimed that the secret society was founded before the birth of Christ in Egypt and was therefore essentially an Egyptian mystical system that predicted and then flourished through Christianity.

Regardless whether the Rosicrucians existed prior to the 1600s or not, the idea of secret magickal societies took hold in the public imagination. Before long, groups appeared claiming to be Rosicrucians, and other groups were formed drawing on the inspiration of the mythical Rosicrucians. Magickal groups were established across Europe and into the Americas. Some of the groups flourished while others disintegrated from a variety of factors.

One of the most influential magickal societies whose influence is still strong today is the Hermetic Order of the Golden Dawn. Dr. William Wynn Westcott, Dr. William Robert Woodward, and Samuel Liddell MacGregor Mathers and his wife Moina founded the Golden Dawn in the late 1800s. The founders all had prior membership in other groups such as Rosicrucian and Mason organizations, so it is not surprising that the new Golden

Dawn philosophy would include these organizational structures and myths. Few if any systems are truly unique or divorced from prior influences. It is perfectly natural for a new tradition to be based on an assortment of concepts and practices drawn from other sources.

The Golden Dawn's origins are traced to Samuel Mathers' translation of a mythical and probably forged document passed to him by Westcott and Woodward, who claimed they received it from a Mason friend. Mathers asserted this mysterious document led him to contact a woman named Ann Sprengel in Germany who directed him to found the Golden Dawn as a new occult society exploring magick, spirituality, and personal and societal development.

The Golden Dawn proved to be quite popular, attracting such notables as the famous stage actress Florence Farr, the poet William Butler Yeats, and the occultist Arthur Edward Waite. It was also the launching point for Aleister Crowley's occult career, and was Dion Fortune's start as well.

Around the turn of the twentieth century Aleister Crowley and Mathers were involved in a conflict with other high ranking Golden Dawn initiates over leadership of the organization. This was the beginning of the end of the Golden Dawn and the group ended up splintering into factions, with a number of the former members going on to establish their own magickal societies. Dion Fortune, for instance, went on to found the Fraternity (now Society) of Inner Light, and Aleister Crowley ended up joining and later leading the Ordo Templi Orientalis.

There are competing groups still in existence today that attempt to continue the Golden Dawn traditions and name. A large amount of the original Golden Dawn material has been put into print, most notably in 1937 by the talented occultist Israel Regardie. Golden Dawn influences are easy to spot in many modern magickal systems including Wicca. The Golden Dawn has played and still plays a very important part in modern occult, magickal, mystical, and religious history.

Wicca As A Mystery Religion

When Gerald Gardner first started promoting Wicca in the 1950s the religion met all three of the basic criteria for a mystery cult. Gardner's religious system included formal initiations of members into working groups or covens, there were oaths of secrecy regarding the content of the spiritual teachings and even the identities of other members, and worship focused heavily on ecstatic practices such as ritual flagellation, chanting, and dancing.

Gardner made it clear in his books "Witchcraft Today" and "The Meaning of Witchcraft" that he felt his religion was at least inspired if not derived from mystery cults like that of Eleusis.

Scholars such as Ronald Hutton in his classic study of witchcraft history, "The Triumph of the Moon," also provide details of other mystery religions or mystery groups that were influential in the development of Wicca. For instance, Gardner was known to have been involved with both Masons and Rosicrucians, and was familiar with Aleister Crowley's OTO. Gardner even went so far as to meet with Crowley in the late 1940s and was granted a charter to start up an OTO lodge and grant the first three degrees to students. With all of these influences it is not surprising to see traces of them in Wiccan practice.

Gardner did take mystery religion back to its roots in many ways, though, by focusing on pagan deities and mythology rather than on Christian and Jewish mysticism as was predominant in most of the other magickal and mystery groups of the time. His rituals and celebrations were also more earth-honoring than was generally prevalent and the emphasis on a Goddess brought in feminist elements that were largely absent in other groups. While other mystery groups of the time were mostly ceremonial magick systems, Gardner's mystery religion was very down to earth, leaning heavily towards the hearth rather than the chapel in its cultural emphasis.

As Wicca developed and spread it was inevitable that the religion should change in ways that some feel dilutes Gardner's original spiritual system. Some of these changes were introduced or at least acknowledged by Gardner and others who were instrumental in founding Gardnerian Wicca. One example of this type of change was encouraged by the recognition that it was possible to be a Wiccan and practice as a solitary or to be self-taught without formal initiations by a coven. Gardner and others often spoke too of the possibility of other Wiccan groups out there who were practicing without contact with any other Wiccans. These sorts of public statements make it harder to discount others who came forward as being somehow less authentic that the Gardnerian tradition.

Some imitators who appeared on the Wiccan scene claiming to be Wiccan based their material on Gardnerian ideas and sometimes privately circulated documents without the formal connection to Gardnerian Wicca through initiatory lineage. This allowed for greater variety in Wiccan practice and encouraged shifts in the emphasis among the different groups and individual practitioners. Some groups shifted away from ecstatic ritual practice and more towards ceremonial magick practices while others embraced ecstatic and shamanic practices to a greater extent than was common in Gardner's own group. Others placed less emphasis on formal initiations and some created a more complex hierarchy than the Gardnerian three-degree system. Many groups maintained oaths of secrecy as a requirement for membership. With more solitaries appearing, though, and with groups desiring to share information with other groups, oaths of secrecy started to become less important. It has gotten to the point where there are very few real secrets in any Wiccan group that are not in print somewhere.

Is Wicca still a mystery religion then, or has it changed sufficiently that it no longer meets the criteria?

The first criterion, secrecy, is still very evident in Wicca. Wicca in most of its forms does include secrets although most of what was once considered secret is now hidden in plain sight. It has developed to the point where the secrets are really about what particular practices a particular group or individual employs and how they are integrated into their spiritual system. Often the specific deity names employed are not revealed except to those who are official members of the group. It doesn't matter that those same practices and deity names are described in minute detail in various published sources. The point is that Wicca is maintained as a personal spiritual path where practitioners are not required to divulge the specifics of their individual path unless they choose to do so. A form of secrecy is maintained.

Wicca is also very much a religion of personal connection with the Divine. It is often described as religion without the middle-man. In Wicca each practitioner is capable of serving as their own priest or priestess interacting with deity, while in many other mainstream religions the average worshipper is considered to be a congregant who must go through an authorized priest to participate in ritual contact with the Divine. Wiccan groups do tend to have high priests and high priestesses that lead their particular groups, but they serve more as organizers and elders rather than as intermediaries. In most Wiccan groups every initiate is expected to have the potential to fill the role of high priest or high priestess at some point in their spiritual life, if only for themselves in solitary practice.

As a religion of personal identification and connection with the Divine, Wiccans tend to frequently focus on ecstatic techniques like singing, chanting, dancing, and meditating. Ritual use of food, drink and incense are commonly used to encourage ecstatic states, to facilitate connection with the Divine. Some Wiccan groups, but not all, also employ more strenuous ecstatic techniques such as flagellation (which is a feature of Gardnerian Wicca in particular), fasting, techniques of binding the body to restrict blood flow, sexual practices drawn mostly from Tantra, and the ingestion of mind-altering substances. Different individuals and groups have their own preferences so they tend to use the techniques that work best for them.

Initiation is perhaps the most controversial criterion of a mystery religion when examined in a Wiccan context. Some groups, such as Gardnerian and Alexandrian Wiccans, only admit members through formal initiation ceremonies so are easily counted as being in agreement with the definition of a mystery religion on this particular point. Some say it is not a mystery religion for Wiccan groups who do not require formal initiations or who practice as solitaries. If initiation is seen exclusively as a formal admittance to an existing group this is correct. If initiation is seen as something more than just a formal admittance ceremony then it's not as easy to dismiss those outside the formal initiation framework.

Gardner and other early Wiccan writers drew heavily upon the lore of witchcraft available to them in the UK as well as from across Europe. While the lore does refer extensively to groups of witches or covens it also frequently mentions witches who work alone. Gardner did not ignore these solitaries but acknowledged them as valid witches, keeping the occult traditions alive even without contact with formal groups. Regardless whether covens or solitary witches existed or not prior to Gardner, the stance was presented by the founders of Wicca that both coven and solitary practice was valid.

We must consider carefully what really makes a particular religion a mystery religion. Are outward manifestations such as formal acceptance rituals and the keeping of secrets from non-initiates the most important parts? Or are the key elements the direct relationship with the Divine, the use of ecstatic techniques, and the idea of a spiritual initiation?

If initiation is considered to be primarily a spiritual milestone, a personal contact with the Divine, then solitary practitioners are just as likely to be participants in Wicca as a mystery religion as those in a coven. It's probably more accurate to disqualify a spiritual practice from being considered part of a mystery religion even though they might practice secrecy and some form of formal acceptance rite if there is no emphasis on initiations as a spiritual milestone or do they not use ecstatic techniques to connect the worshipper with the Divine. If we consider the important part of a mystery religion to be what many initiates call the Mystery, the direct experience of the Divine, then perhaps the key component to a mystery religion is essentially mysticism.

In mainstream religions some religious devotees, often priests, nuns, or monks, but also sometimes just particularly devoted worshippers, achieve a sense of special closeness with the Divine. This closeness is frequently described using the language of love, peace, and serenity. It is most often described as a direct, individual, and intensely personal connection with a greater reality, with the focus of all worship, the deity. In eastern religions this experience is described as achieving Nirvana or enlightenment. In western religions this is more often described as mystical union, and the worshipper described as a mystic.

The core of the mystical experience is the all-encompassing and often overwhelming transcending of one's sense of self to encounter first-hand an entity, energy, or sense of oneness that is described as the ultimate reality, the Divine light, or merely God/dess. Different religions give this being different names. Christians know it as God or Jehovah or Yahweh. In Judaism, it is sometimes described as G-d, the ultimate deity whose name is not spoken aloud. In Buddhism this Supreme Being is Buddha and in other eastern religions it is an abstract state called Nirvana. Pagans the world over use a multitude of names for the Divine and will at times describe a particular manifestation of the Divine as their matron or patron deity. The mystical experience appears to be universal although it is one that is perceived in a myriad of ways.

Characteristics Of A Mystic

The word *mystic* derives from the same source as the word *mystery*, so in many ways an initiate of a mystery religion is the definition of a mystic. The word mystic however has come to focus more on the ecstatic union with the Divine rather than the other external elements often associated with mystery religions. A mystic is not necessarily bound by oaths of secrecy, nor needs to receive any sort of formal initiation performed by human hands. Mystics in mainstream religions are more often solitary worshippers than members of groups that focus on communal worship. The stereotype of a Christian mystic, for example, is often described as a worshipper who is isolated from others, sacrificing normal human contact in order to focus on contemplation and prayer. Ecstatic experience is at the core of the mystical experience though, which is also the core of mystery religions in their traditional form. The mystic's ecstatic techniques can include gentle but long term methods such as meditation, contemplation, and prayer, but also sometimes include harsh methods such as extensive fasting, denial of bodily needs, and infliction of pain through techniques such as flagellation.

Scholars of mysticism such as Evelyn Underwood and Wayne Teasdale identify some characteristics that appear to be universal in true mystics. These characteristics include an honest practicality, awareness of a transcendental realm that they associate with the Divine, an overwhelming focus on love, and a core objective of union with the Divine.

A mystic is not someone who divorces themselves from awareness of physical reality but someone who recognizes this realm as necessary and definitely present. This acceptance allows the mystic to see physical reality without the tainted filters through which we often perceive our world. The mystic's senses are cleansed, heightened in the pursuit of the Divine and thus attain a clearer vision of the physical realm. Illusions and distractions that make up our everyday world are obstacles to be dismissed or overcome. The mystic is instead able to focus on what really matters, avoid the superfluous, and maintain a healthy balance in their mundane lives.

Mystical pursuit is predicated on the idea that there is something beyond the physical realm, something that transcends the mundane world in a higher plane of existence. While some schools of mysticism encourage initiates to focus exclusively on the transcendent this is not universal to all mystical paths. Some Buddhist mystical systems, for instance, encourage initiates to attain enlightenment and then return to focus on the mundane world in order to bring back the gifts of enlightenment and to make the world a better place. Mystics in Buddhism who have attained enlightenment and who return to charitable work in the mundane are referred to as bodhisattvas and are considered selfless examples of the Buddhist ideal.

Love is considered the purest and most Divine of emotions. Some religious philosophers even go so far as stating that God, the ultimate essence and totality of the Divine, is Love. Many mystics turn their attention to examine love in intellectual and emotional ways in order to better understand and experience it personally and therefore come closer to the Divine. By focusing on love they come to see other emotions such as hate as obstacles to achieving understanding and union with the Divine. In this philosophy to be alienated from love is to be alienated from the Divine.

Some Christian mystics describe Divine love in terms of grace. Whether they call it love or grace, however, descriptions of it sound rather familiar when compared with descriptions of initiatory ecstatic experiences in mystery religions. For example the Christian mystic Hildegard von Bingen, who lived from 1098 to 1179, wrote in her Latin plainchant song "Columba Aspexit" the following verse, translated to English: "The heat of the sun burned/ dazzling into the gloom:/ whence a jewel sprang forth/ in the building of the temple/ of the purest loving heart." The description sounds very similar to the accounts of ecstatic surrender, where mundane perceptions and emotions are overwhelmed by the strength of Divine love. Hildegard von Bingen was noted for her lush descriptions of the mystical experience and is revered in the Catholic church today as a saint. Wiccans also like to use her works for inspiration; her texts on healing and mysticism are very popular today.

One of the most common descriptions of the intense mystical experience is that you find your sense of separation or individuality becomes blurred, and you feel like you are truly at one with something larger than yourself. It's like your sense of self is allowed to retreat, so that identification with the Divine can move in to take its place. This experience has been described in terms of nirvana or spiritual bliss, enlightenment, being engulfed with Divine light, becoming one with the universe, or achieving cosmic consciousness. Others talk about it as being a union with one's higher self, or achieving knowledge and conversation with one's Holy Guardian Angel. All these terms appear to be describing the same essential experience though, where one's everyday sense of self expands to include something much greater, in most cases a sense that you are truly one with everything that exists.

Descriptions Of A Mystical Experience

A typical mystical experience, if we can imagine such a thing, tends to involve some common experiences.

Mystical experiences can creep up on you and overtake you when you least expect them, while you're involved in everyday routines, engrossed in a complex task, or during an out of the ordinary event such as an accident or illness. In these cases it's like the conscious mind has been sufficiently distracted for the Divine to sneak into our awareness through a crack in our perceptions, and then the Divine steps forward to be noticed.

People who devote themselves to seeking mystical experiences also tend to find Divine communion happens in moments of prayer, meditation, or when involved in religious ritual. These cases involve preparing yourself for the possibility of Divine communion so that when it does happen it is encouraged and welcomed.

The experience itself frequently involves the sensation of one's awareness expanding beyond the boundaries of one's physical body, often to the point where our awareness encompasses the whole universe, everything that exists. This is such an unusual sensation that our normal sense of self dissolves and we become aware of a greater consciousness which we call Deity.

Many describe this contact as being engulfed with a glow they call the pure light of holy love. It is such an intense feeling that the light and emotion penetrates every molecule of our being. Later on, as our awareness contracts back into our physical form, it feels as though the light has condensed in us as well so that our physical bodies are radiating the warm light of Divine love.

There are many theories that try and explain this experience according to various philosophies and theologies. Some explain the experience as reaching enlightenment, or traveling to Nirvana or feeling Divine bliss. Others call this achieving cosmic consciousness or being in the Divine presence. Still others rationalize it as coming into awareness of one's own soul or Divine spark, or contacting one's Higher Self, or one's Holy Guardian Angel. Despite the differences in explanation, the experience itself seems to be remarkably constant.

Results From A Mystical Experience

People who have mystical experiences often find that they gain a new perspective on life and its complexities. Some consider the physical realm to be an illusion distracting us from the perception of the Divine and strive to turn their attention away from the physical. Others, including many Wiccans, feel that the experience confirms the theory that the Divine is omnipresent and thus embrace the physical realm as an expression of Deity. Most who undergo mystical experiences come away with an understanding that mundane difficulties are obstacles that can be overcome, and that love is much more important than these minor annoyances no matter how intrusive they might be in daily life.

Some mystical schools teach that these encounters with the Divine are to be used as inspiration for making the mundane world a better place. The gift of Divine love is to be drawn into one's self, then brought back and shared with others in this realm. Love, to be honored, must be nurtured and shared rather than hidden away and rationed for one's self. True mystics, it is argued, are practical and grounded. They do not ignore the mundane world in favour of fleeting encounters with the numinous.

Mystics In History

History is filled with stories of mystical experiences. No one culture has exclusive claim to mystical practitioners either – everywhere we look, there are mystics! Here are a few well-known mystics from a variety of cultures and historical periods:

Buddha (c 563 BCE - 483 BCE): Born Siddhartha Gautama in Nepal, he was a wealthy young man raised in opulence. He left his wife and family when he was twenty-nine to live the life of a religious hermit. He had visions and achieved enlightenment while meditating under the Bodhi tree. His teachings are the foundation of Buddhism.

St. Paul (c. 10 - 67 CE): Saul the Hebrew had a vision of the resurrected Jesus around 36 CE while en route to Damascus to arrest Christians. He converted on the spot to Christianity, took the name Paul, and became a leading Christian figure.

Muhammad (c 570 CE): Born in Mecca, he lived a normal life with his wife and family until he had a vision around the age of forty. His vision involved meeting an angel that commanded him to write the Koran and preach this gospel. Today the Muslim religion is one of the largest.

St. Hildegard von Bingen (1098 - 1179): Born to a noble German family, she experienced visions throughout her life. She became a nun at age eighteen and by thirty-eight was a prioress. Her most intense visions occurred when she was in her forties. She felt compelled to describe her visions on paper, often in beautiful poems and illuminated calligraphy texts. She was known as the "Sibyl of the Rhine" for her visions.

St. Teresa of Avila (1515 - 1582): A Spanish mystic who became a nun in her early twenties. She had visions and experienced ecstasy, which she described as her senses awakening as if from being dead. Her prayer methods sound suspiciously like trance methods.

R. M. Bucke (1837 - 1902): Bucke had episodes of mystical insight that triggered what he came to call cosmic consciousness. Bucke wrote about the topic in his book "Cosmic Consciousness" which many consider a classic. Other mystical writers use terms like enlightenment, nirvana, or Samadhi to describe the same experience.

Alexandra David-Neel (1868 - 1969): One of the early western explorers to go to Tibet and document the mystical and magickal traditions practiced there, David-Neel was herself considered to be a mystical adept. One account describes how she was able to produce a thoughtform using psychic energy that was so successful it appeared as a flesh-and-blood person others mistook for a real human.

Mystical Occultism

Mystical pursuits are not just the stereotypical work of solitary scholars. There are quite a number of examples of magickal systems or groups that were established with the primary purpose of helping members work towards mystical experience or communion with the Divine.

Perhaps the most famous of these groups is the Rosicrucians, a Christian mystical sect that focused on the study of hidden or suppressed information as a path to enlightenment. The Rosicrucians were also one of the most influential of the modern secret societies or new incarnations of the old mystery religions. Many subsequent occult organizations drew on Rosicrucian ideas of occult study, overall philosophy, and even organizational structure. The Rosicrucians were also one of the earliest modern groups to popularize questionable but highly romantic origin claims in an effort to establish themselves as authorities.

Other groups that followed the Rosicrucian model include the Hermetic Order of the Golden Dawn established in the UK in the late 1800s by Samuel Liddell Macgregor Mathers and a few of his Rosicrucian/ Freemason associates. The group was highly popular, attracting such celebrities as the poet W. B. Yeats, Maude Gonne, and the actress Florence Farr. Other notable members who went on to run their own highly popular occult societies include Aleister Crowley and Dion Fortune.

These occult societies worked as training centers to provide an organized method for working towards mystical experience. Complex philosophies involving elements of the Jewish Kabala, pagan theology, and usually a large amount of mainstream Christian mysticism were blended in various proportions. The groups, being products of their times, were structured around strict hierarchies with ritual initiations performed to acknowledge progress from one grade or class to another. Some groups, such as Dion Fortune's Society of the Inner Light, incorporate psychological theories into their systems while others tend to focus more on a religious approach.

Mysticism In Wicca

Wicca is a mystical religious system. At its core lies the belief that *each and every one of us is capable of experiencing a direct relationship with the Divine in some form.* Even in the emphasis on magick there is the underlying assumption that to be effective the practitioner must have some sort of connection with the Divine. The energy that many believe is the force at work in magick is often described as Divine energy. To tap into Divine energy one must have a connection with the Divine.

Wiccan spirituality and indeed magickal practice in general requires the practitioner to develop a secure awareness of themselves, their environment, and how choices are connected to consequences. Magick is about manipulating circumstances and making choices in order to bring about specific results. Gaining an awareness of one's place in the universe, expanding one's consciousness beyond the mundane, is another way of describing what others call enlightenment or cosmic consciousness or oneness with the Divine.

The work involved in practicing Wicca is not about being able to recite lists of correspondences, being able to perform specific rituals precisely, or wearing the right clothes or jewelry. It's a spiritual system that is centered on balance. We learn about ourselves, the world around us, and how we fit into the balance of things. We learn about how each of us is a strand in the vast tapestry of life and how each of us is able to make a difference through our choices. We learn how to work harmoniously with all of existence, the seen and unseen, the inner and outer. We learn that "as above, so below" is not just a pretty phrase but also a crystallization of magickal philosophy and spiritual understanding.

Wicca has autonomy at its core too. Even in group work each participant is responsible for doing their own very hard work to gain understanding and seek appropriate balance in order to be effective. We learn that in Wicca, as in many spiritual traditions, all the teachers and books and lessons taught by others mean nothing if we don't do our own work and take responsibility for our own progress. Others can't do the work for us and hand us spiritual awakening as something for us to consume. They can show us how they do things, talk about the insights they've had, but in the end we must have the realizations ourselves and discover and strengthen our own individual relationships with the Divine and with our inner selves.

Chapter 2:
Initiation, and Being An Initiate

Initiation: What's It All About?

ne of the most frequently cited characteristics of a mystery religion is that initiates perform rites in private. Wiccan groups that involve formal initiation of members, maintain oaths of secrecy, and which focus on the goal of achieving direct experience of the Divine through the induction of altered states of awareness, do fit quite well into this definition of a mystery religion.

Initiation, however, isn't merely a matter of being formally inducted into a group. Another meaning of initiation, and perhaps a more important one from a spiritual standpoint, is that of a spiritually transformative experience undergone by an individual. Initiation in this sense is a significant moment marking a step in one's growing spiritual maturity. It indicates one has progressed along one's journey towards self-knowledge and knowledge of the Divine. In the occult community to be considered an initiate often means being acknowledged as one who has attained or exhibits a level of spiritual or occult mastery that is greater than the norm among the general population. This does not mean the initiate necessarily has acquired any formal degrees or titles or even belongs to any formal associations or groups. Rather, it is about exhibiting spiritual maturity.

Two Types Of Initiation

Initiation Into a Group

One meaning of initiation is formal acceptance or induction into an established group. Within many Wiccan traditions, there are specific requirements or training that must be achieved before an initiation ritual is conducted. Almost all Wiccan traditions have an initiation ritual to formally accept the candidate as a full member of the group. Many Wiccan traditions also have further initiations, performed after subsequent training and experience within the group, which elevate the initiate to higher status within the tradition. These higher-level initiations often grant such titles as High Priest/ess or Elder. Holding a higher-level initiation is intended to indicate a greater level of knowledge, and usually experience and responsibility, within the group.

Wicca is a religion of autonomous groups. This means that there is no central authority to establish standards for initiation or training. Some groups might grant different initiations to members quite freely while other groups require long periods of rigorous training for the same titles within their traditions. A third-degree initiate from one group is not necessarily as experienced or knowledgeable as a third-degree initiate from another group, or for that matter, as mystically experienced. As well, a rigorous training program in one group might mean very focused study on very limited topics while in another group a just as rigorous training program might encompass a much broader curriculum. There is no guarantee that training which takes the same length of time or effort will produce equally broad or equally focused training any more than a specific title always means the same level of experience or training in all groups.

Wicca is not unique in this confusion over titles, however. In the Christian community different groups or denominations have different requirements for clergy. A preacher in one denomination, for instance, could be an individual, regardless of their educational background, who is elected by their congregation to the role. A preacher in another denomination, on the other hand, might have to hold an accepted university degree and also have completed a program in specific approved seminary colleges.

Specific titles really only mean something within the tradition or denomination where they are granted. To argue that all Pagan traditions or denominations should adhere to a standard would require giving up some of the autonomy that those traditions or denominations currently enjoy. It's a tradeoff which we must consider carefully as a community and which to date has not been resolved. The Wiccan and Pagan community is so diverse that it is doubtful our cherished autonomy will be compromised in favor of centralized standards because that would require establishing a centralized authority.

Magickal groups that perform formal initiations often consider there to be another important purpose for the ritual besides conferring a title or recognition of formal membership in the group. Initiation can be seen as an introduction of a new member to the magickal "group mind" of the specific group or tradition. Initiation in this sense is more than just an introduction to a group but a formal entrance into a carefully cultivated shared future. Some believe that this spiritual union lasts beyond the boundaries of physical death and so should not be considered frivolously.

Initiation as a Spiritual Milestone

Initiation defined as a significant milestone in an individual's spiritual maturation is the more esoteric, and less easy to outwardly confirm, form of initiation. Initiations into a group are straightforward — there is little doubt when they are performed, and witnesses can confirm them. Spiritual initiations, however, are not always easy for other people to recognize. Some steps in spiritual maturation might be highly significant but aren't externally visible. The same spiritual illumination might be more significant and visible in one person than in another, even though the jump in spiritual maturity is identical in both. Other people might or might not themselves be spiritually mature enough to recognize spiritual changes in another, so that external confirmation of growth might not happen.

The only person who can truly tell if spiritual growth has occurred is the one who experiences it. If a change is very subtle or gradual it is easy to miss noticing the change. When it comes down to it each person is really concerned primarily with their own growth and isn't necessarily paying close attention to changes in others. Others who are paying attention will likely notice big changes but it isn't always the big changes that are the most meaningful or the most common. Small changes are more likely to be lasting changes; big jumps are frequently accompanied by backsliding, additional smaller jumps forward, and overall upset until things settle down and stabilize at the new level. Small steps are more gradual yet just as important as big steps.

It could be argued that for a person to have the determination to call themselves a Witch or Wiccan they must have been touched by the Divine in some way or else they wouldn't be on the path they have chosen. Other formally recognized members within a specific group might be required to bestow an initiation into a specific Wiccan tradition, but only the Divine can perform the spiritually significant initiation that marks the individual as changed. The Divine is not bound by human rules or philosophies but chooses to grant those initiations in Their own ways and times. All we humans can truly do is work to open our senses to awareness of Them and struggle to make ourselves ready for Their communion.

The Occult Initiate As Mystic

In a spiritual and occult sense one of the assumptions made about those who are considered to be initiates is that they are somehow more in tune with the Divine than average people. Occult and spiritual power is usually seen to come from a Divine source to be manipulated or expressed by the initiate. It takes a special person with a close connection with deity to be able to consistently demonstrate occult faculties.

In occult philosophy the ultimate goal is often described as the Great Work, attaining the Knowledge and Conversation with one's Holy Guardian Angel, manufacturing the Philosopher's Stone, or achieving Cosmic Consciousness, Nirvana, or Enlightenment. Another way to describe this is that the ultimate goal is to achieve communion with the Divine or to attain a degree of close personal relationship with deity. This goal is also the primary goal of the mystic. In many ways it is accurate to say that the quest to become an occult initiate is ultimately the same as the quest of the mystic.

Differences Between the Occult and Mystic Paths

While both occult initiates and mystics have the ultimate goal of achieving communion with the Divine, secondary goals set the two paths apart. Some authors, such as Dion Fortune[3], believe that the two paths are irreconcilable despite the fact that they both seek similar ultimate goals.

Mystics generally favor turning one's complete attention to the Divine and consider the physical plane a distraction to overcome. Occultists generally favor drawing the benefits of Divine communion into the physical plane, manifesting Divine influence in ways to make the world better. Mystics frequently practice mortification of the physical body as a way to escape from the physical into the purely spiritual realm. Occultists usually practice mortification of the body in limited ways as a method of attaining discipline and control over the physical.

The apparent conflict between the occult and mystical paths can be attributed to something else, though. In a philosophy where the Divine is seen as exclusively transcendent, separate from the physical realm, it makes sense that the physical realm would be considered a distraction. However, not all spiritual philosophies require acceptance that the Divine is solely transcendent. Pantheists, for instance, believe that the Divine is actually present in everything that exists, in everything that is present and thus the Divine is said to be immanent in the physical plane. Panentheists agree with pantheists in the immanence of the Divine but also incorporate the idea that the Divine is transcendent or beyond the physical plane as well. If one's religious philosophy is either pantheist or panentheist in nature it does not make sense to reject the physical plane in an attempt to achieve union with the Divine. In a pantheist or panentheist worldview working to honor the physical realm is very much a part of communing with the Divine.

Many monotheist religious groups teach that the Divine is exclusively transcendent. In contrast to this many Pagan religious groups, including many Wiccans, see the Divine in either pantheist or panentheist terms. This means that there does not need to be an inherent conflict between the mystical and magickal paths in one's spiritual practice unless one is following an exclusively transcendent philosophy. For Pagans and Wiccans in particular, it is very possible for one's spiritual journey to be both mystical and magickal at the same time.

Characteristics Of A Mystical Initiate

There are a number of outward signs that often accompany an initiation when it's considered to be a spiritual milestone in an individual's developing maturity. Wiccan initiates, for instance, usually discover a growing awareness of the presence of the Divine and elemental or other non-corporeal forces, sometimes perceived as other planes of existence. They are able to sense and direct energies to specific goals in ways that are usually considered magickal. Their view of the world becomes more attuned to the hidden connections between things, an awareness that all is ultimately One.

Pantheists and panentheists, who consider the Divine to be immanent in the physical realm, experience first-hand that the Divine is omnipresent. It is like doors have opened in their lives leading to new spiritual landscapes that they may not have known existed.

As their attention moves to more spiritual things Wiccan initiates often find that old hurts are healed. In the most dramatic cases an initiate might find that they are no longer the person they once were, that nothing in their life or their outlook has carried over from their previous existence. In these instances they are described as being transformed by the experience. Initiations of all types are often described as being a form of spiritual rebirth and renewal.

Authors who wrote extensively on mysticism such as Evelyn Underhill describe similar qualities in those who have undergone a mystical initiation. A mystic, for instance, has a new transcendental awareness, an ability to perceive beyond the surface of the physical realm. In the most advanced of mystics this heightened awareness dominates their conscious life. Their awareness has been transfigured so that they no longer dwell merely in the physical plane as do most non-mystics. The transfigured mystic perceives and is immersed in hidden rhythms of nature. They react to this spiritual world, operating under its rules and requirements, apparently beyond what the non-initiate can grasp.

Another major part of the mystical initiation is learning to surrender one's self to the embrace of the Divine and to accept and revel in one's part in the elaborate dance of reality. The mystic who has truly become an adept in this way has achieved much more than just a momentary glimpse of holy oneness but has learned to perceive the eternal Divine presence and has made it the centre of their existence.

The descriptions of both magickal and mystical spiritual initiates overlap to such a large extent that the two could really be seen as slightly different approaches to the same thing. The magickal and mystical paths might come from different emphases of method or perhaps different philosophical outlooks regarding the nature of the Divine. Despite these differences they both hold essentially the same ultimate goal: knowledge of and communion with the Divine.

Chapter 3:
Wiccan Mysteries and Magickal Spirituality

Is Wicca A Mystery Religion?

Wicca is often described as a modern mystery religion. When asked to explain, though, few Wiccans can really describe what this means.

A mystery religion, if we go by the definition used by scholars who study ancient Greek, Roman, and Egyptian religion, has a few distinguishing characteristics: it is a religion where one must be formally initiated into the group to be considered a member, there are secrets which are only revealed to those who are within the group, and worship tends to focus on ecstatic communion with the Divine. These characteristics are all descriptive of the Eleusinian mystery cults of ancient Greece, the cults of Mithras, and some of the cults of ancient Egypt. But do these characteristics describe Wicca?

The Wiccan tradition Gerald Gardner promoted in the 1940s, 1950s, and into the 1960s included these three key characteristics of a mystery religion. First, new Wiccans are made through formal initiations performed by a Wiccan who possesses a second or third degree initiation themselves. Second, the tradition's rituals, mythology, and teachings were kept secret, written down in the Book of Shadows and only shared with other initiates. Third, communion with the Divine is sought through ecstatic methods. Gardnerians made use of ritual flagellation, chanting, and dancing as key methods to raise power and contact the Divine; all these are methods of achieving ecstatic states. There is no question that Gardnerian Wicca is definitely a type of mystery religion.

Gardnerian Wicca is just one sect within the Wiccan community. Other forms of Wicca, including that practiced by solitaries, could be considered mystery religions if we look at the key characteristics with an eye to what is most important. Real life, including spiritual life, isn't always easy to pin down with clearly defined labels.

Initiation

Initiation was the only way to become a Wiccan at the start, and is a nice tidy way to control access to official status. Unfortunately there are problems with this in Wiccan history, the primary difficulty being Gardner's claim that he was merely passing on an intact tradition rather than starting something new. By claiming that he was but one initiate of an existing intact tradition the door is opened for there to be others out there in this same tradition, or perhaps in offshoots, who have just as much (if not perhaps more) claim to lineage and therefore authority. In the introduction to the Mercury Publishing edition of Gardner's book "The Meaning of Witchcraft," Dr. Leo Louis Martello brings up a rather telling point: Gardner may have never received more than one initiation into Wicca. Gardnerian teachings are quite clear that only a second or third degree Wiccan is permitted to initiate others. We may never know for sure whether Gardner really was initiated into an existing tradition and what degree he had achieved as no independent proof has been uncovered to back up Gardner's claim of lineage. Additionally, if the lineage was valid and if Dr. Martello is correct that Gardner had only ever been given his first-degree initiation, how could his line of initiatory descendants be considered an intact transmission of the Wiccan mystery? Gardner was quite clear in his insistence that only second or third degree Wiccans were authorized to initiate others. On the other hand, if Gardner was really starting up a new religion based on older material or made up completely new it is irrelevant whether Gardner had been initiated or not himself. The founder of a system has the privilege of making up the rules for their system as they see fit.

Gerald Gardner was not the only one to start a Wiccan line under rather questionable circumstances. Alex Sanders, the founder of the Alexandrian denomination, had just as murky a start to his Wiccan career. Like Gardner, Alex claimed to be merely passing on an intact Wiccan mystery tradition and produced a robust enough initiatory lineage to follow him that the tradition is still quite healthy today. And since the Gardnerian and Alexandrian traditions are arguably the two oldest of the Wiccan denominations, they are rightfully recognized as the templates that the majority of subsequent Wiccan sects are based on.

Alex Sanders' was perhaps the most well known Wiccan "grandmother story." He claimed that he had a grandmother who was a Wiccan, who initiated him in a naked ritual performed in the kitchen when he was all of seven years old. Alex claimed that he was therefore an hereditary witch and had learned the Craft from a blood relative, years before Gardner was initiated into the New Forest coven.

The details of Alex's start in Wicca weren't quite that romantic as later research proved. Alex didn't appear on the Wiccan scene until the early 1960s, well after Gerald Gardner's books on modern witchcraft had been published, and well after various Gardnerian covens had started to spread around the UK and outside its borders. Alex, it seems, wanted desperately to join one of the existing Gardnerian covens. After being turned down by High Priestesses such as Patricia Crowther, he managed to get a copy of the Gardnerian Book of Shadows and shortly after started enthusiastically initiating others into his own version of Wicca.

While both the Gardnerian and Alexandrian traditions have proven their worth, withstanding the deaths of their founders and spreading all over the globe, the details of how they were started raises serious doubts whether a formal initiation is necessary for a modern mystery religion to be meaningful to its practitioners. Traditions have to start somewhere and a tradition can be just as meaningful for the first-generation practitioners as for subsequent generations.

Witchcraft lore in the UK is also rife with mentions of lone witches and sorcerers, practitioners of magickal arts who are completely self-taught and just as effective as the most skillful coven member. If Gardnerian and Alexandrian Wicca were truly intact continuations of a previous system then it is highly likely that solitary witches could be considered authentic Wiccans even though they have never undergone formal initiations. It is more likely, in fact, that the traditions sprang up when solitary practitioners decided to share their methods with others and practice in groups. Coven work, then, might very well be the descendant of solitary witchcraft rather than a distinctly different religious system as some might suggest.

If Gardner or Sanders had instead claimed that they were starting up brand new religious systems then they could have established rules denying the title of Wiccan (which did originate in its current usage with modern witchcraft) to non-initiated solitary practitioners of witchcraft. Since they claimed they were merely passing on an intact tradition, an existing tradition of witchcraft which did include solitary uninitiated practitioners within the body of lore, it becomes much more difficult to exclude solitaries from being considered Wiccans.

Another way to look at the question of initiation as a requirement for a religion to be a mystery religion is to consider that initiation means a number of things. When scholars identified initiation as being a requirement for ancient mystery religions they were speaking of formal acceptance into the group through a ritual of welcoming. In ancient times many religions were open to all, considered part of community life and culture, without any requirement for participants to formally join the faith. In those times, when religious groups like the cults of Eleusis sprang up, it was rather distinctive to have an exclusive membership.

Today, however, many if not most religions require formal acceptance into the group for a participant to be considered a part of that religious sect. In Christian terms this is accomplished through confirmation or baptism. Now it is much more rare for a religious group to accept anyone who wanders in off the street as a full member without any form of acceptance ritual. But despite the popularity of initiation rites not all religions that use them are really mystery religions.

So initiation as a formal acceptance to a group probably isn't a key characteristic in identifying a mystery religion. It might have been key in the past but it is no longer a distinguishing factor that sets a mystery religion apart from other religions that are clearly not mystery faiths.

Initiation has another meaning however which does fit in well with the idea of a mystery religion. If initiation is considered to be a spiritual experience of a very real and personal contact or communion with the Divine then it fits in well with the mystery religion idea. In the ancient mystery religions the ritual of acceptance into the group was more than just a formal acceptance but an attempt to trigger a spiritual awakening experience or spiritual initiation. It is the spiritual initiation, the direct contact with the Divine, which makes the religion a mystery religion.

In Wicca initiation ceremonies are patterned after the ancient mystery religions with the ceremony designed to try and fulfill both functions. Initiations act as a formal acceptance into the group and also attempt to trigger the spiritual awakening or spiritual initiation. It is important to note, though, that the spiritual initiation is encouraged by ritual but not necessarily caused by ritual. Spiritual initiations are bestowed by the Divine and not by mortals no matter how determined we might be.

In her book "The Training and Work of an Initiate" Dion Fortune discusses at some length the fact that spiritual initiations are the ultimate goal of magickal work but are not at our beck and call. A person can receive a spiritual initiation before, during, or after a ritual initiation into a group. Spiritual initiations might come to a person who never joins a formal group and members of formal groups also might never receive spiritual initiations.

If it is really spiritual initiations that are the important type of initiation within mystery religions, it follows that a religion could be a mystery religion without rituals of formal acceptance into a group. Solitary practitioners who are self-taught, then, can be practitioners of mystery religions if they have a focus on seeking spiritual initiation. Solitaries can and do seek direct contact with the Divine and thus could achieve a spiritual initiation as can someone who is an accepted member in a formal group.

Secrets

When Gerald Gardner first started promoting Wicca the only way to gain access to the Book of Shadows, the ritual and theological sourcebook handwritten by each member, was to become a formal initiate. The only way to learn how things were done was to be accepted as a member.

As often happens, things changed as the religion grew. Different factions started to appear as different traditions or sects that practice Wicca in their own ways. Some Wiccan spokespeople, including Gerald Gardner and Alex Sanders, were quite willing to share information with the media that other Wiccans considered secret. Alex Sanders, for one, was quite willing to invite news reporters and cameras to be present at various rituals. Gardner, a bit more reserved, did quite a bit of publicity work himself in letting the world know about Wicca. His various books set the example by describing bits of lore and in some instances provided almost complete rituals including the first-degree initiation rite. Other Wiccan authors followed his lead and over time ended up publishing pretty much everything that was in Gardner's personal Book of Shadows, which was the original all later copies drew from.

While it is true that most of the secrets of Wicca are published now, the information is still considered occult, that is, hidden, and not much use to a person unless they actually put it into practice. A person who is learning on their own exclusively has to do a lot of research and needs to be determined in order to learn Wiccan philosophy and practice. To put it into daily use and make it one's spiritual path requires a lot of work.

As with initiation, considering a mystery religion to be a spiritual path where there is secret knowledge might have been accurate when examining ancient faiths. If the basic knowledge in a religion was once secret but is now publicly available does the religion stop being a mystery religion? Do vows of discretion regarding the discussion of specifics count as secrecy? Is secrecy really a determining factor for a mystery religion?

Ecstatic

The American Heritage Dictionary (Fourth Edition: 2000) lists the word *ecstasy* as traced back to the Greek *ekstasis* which means astonishment, distraction, or displacement. In more modern usage *ecstasy* is often considered to be a state of intense joy or delight, and in spiritual terms is a mystical trance where one is engulfed in direct union with the Divine. The word *rapture* when used to describe an emotional state is similar in many ways as it too has mystical overtones. When one is in a spiritual ecstasy one's perceptions open to a direct awareness of the Divine presence and heightened emotions of love overwhelm and overflow to touch everything.

The use of techniques to induce spiritual ecstasy is probably the key characteristic of mystery religions that truly distinguishes them from other religions. The ancient mystery cults were religions of individual and very personal communion with the Divine. They were religions where deities were not just abstract concepts to be discussed in dry dialogues but were living entities and forces that worshippers experienced first-hand. Mystery rites involved lifting the celebrants out of their routine existence, their mundane perceptions of life and existence, to a new awareness and identification with something greater than themselves.

Celebrants of Bacchic rites were often described as being in a divine frenzy; Eleusinian initiates underwent a personal spiritual rebirth; devotees of Mithras re-enacted the sacred myths and subsumed their personalities in that of the Divine. In pre-modern stereotypical witchcraft lore the infamous witches' sabbath or sabbat is depicted as an orgy of feasting and dancing and often sexual revelry with other witches as well as nonhuman supernatural entities. Modern Wiccans are more like followers of Voudou than they are like stereotypical Satanists. Wiccans conduct rites to channel

Divine energy and knowledge in rituals such as Drawing Down the Moon and seek to commune with various spiritual forces in meditation and pathworking. There is also a strong encouragement to enjoy life for as it says in the Wiccan Charge of the Goddess "all acts of love and pleasure are My rituals." The Divine is believed to experience things through worshippers and indeed through all existence so Wiccans frequently perceive even mundane life as flooded with the Divine presence.

Wicca is an experiential religion where one is expected to actively seek out contact with the Divine through a multitude of methods. It is not a religion where the worshippers' access to the Divine is exclusively maintained through the intermediary of authorized clergy. In Wicca each participant is a witch and priest/ess in their own right. Wicca is often described as religion without the middleman; the idea of a direct relationship between worshipper and the Divine is drawn specifically from the classical mystery religions.

The criterion of ecstatic practice is therefore met in Wicca just as it was in ancient mystery religions. It is likely that this characteristic is the essential core, the Mystery, of mystery religions. It is also likely that the ecstatic experience of communion with the Divine is the essence of the path of the mystic. There is a lot of overlap between the path of mystery and the path of the mystic. Perhaps they are merely different methods of achieving the same goal.

Mysteries In Wicca

Some Wiccan authors insist that mysteries can't be verbalized but must be experienced. This is perhaps a bit of an evasive attempt to try and maintain that elusive secretiveness, a sense that Wicca is still an exclusive group outside the realm of the mundane.

In mystical religious systems those who have attained even a glimpse of Divine communion seem to have no problem with attempting to describe their experience, to share it with others through self-expression. In fact it is often those considered to be mystics who produce the most compelling art. A poet, painter, or sculptor who attempts to express their mystical experience is not usually actively discouraged from sharing their experience. It is true that at one time, and still in many circumstances today, keeping one's spiritual path a secret was necessary to avoid persecution or discrimination. Western society is changing though and it is becoming more common for Wiccans and other Pagans to admit their faith openly. It is also possible to express one's spiritual insights through art without specifically identifying your religious affiliations or titles. Perhaps the rationale behind the Wiccan code of silence regarding mysteries needs to be evaluated and reconsidered at least for some instances. There are varying forms of secrecy regarding the mysteries that work quite well for other spiritual groups. Why should Wiccans insist on total secrecy even when talking with other Wiccans? This policy ignores the benefits of sharing and attempting to express the inexpressible.

Mysteries, whether mystical, occult, or mundane, are appreciated best when they are experienced directly. We can and should seek inspiration from whatever source we find appropriate and should value direct experience over second-hand exposure. We try to trigger direct experiences of the Divine so we can see for ourselves what it is that the adepts and mystics are all talking about. We can read all about friendship, for instance, but until you have found a friend and have been a friend to someone else through the good times and the bad you won't really appreciate what the mystery of friendship is all about. However, to insist that we should not examine friendship in a scholarly way, to forbid attempts to express what friendship is all about in words and art, seems rather misguided and in fact could be seen to lessen the impact of the experience.

Some of the greatest works of art are the result of efforts to explain or embody mystical experience. No one seriously suggests the art replaces the actual experience. In fact when art is successful it is often recommended as a way to educate the mind, heart, and soul and prepare the observer for greater spiritual understanding. Art can be a trigger to spiritual awakening. If we were to insist that spiritual insights or experiences must never be expressed because they can't be contained in such an expression then the world would be a rather sad place. We would be denying the possibility for mystical experience to be reached through the catalyst of art.

Within overall Wiccan philosophy there are some concepts or mysteries that tend to predominate. The fact that we can give general names to them means that they can and will continue to be discussed. Some of the most common themes are birth, life, death, and rebirth. Other mystical themes that many Wiccans explore and experience include communion or union with the Divine, perceptions of the Divine as immanent, Divinity as being both male and female, the existence of nonphysical realms and beings, and sensing and working with spiritual or psychic energies.

Communion with the Divine

This is arguably the ultimate purpose of Wicca or any religion: the bringing together of the worshipper with the Divine. Within Wicca a large amount of the spiritual growth and ritual work is directed towards encouraging one to expand awareness beyond our everyday boundaries to perceive and identify with the Divine, whether in the form of a specific deity or force or with something more abstract. In mystical literature this is often described as bathing in the light of the Divine, being in the direct presence of the Divine, finding nirvana, or achieving enlightenment or illumination. In occult and magickal literature this is described in terms of attaining cosmic consciousness, peak experiences, invoking or evoking deity, attaining knowledge of and conversation with one's Holy Guardian Angel, or meeting one's Higher Self.

Mystics and magickal practitioners who are seen as being true adepts, the highest level initiates, are those who have practiced and grown to the point that they are able to achieve this direct experience of union with the Divine for more than just brief glimpses, where they are considered transformed and usually in a state of permanent communion.

Divine as immanent

Mainstream Judaism, Christianity, and Islam tend to teach that the Divine is transcendent. In an exclusively transcendent worldview, the Divine is separate from the physical plane, usually existing in a separate realm known as heaven. This worldview often reinforces an attitude of duality or conflict between the spiritual and the physical realm. Nature and flesh are seen as tainted and weak, while the spiritual is perceived as being the only thing of worth. Worshippers are encouraged to reject the physical realm in favor of an invisible spiritual realm that they will often only get to perceive after death.

Wicca, however, tends to encourage a pantheist or panentheist worldview. In pantheism, the Divine is seen as being immanent, present in everything, in the physical realm in all its manifestations. Panentheism sees the Divine in everything, but also sees the Divine as including a nonphysical level that is beyond the physical.

One common ritual goal in Wicca is to perceive and attune with the spark of Divinity which is in each of us and also to learn to recognize and honor that holy presence in everything around us from the trees, to rocks, to animals, lakes, sun, moon, sky. When the Divine is considered immanent, present in everything, then we must strive to learn to see the holiness in everything.

Divine as both male and female

Many Wiccans are at heart polytheists. The Divine manifests to us in a multitude of names and forms. Regardless whether we see the multiplicity of deities as independent entities, or whether we consider them to be different faces of One Supreme deity, we at least acknowledge there is more than just one valid deity name and form.

Since there are many deity names and forms that are each worthy of respect and worship Wiccans have no problem with acknowledging that deity can manifest in male, female, or some other gender configuration. Since we see frequent examples of a male-female sexual dynamic in nature it is perfectly normal for Wiccans to worship a paired Goddess and God.

As we explore and grow in our relationship with the Divine we discover how deity manifests in our lives through male and female characteristics and qualities. Balance is a key tenet of Wicca. We tend to seek out those things in our Divine worship that remind us of the magnificent complementary dance of energies that is existence. Many Wiccans consider polarity to be a primary concept in their philosophies; polarity is essentially the interaction between different forces, at its most basic level between Goddess and God.

Experience of realms other than the physical

Wiccans tend to see the world as much more than just solid objects in physical interaction in mathematically predictable ways. We are gifted with imagination, intellect, and emotion as well, which we consider to be both magickal and Divine.

We all experience other realms through dreams and as practitioners of magickal arts we work with our dream-capacities to explore inner and outer realms, to learn more about the surrounding world and ourselves. We see the cultivation of imagination and its expression in the physical realm as partaking of Divine creation.

Meditation, deep prayer, pathworking, and dream work are just a few of the methods Wiccans tend to use in order to experience nonphysical realms.

And like all mysteries there is much written and said about it but it's best when one does the work and gains first-hand experience.

Tapping into energy within and without

Wiccans work to perceive and when appropriate manipulate the ebb and flow of energies that are all around us. Seasonal tides, influences of the moon, sun, and heavenly bodies, the power of emotions, the energy that courses through our bodies and keeps our hearts pumping and our breath flowing in and out, are all as much a part of us as our skin, our blood, our bones. Learning about the cycles of things, the peaks and lows, allows us to take advantage of these things and use them to our advantage.

There are a number of occult theories that attempt to explain these energies and in many cases teach how these energies can be perceived, nurtured, and directed. These energies are called different things in the competing theories: mana, Odic force, prana, Kundalini energy, etheric energy, astral light, chi, auric energy, ki. It is not uncommon for some Wiccans to undergo martial arts or yoga training in parallel with their Wiccan training as a way to better understand and manipulate these energies. It is also quite common for Wiccans to incorporate one or more of these basic theories into their philosophy and work a Wiccan variation of the standard methods taught within that energy system.

Probably the most common energy theory that has been incorporated into Wiccan practice is the Indian theory of chakras or energy centers in the body carrying what is known as Kundalini energy. In this theory there are various locations in the physical body (and some outside the body) that act as accumulators and channels for this mystical life-force energy. The seven commonly used chakras are identified as:

1. the root chakra, at the base of the spine (the end of the tailbone)
2. the procreative chakra in the genitals (testicles in the male, ovaries in the female)
3. the solar plexus chakra, around the belly area
4. the heart chakra
5. the throat chakra
6. the third eye chakra, in the forehead between and just above the eyes
7. the crown chakra, at the top of the head

Kundalini energy is often thought to originate in the human body in the root chakra and then pass upward in sequence through the other chakras to finally reach the crown chakra. Other energy paths identified essentially as male and female are also believed to rise up from the earth and through the chakras or down from the heavens and through the chakras. In Wiccan chakra exercises it is common for the energy to be perceived as rising up from the depths of the earth, into the root chakra, and then through the other chakras to the crown chakra often using the visual metaphor of a tree. It is also common to perceive stellar energies being drawn down from the skies and into the body through the crown chakra, essentially going in the reverse direction of the earth energy coming up from below. If both earth and stellar energies are being drawn in during a single working, they can be drawn up and down respectively to meet and mingle in the heart chakra located in the middle of the seven-chakra sequence.

Each chakra has a series of correspondences or images associated with it. One common set of correspondences assigns a colour to each chakra, going through seven colours of the rainbow with red linked to the root chakra, orange to the procreative chakra, yellow for the solar plexus, green for the heart, blue for the throat, indigo for the third eye, and then violet for the crown chakra. Imagining the chakras glowing with their respective colours in sequence is one very useful way to activate the chakra energies through visualization.

Some sophisticated chakra theories postulate more than just seven chakras located in the body and offer more detailed exercises and associations with each center. For example, some describe energy centers in the hands, in the feet, and associated with other parts of the body and specific internal organs, or even located outside the body. One commonly mentioned external chakra is located about eighteen inches above the head and is known by some adepts as the Transpersonal Point. This chakra is believed to be a point of pure white light that connects us to the Divine and also to each other. Most Wiccans, however, use the simplified seven-center theory with great success.

Directing energy to achieve goals

In life we can choose to be the protagonists of our stories or we can linger back and let circumstances carry us along. People who use magick, including Wiccans, are usually those who desire to control their own destinies. They are not content to let things just happen to them. When they decide they want to achieve something they work towards that goal until it is achieved.

Working magick is all about determining one's goals and then actively manipulating circumstances and forces in order to attain those goals. Magick is about doing, reaching, directing, bending. The word *Wicca* is etymologically related to the word *wicker*, which is bent and shaped to produce useful objects. Some Wiccans describe magick as the art of bending consciousness or reality to conform to one's will. Sometimes the changes we induce are in our surroundings, in things outside ourselves. Other times the changes that occur are primarily within ourselves. Sometimes reaching a goal means we must grow rather than expect outside forces or objects to change at our command.

Magick tends to work by following the path of least resistance. There are many stories told about a witch or magician who performs a spell to achieve a goal only to find the method by which the goal comes about was not quite the way they envisioned it. For instance, a person who does a spell for money might find that they do get the money requested but in the form of an inheritance resulting from the death of a loved one. A wise magician or witch knows how to accurately assess the situation and then focus on changing the most appropriate energies, objects, circumstances, or ideas. A successful witch or magician strives for the wisdom to know how and when to be flexible in order to achieve goals, to know when and how to act, and also to know when it is wisest to not act. When we attempt to bring about change we must be willing to accept the consequences of our decisions even when those consequences were not exactly what we expected.

Witches and magicians who study energy systems such as the chakra system from India, the chi or ki systems of China, or theories of mana or orgone energy usually incorporate these ideas into their spellwork. Magick ritual and spellwork frequently involve tapping into these energy systems, building the energy, and then directing the energy towards specific goals. Items can be consecrated and charged, runes and sigils drawn with mystical energy, cones of power raised and released at their targets. Identifying circumstances and influences affecting a goal is the intellectual part of spellworking but actively raising and manipulating energy and knowing how and when to act is the practical part that gets the work done.

Categorizing Magick

Magickal work can be classified into two categories based on the types of goals involved: mundane and spiritual. Mundane goals include attempts to change circumstances of health, luck, love, and wealth. Spiritual goals include attempts to attain contact and eventually establish a relationship with something greater than yourself, usually perceived as a deity or divine force. Mundane magick is practical magick. Spiritual magick is that which tries to help us evolve beyond our human limitations and connect with the Divine.

What Are Thaumaturgy And Theurgy?

Both thaumaturgy and theurgy derive from Greek and relate to magick. According to The American Heritage Dictionary of the English Language (Fourth Edition: 2000) *thaumaturgy* is from the roots *thauma* which means wonder, and *ergon*, work. The same source lists *theurgy* as originating in the Greek word *theourgia*, which translates as sacramental rite or mystery. The definitions of both thaumaturgy and theurgy are given as working miracles usually with the assistance of the Divine.

Within the magickal community thaumaturgy is a label usually applied to mundane or practical magick while theurgy refers to spiritual magick. In occult literature thaumaturgy is sometimes described as black or grey magick and theurgy as white magick. Thaumaturgy is also sometimes referred to as low magick and theurgy as high magick. It is important to realize that value judgments associated with the terms *high* and *low*, *black* and *white* are misleading.

The goal of theurgy is described in a number of ways in occult and religious literature but all essentially explain the same thing. Ceremonial magicians speak of theurgy as the "Great Work." Aleister Crowley describes the goal of high magick as achieving knowledge of and conversation with one's Holy Guardian Angel. Cabbalists attempt to work their way through their theoretical magickal structure of the universe, the Tree of Life, to experience and integrate with the various spheres or sephiroth until they attain the highest, Kether, the Crown, which represents the most pure form of the Divine. Among followers of Voudou the fortunate faithful achieve a state of divine possession in which they are "ridden" by gods, ancestral spirits, or entities that are considered to be both. In traditional Wiccan ritual, core rites include invocation of deity into the bodies of the high priest and priestess, such as in Drawing Down the Moon, Drawing Down the Sun, and the performance of the Great Rite, a symbolic reenactment of union between Divine forces.

The goal of theurgy is also the goal of mysticism: union with the Divine. Where the ceremonial magician traditionally seeks Divine union through religious rites the mystic follows a more individual, meditative, and down to earth philosophy. The ceremonial magician works through ritual to exalt their consciousness to a more pure level and therefore come into communion with a greater reality. The mystic seeks to overcome our customary alienation from individual awareness of the Divine Presence by conscious immersion in a daily cycle of living, contemplation, and tranquility.

Thaumaturgy is magick performed for practical ends. Working magick to heal, to glimpse the future, to resolve everyday concerns are all thaumaturgical. Since most charms, spells, and forms of divination are focused on dealing with the problems of living, they are thaumaturgical magick. Summoning spirits, deities, or ghosts for advice or to assist the magician is thaumaturgy unless the assistance requested is to help induce Divine communion.

Many modern practitioners of magick consider spells to be a form of elaborate prayer enacted for specific purposes. The reverse is also therefore true: prayer is a form of simplified spellwork. By looking at the goals of specific prayers, they can be classified as either theurgical or thaumaturgical. Prayers whose sole purpose is to help the worshipper identify with and commune with the Divine are theurgical. Prayers designed to ask for assistance are thaumaturgical. To say that thaumaturgy is by definition evil magick is a gross oversimplification and does no justice to practitioners' intentions that are typically good or neutral rather than evil.

Thaumaturgy And Theurgy in Wicca

Wicca is a religious form of witchcraft and therefore is a system of religious magick. Like most religions, one of the major goals of Wicca is to help the worshipper develop a close personal relationship with the Divine. While this theurgical emphasis is dominant, Wicca is also a very practical religion. Wiccans see personal development and fulfillment as an expression of reverence for the gift of life. Working to improve one's self or to improve the conditions here on the physical plane is a very real way to honor the

Divine that is present in this world. Thaumaturgical magick is therefore just as integral to Wicca although sometimes of secondary importance when compared to theurgy.

A number of standard practices in Wicca can be identified as theurgical while others are thaumaturgical. Casting the circle, identifying and consecrating holy space, is theurgical. It is an act of focusing one's attention on a personal connection with the universe and with the Divine. It is a conscious act of setting aside time and space to commune with forces greater than us.

Drawing down the moon or drawing down the sun and indeed any ritual that involves requesting a Divine force to be expressed through the body of a worshipper is inherently theurgical. Similarly, prayers or invocations requesting a deity to be present are theurgical so long as specific favors are not the primary goal of the petition.

Celebratory rites such as sharing of cakes and ale are also theurgical as they are symbolic communion with the Divine. Some Wiccan cake and ale rituals mimic the Christian idea of the ritual meal representing the essence of the Divine that is then consumed and absorbed by the participants. In other cases, though, cakes and ale are seen as sharing the bounty of the harvest among worshippers and the Divine in equal measure.

Consecrating ritual tools is a thaumaturgical act. It is the process of purifying and charging ritual objects for the purpose of magickal use by a specific person or group. These ritual objects are used in both theurgical and thaumaturgical magick but the consecration process itself is thaumaturgical.

The vast majority of spells are thaumaturgical in that their goals are to heal, to protect from harm, to inspire, or to bring about changes in the physical world. Spells are eminently practical and are thus thaumaturgical. It is possible to perform spells with the purpose of opening one's perception to communion with the Divine, but this goal is usually sought through direct acts of worship and celebration rather than through spellwork.

Why Both Are Important

Thaumaturgy as a form of magick is just as valid and important as theurgy. The differentiation in terms is meant really to illustrate the difference in goals rather than value of the magick itself. Magick itself is neither good nor evil, and both thaumaturgy and theurgy can be conducted in both ethical and unethical ways.

Wiccans and Witches as a whole are not bound by the dogma of either mystical or ceremonial magick philosophies that hold the unseen world as more valid than the physical realm. Many Wiccans in particular hold as a central tenet of their philosophy the concept of pantheism, that Deity is in everything, or panentheism, that Deity is in everything and Deity is much greater than the sum of its parts. To Wiccans, the rejection of the material world is a rejection of part of Deity. If the Divine is present in everything, then rejecting the physical world is an insult to the Divine. Thaumaturgy might be concerned with material goals, but to pantheists and panentheists thaumaturgy can be just as valid a form of reverence as theurgy. By trying to make the physical realm a better place for others and for ourselves we are showing reverence for the Divine. The physical realm is a gift the Divine has honored us with and we are honor-bound to show it reverence. A balanced outlook including both the material and spiritual realms is truly the position of the Witch, one who is in-between: we are dwellers of that space that is not a space; in time that is not a time.

Chapter 4:
Sources of Inspiration

Historical and Other Sources of Inspiration

Knowing Where We Come From

Ideas rarely ever spring up disconnected from everything else. Sometimes the influences that lead to an idea are obscured, but if we examine history and the circumstances around the idea's appearance, we can usually discover where the idea came from. Groups are the same: they rarely spring up from nothing. People who form groups draw their ideas from somewhere although they might combine those ideas in new ways. By looking at the origins of groups and ideas we can see how they developed and also start to truly see the unique and new elements that were previously unknown.

Gaining an appreciation for history helps us to perceive strengths and weaknesses that we might not have realized existed. Being aware of the possible weaknesses helps us to plan around them or correct the fault that lead to the weakness. Knowing about the strengths allows us to build them up even more and provides a solid foundation to build new strengths.

Groups that are ignorant of their own history have an unfortunate tendency to repeat the same mistakes over and over again. Weaknesses can grow and in some cases prove to be so great that the group collapses as a result. Unacknowledged strengths, too, can prove to be a problem if allowed to grow unchecked. A group that does not consciously examine its own strengths might find that it ends up evolving away from its original foundation and is no longer what it originally set out to be. If magick is primarily about conscious awareness and manipulation of circumstances, then magickal groups must strive for conscious understanding and control of their own group process and development.

The Web of History: All Is Connected

Except in extremely rare circumstances, cultures develop in relation to other cultures in their general area. Even cultures that are located at a distance can be an influence through trade and through secondhand exposure through other cultures that are closer geographically.

For example, the culture of English-speaking western nations has been influenced by a wide variety of societies through history. Our language is a descendant of Anglo-Saxon, with French and other romantic language influences mixed in and still quite evident. Our alphabet is based on the Latin predecessor, which is drawn from the Greek alphabet. Our numbers come from Arab sources. Christianity, the most common religion currently in English nations, is a Semitic faith that originated in the Middle East with an Egyptian influence.

Genetically there is Celtic heritage flowing through English veins and many remnants of Celtic folklore survive in family and community life even today. Our calendar of annual celebrations, whether Christian or Pagan, are drawn from Germanic, Norse, and Dutch origins melded with Roman, Celtic, and Christian ideas. Culture is eclectic at its very core.

The human family tree is interrelated with distinct branches springing from common sources with frequent instances where diverse branches come together and branch away again weaving into a complex and beautiful pattern. In such a structure is there really such a thing as a pure lineage? Which branch can truly claim that it is not connected to the others and has no external influences that have been drawn into its identity?

It seems that we humans have a desire to make easy classifications of the things around us as though pinning labels on things allows us to control our world and creates some stability. Labels are useful tools that allow us to communicate but we have to be careful to not force the things we are labeling to try and conform to our arbitrary classifications. If we must force labels upon things we should do so with a real awareness of what it is we are doing and at least an inkling of the consequences. We must also strive to realize that labeling is an artificial distinction that we use to enable communication and our labels are merely conveniences and not necessarily the hard reality of things.

Historical religious eclecticism

Students of religious history are usually quite familiar with the idea of tracing sources. They can usually recite standard identified influences that lead to the formation of major religious groups. For instance, it is no secret that the Christian church drew upon a Jewish base, adding in many ideas and practices from Rome, and also included many things from other cultural groups in the Mediterranean and United Kingdom as the religion spread. Authors such as the Episcopal bishop John Spong have produced many interesting volumes tracing the diverse historical and ideological influences that are firmly embedded in mainstream Christianity. Religious and historical scholars have done the same for many religious and cultural groups as a matter of the normal course of study and research. Very few groups have truly developed their spiritual and societal systems in isolation.

Scholars such as the popular historian Ronald Hutton have done a lot of excellent work in researching and presenting the historical roots of modern Wicca in particular and the Pagan movement in general. Hutton's "The Triumph of the Moon" is considered by many to be a classic although at the time it was published it was considered controversial as it firmly debunked many long-standing assumptions and myths about Wiccan history. Hutton does a solid job of showing the sources that Gardner drew upon and shows how Gardner happened to be the right person in the right place at the right time to tap into a spiritually and ideologically eclectic trend that made the rebirth of Pagan spirituality possible in the English-speaking world.

Scholars such as Joseph Campbell have spent a lifetime exploring common themes in mythology and religion across diverse cultures. In some cases it is possible to see how an idea started in one group and then was picked up by other groups that came in contact with the originators. As an idea spreads it often changes, taking on new emphases or sometimes getting turned completely around to mean the opposite of its original significance. Some of the changes are a result of modifying the idea to make it fit in with other ideas, and some changes are more a result of fashions or fads or political influence rather than logical consistency. Tracing the evolution and expression of a particular idea across cultures and groups can reveal a lot about the goals and ambitions of those groups.

Historical magickal eclecticism

Magickal practice has always had a strong eclectic element. Every new magickal system that develops builds on the ideas of predecessors, and while there are often new and innovative techniques and ideas in new systems there are also very clear links to past systems. Many systems provide a new way of looking at old and diverse material, innovating rather than inventing whole new techniques of magick.

Some of the most obvious examples of magickal eclecticism through the ages is documented in "The Greek Magickal Papyri in Translation" edited by Hans Dieter Betz. This book, published by the University of Chicago Press in 1986, is a handy compilation of the hard work of various scholars who have been translating ancient tablets and manuscripts that date back as far as the second century BCE and up through the fifth century CE. The interesting thing to note is that it is quite common to see spells or incantations that are directed at a variety of deities drawn from a number of different cultures. One love spell[4], for example, requests the assistance of Kore (Greek), Adonis (Greek, adopted from Semitic), Ereshkigal (Assyro-Babylonian), and Anubis (Egyptian) along with others. The ancient magician who wrote this spell obviously didn't think it was a bad idea to draw on a variety of sources to accomplish magick.

More recent magickal groups have also felt quite free to borrow ideas from other cultures. Helena Petrovna Blavatsky, who founded Theosophy in 1875, wrote her epic "Isis Unveiled" as a cross-cultural examination of spiritual and magickal ideas with an overall synthesis to try and draw it all together into a coherent whole. She took a large amount of her inspiration from the philosophies of India, combined them with Christian and Jewish mysticism, and presented the result to her mostly English-speaking audience as Theosophy.

Another prominent organization with mystical and magickal overtones was the Freemasons. They, too, are a predominantly Christian organization but have strong elements drawn from Egyptian and Greek mythology and philosophy. Freemason imagery is evident in such mundane things as the printed currency of the United States of America: the back of the one dollar bill shows the Great Seal of the US depicting an eye in a triangle at the top of an Egyptian-style pyramid.

In the latter half of the 1800s William Wynn Westcott and Samuel Liddell Mathers founded the Hermetic Order of the Golden Dawn as an overtly magickal organization offering training and a structured degree system of initiations. Both Westcott and Mathers were previously involved in Freemasonry as well as a number of occult organizations. Israel Regardie published the bulk of the Golden Dawn materials in 1937 years after the organization had officially folded. It is clear from the published documents that the Golden Dawn system drew from pretty much anything that was available including Theosophy, Freemasonry, Indian spiritualism, as well as grimoires of ceremonial magick that were available at the time. The Golden Dawn was highly successful in its time and produced a number of members who went on to run other occult organizations that still operate today. Dion Fortune (whose led the Society of the Inner Light) and Aleister Crowley (who headed the Ordo Templi Orientalis, or OTO) are two examples of Golden Dawn initiates who continued the occult traditions through surviving organizations.

Gerald Gardner and other early Wiccans are known to have been familiar with trends and thought within the larger occult community. Doreen Valiente, one of Gardner's earliest and probably most influential high priestesses, openly acknowledged her familiarity with both Aleister Crowley's work as well as her admiration for Dion Fortune's work. Valiente frequently recommended their books to Wiccans, along with a diverse selection of other books on spirituality, mysticism, history, and occultism. It is not a secret that Gardner was acquainted with Crowley either. He visited Crowley in person not long before Crowley died in 1947 and obtained permission from Crowley to form a branch of the OTO. Gardner apparently didn't follow up on this, instead putting his energy into promoting Wicca.

Philip Heselton has published a lot of the evidence for Gerald Gardner's influences and sources in "Gerald Gardner and the Cauldron of Inspiration" (Capall Bann: 2003.) There is very little doubt that Gardner had the opportunity to explore many of the occult trends in the UK prior to settling on Wicca and putting energy into promoting it as a viable spiritual and magickal path.

Drawing on a variety of sources to produce an eclectic whole is actually quite common within the magickal community, and has been going on for a long time. It is not surprising then that many modern practitioners should also select an eclectic variety of sources in their own magickal work. If drawing from multiple sources worked well for the first Wiccans and pre-Wiccan magicians, then it should certainly be just as effective for Wiccans today.

Drawing On Your Ethnic Background

Each of us is born into this life with a complex web of ethnic and cultural connections. Our biological families provide us with a genetic heritage, sometimes predominantly from one particular culture or ethnic group, but just as often with a mix of ethnicity. Depending on where we are born geographically, where we live as we grow up, and where we live as adults we are also surrounded and included in a cultural group. This might mirror that of our own biological ethnicity but it might not. People move, families migrate to new homes. It is common now for people to live in geographic areas that are different from their ethnic homelands. We are influenced by all of these things as they contribute to our identities and how we live.

Drawing on one's ethnic or genetic background, as well as the culture where you grew up even though you might not have strong genetic ties with this culture, has the strength of immediate ties to support you. It's easier to immerse yourself in a culture and mythology when that culture and mythology is around you in everyday life. Often we take our own ethnic and geographical culture for granted because we see it all the time, and therefore tend to miss the sense of mystery and the exotic that people from other cultures or areas feel when they come to visit. It's an old truism that we rarely visit the tourist attractions in our hometowns. If we allow ourselves to see where we live, our own immediate culture and ethnic environment, with the perspective of an outsider we can discover a wealth of valuable insight. Living within an ethnic or geographical culture provides us with added insight into that culture that outsiders will rarely see. We can perceive the subtleties as well, which might be lost in the distraction of more visible elements that tend to attract the notice of tourists.

Many cultures base at least part of their spiritual systems on a reverence for ancestors. This is one way to help us to understand our individual place in the larger human family. We are able to trace the links we have with the past and hopefully also see the connections we have through blood to other families, clans, tribes, and ethnicities. We are never truly alone: we have thousands of years of bloodline coursing through our veins. Acknowledging and showing reverence for our ancestors strengthens our connection through space and time with the whole human race.

Drawing On Other Cultural Sources

Many modern Pagans feel affinities towards cultural or ethnic groups with which they don't have any obvious or immediate blood ties. Many in the UK and elsewhere in English-speaking communities feel drawn to ancient Egypt, for instance, or ancient Greece, or Rome, or the Middle East. Some are so attracted to these cultures that they devote their spiritual lives to worshipping deities from these genetically-foreign cultures.

Some people insist that one should only worship the deities of your genetic ancestors. This raises the problem of so-called "genetic purity;" is there anyone who truly has no ancestor in their past from a different ethnic background? Many in the British Isles, for instance, will have mixes of Celtic, Saxon, and Norse blood coursing through their veins, which historians note are all invaders who came to the British shores. This contact with other cultures often remains in the form of place names and archeological remnants; there is a very Egyptian-sounding River Isis in England, for example, and evidence that there was a temple of Isis in London. Only the most isolated communities can honestly claim to any sort of ethnic or genetic purity. In the English-speaking world in particular we are pretty much guaranteed to be of mixed ethnic backgrounds.

Other religious paths have survived quite well and are accepted as mainstream despite the fact that they are specific ethnic traditions that spread outside their original cultures. Christianity, Buddhism, and Islam are three very popular examples. Christianity and Islam are both offshoots of Judaism, which arose originally within a particular ethnic group in the Middle East. English-speakers tend to think of Islam as a Middle-Eastern religion still, without noticing that there are actually many ethnic groups under the Islam umbrella. There are also many vibrant Muslim communities around the world including in Asia particularly in the Philippines and Indonesia.

Buddhism is another excellent example of a religious tradition that quickly spread beyond its original ethnic group. It started in India as an offshoot of Hinduism, which itself is a very heterogeneous mix of different ethnic traditions. Buddhism spread across Asia, mingled with other traditions, and developed into a variety of different schools of thought and practice. The Dalai Lama is one well-known Buddhist leader and is head of the Tibetan branch but not necessarily the leader of all Buddhists. Buddhism, like Christianity and Islam, is found all across the world today in large and small communities.

If one's spiritual path is supposed to be about our individual and very personal relationships with the Divine then it does not make a lot of sense to judge others based on how the Divine has chosen to manifest to them. I might find the Divine appears to me as a Celtic goddess while my neighbor might find the Divine connects with them in the form of a Jewish prophet. The Divine touches our hearts and lives in ways we can't control regardless which forms we think It should take based on our ethnic or genetic heritage. It would probably be an insult to the Divine to reject a particular manifestation because of some arbitrary cultural political correctness. When we strive to listen to the Divine we should take note of when It speaks to us.

Drawing On Current Sources

All religious systems and spiritual traditions are new at some point in their lives, and if they have enough appeal, can last until they are considered to be so old that it's hard to remember a time when they weren't entrenched. But does the age of a particular system or practice make it more worthwhile?

Ideas that have been around for longer certainly have the advantage of being tested by others before us. If we trust what we are told it can save us time in trying to find workable practices or a coherent system. However, as a practice is transmitted through time it often gets changed to suit the various practitioners and can end up becoming a diluted and tamed down version of the original. At some point a practice that continues to be diluted will reach a point where doing nothing can produce the same results.

Even when we are considering ancient practices we still have to test them out to see if they are going to work for us. Not every practice will work for every person every time. Each of us needs to decide for ourselves whether the effort required for a particular practice justifies the potential reward. Does it fit in with our own experience and our own understanding of our relationship with the Divine? Does it bring some new understanding or a new way of relating? Does this practice, no matter how old or young, help us to grow?

Systems that were invented recently can actually have the advantage over older systems as they can be built on more current (and hopefully more accurate) understandings. With a healing ritual, for instance, an old method might be based on the assumption that illness is caused by demonic possession; a new method might be based on the assumption that illness is caused by a combination of biological sources (viral or bacterial infection, for instance) and bodily imbalances. Just because a method is older does not necessarily mean it is more accurate or effective.

Chaos magick is a perfect example of a modern magickal and spiritual system that in many ways can prove to be more effective than older established systems. The base philosophy is simple: if it works, use it! Practitioners strive to critically evaluate magickal techniques and theories and feel free to modify them to suit their own preferences or circumstances. If an idea would work better for them with a bit of adaptation then a Chaos magician sees nothing wrong with making the necessary changes. Exploration and results are primary with answers to the question "Why" being seen as helpful and interesting. Ideas are always open to evolution or extinction. If an idea should evolve into an obstacle then it is evaluated, possibly changed, and eliminated if necessary. As a result Chaos magicians are not as restricted by dogma or political motivations for maintaining ideas in a system and are flexible enough to change easily with new evidence.

Wicca is a religious system that as a whole is not plagued by dogma the way other established religions are. The Wiccan Rede's simple choice-positive statement "An it harm none, do what you will" expresses a commitment to autonomy inherent in Wicca. The Charge of the Goddess reinforces this with the statement that "all acts of love and pleasure are My rituals." Various sects within Wicca might establish their own rules and dogma but overall those restrictions do not apply outside that particular group. So long as this basic freedom is respected within Wicca at large there will be room for glorious variety. Those who wish to innovate are free to do so and those who wish to limit themselves to particular ideas or practices are also free to decide things for themselves.

Spirituality is not divorced from mundane concerns, everyday stresses and events, and psychological or physical well-being. New ways of looking at the mundane world are a reflection of things in the spiritual realms as well. We can use our new insights into mundane things to help us better understand the spiritual. We can use these insights to fine tune old spiritual ideas or practices or invent new ones that are more effective. Spirituality is not a dead science that has been completely explored and explained. Spirituality is a living part of our existence and as a living thing it changes and evolves as we do.

Drawing On Fictional Sources

Mythology is a tale that holds some spiritual truth or insight even though the story itself might not be literally true. Some myths start out as true events but become inflated with fictional details. Many myths have kernels of literal truth in them but the overall story is clearly fictional. Regardless whether the details of the story can be proven as literally true, the myth overall imparts some meaning that teaches us about some aspect of life, death, existence, and the Divine.

We often hold a rather peculiar opinion regarding myth today even among modern Pagans who use myth as a source of spiritual inspiration. We assume that to be valid as a myth a story has to have been told by some long-dead group of people or has to have come from a firmly established religion. It's as though our own myths, or myths which have been invented more recently within our own peer groups, could not possibly be as valuable. In many ways it's a manifestation of the cliché that the grass is always greener on the other side of the fence. Things from "somewhere else" are considered to be more valid than things that originated right here with us.

The myths of the ancient Greeks were originally told as brand new stories. Were they less meaningful when they were new? Perhaps the fact that they have withstood all these years, all the retellings, does say something about how the meaning transcends time and place. Are stories invented now, within our own families, neighborhoods, and tribes inherently less meaningful? Is it impossible for a new story to be invented that will eventually prove to be just as meaningful as the stories told by the ancient Greeks, Egyptians, or Mesopotamians?

When we look through history at how artists were treated in their time, whether they were sculptors, painters, musicians, or dramatists we can see that things really don't change that much. Mozart was a superstar of his time with fawning fans eager for a glimpse of the musician. His compositions have lived on well past his death testifying to his talent and the meaning in his work.

Today we have different media by which the creative tell their stories. Television is an ubiquitous medium, found in most homes, and bringing all sorts of fictional stories into our lives every day. Some people obsess over the stories that touch their lives. Some go to the extreme of patterning their whole waking lives after their favourite fictions. We might have some very extreme examples of fandom today but is it really much different in essence from what has always been the case when creative people touched the lives of their audiences?

Fictional stories of the long-distant past clearly influenced religion and spirituality with some recurring characters transformed into deities of one form or another. Were they ever actual people? Are any of the tales told about them literally true? When is it acceptable for fiction to be used as a basis for a spiritual path, for the founding of a religion?

In the 1960s a group of free spirits in the United States were so moved by Robert Heinlein's novel "Stranger in a Strange Land" that they decided to establish a formal religion based on the philosophy expressed in that book. They founded the Church of All Worlds and today have members all over the world. CAW proved to be quite influential in the larger Pagan community as well; for many years they published the magazine "Green Egg" which served as a key method for building contacts between diverse Pagans and also provided a much-needed forum for the exchange of ideas. CAW may have started as an entertaining way to spend some time but over the years has developed into a full-fledged religious institution just as respectable as any other sect.

Another interesting example of fiction influencing modern spiritual trends is found in George Lucas' "Star Wars" movie series. This fairy tale set in a space opera fictional universe draws heavily on the work of the scholar Joseph Campbell, in particular his famous study of mythology published as "The Hero With A Thousand Faces." Campbell identified numerous primal themes in myth which Lucas woven into an entertaining cinematic empire complete with magick, spirituality, and mysticism. The spiritual path of the Jedi, which forms a key element to the storyline, has touched so many people that thousands have taken to listing it as their religion on official forms. In Australia there was a successful lobby to have Jedi recognized as a valid religious option in the national census. The Jedi religion is still very new and is still likely a joke for many who profess to follow it but over time it could evolve into something more. It has a large enough following and provides inspiring models upon which a mature spirituality could easily grow.

Why should we think that fiction invented recently should be off-limits for use in spirituality when it is clearly acceptable when the fiction was invented in the distant past?

Modern Pagans, in the enviable position of developing their own spiritual traditions and systems, are able to select the myths that best suit their goals. In systems where there is no central authority to dictate for followers we have the freedom and the responsibility to decide for ourselves. We can decide to base our traditions on the myths that speak most clearly to our truths. We can decide for ourselves if the myths that speak to us are ones drawn from ancient times, from yesterday, or are myths that we haven't created yet.

In the end it comes down to our own individual relationships with the Divine. How does the Divine speak to us? Do we feel moved by a particular story, a particular character or myth? Do we see something greater than ourselves in a particular manifestation of the Divine? How does the Divine reveal Its presence to us? Where do we find the most meaningful spiritual truth?

Separating the Wheat from the Chaff: Critical Thinking Skills for Pagans

Information on the occult and on alternative religious paths such as Wicca is readily available now more than ever before. Most mainstream bookstores carry at least a few books with titles like "Easy Wicca" or "Casting Spells in 3 Simple Steps," or might have a wider selection from scholarly philosophical tomes to straightforward how-to books. It's easier than ever now to get your hands on information that used to be accessible only to those who had joined secret occult groups. Not so long ago you had to be lucky enough to find a group nearby and had to go through extensive training before being shown even the basics such as how to read Tarot cards or how to cast a magick circle.

People learn through a variety of methods that depend on the personality, background, and capabilities of both the student and teacher. Some people absorb concepts easily through reading, others through hearing the concept explained verbally, and others learn best through hands-on doing. Different teachers or sources of information have their own presentation styles that might emphasize one learning style over another. Sources of information, whether printed books or flesh-and-blood teachers, are also fallible and make mistakes. A good education is usually the result of the student seeking out a variety of sources so they can hopefully fill in the gaps in their education and correct misconceptions. Lessons that might not be absorbed through one source's teaching style can be picked up when repeated through another source's variation on that lesson. The most valuable lessons can come from the cheesy "Wicca Made E-Z" books just as they can from the densest scholarly tome. When the Divine speaks to us should we refuse to listen because the message is presented in a way other than a university course lecture?

With all this information now freely available it is easy to be overwhelmed with the diversity of choices. Increased diversity also brings a greater number of conflicting theories that attempt to explain the basic ideas. There is a greater need now for those exploring the occult in particular to develop a healthy skepticism. Knowing how to sort the useful information from the less useful is an essential skill for anyone exploring the occult.

One thing to keep in mind is that despite claims to the contrary occultism is more an art than a science. Science is a process where explanations are based on observations that can be repeated and verified, explanations are challenged and tested, and results must be reproduced reliably to justify those explanations. Explanations that are tested and disproved are abandoned. To be truly scientific tests must always produce the same results no matter who is conducting the experiment. Art, on the other hand, is very much a matter of personal preference. What is considered significant art for one person might be irrelevant for another. Things like proof and the ability to always reproduce results exactly are not necessarily important in art. Art is more about self-expression and an interaction between the individual and the environment or the individual and an idea, while science is more about hard and unchangeable facts.

There are certainly elements of science in occultism. There are myriad theories, systems, and explanations that try to describe the universe and the role of humanity. Some of these theories adopt scientific terms in an attempt to impress while missing the important point that to be scientific the theories must be testable and provable. Making a theory sound scientific unfortunately doesn't mean that it is.

Philosophers have identified an impressive list of fallacious arguments that can serve as helpful guards against mistakes. If one of the main points of studying occultism is to discover what really works for us, educating ourselves in how to spot errors in thought will help us to avoid wasting our time examining theories which prove groundless.

Common Fallacious Arguments

This is just a summary of common fallacious arguments. There are undoubtedly more, and are indeed the subject of numerous books.

Just because something is possible doesn't mean that it is real.

For example, it is possible that a species of dinosaur evolved to look just like modern humans, and this species is secretly dwelling among us. This does not mean that it is true unless verifiable proof could be produced. Many things are possible but aren't true.

Just because something hasn't been disproven doesn't mean that it must be true.

This is a common assumption among occultists. There are many people promoting their own occult theories who insist that their theories must be true since they haven't been disproved. To be true, an idea must withstand attempts to disprove it, but must also succeed in tests to prove it.

For example, I could claim that I can teleport from one location to another without physically moving through the intervening space. My claim isn't proven just because it hasn't been disproved; I must still prove that I can actually teleport.

Just because something hasn't been proven doesn't mean that it's false.

This is the flip side of saying something must be true because it hasn't been disproven. Often skeptics will go too far by insisting something could not possibly be true because it hasn't been proven.

For example, the claim that the Earth orbits the Sun was true even before Copernicus proved it mathematically. Proof just confirms the truth of a claim.

Just because something hasn't been explained doesn't mean it's supernatural.

The word *supernatural* means *outside the bounds of nature*. Just because something is not explained does not mean it is not natural. Many things are natural regardless of our inability to understand them.

There are frequent cases where an ill person recovers and doctors are at a loss to explain why the patient was healed. In many of these cases, people claim that the healing was miraculous or supernatural. With enough study, however, it is likely that science will discover a perfectly rational and natural explanation for why the illness was overcome.

Just because something seems real doesn't mean that it is.

Our senses can sometimes be fooled into accepting things that aren't really as they seem. For instance, optical illusions can fool our eyes into believing that in certain locations gravity appears to allow objects to roll uphill, or tall people appear to be the same height as short people. Careful examination of the situation though reveals that a clever use of angles and specific points of view can fool our eyes. Similarly, uncritical observers can be fooled by charlatans into believing they have witnessed occult phenomena when in fact they are seeing sleight-of-hand tricks.

Just because you believe something is true doesn't mean that it is true.

There are many beliefs that were firmly and genuinely held which have proven to be false. For instance, at one time it was common to believe that the Earth was the center of the universe, and the sun and other heavenly bodies orbited us. Many people firmly believed this was true although now it has been quite thoroughly refuted. Sincerity and strength of belief does not make something true.

Something doesn't become more true because more people believe it.

The vast majority of people once believed the sun and planets (and indeed the whole universe) revolved around the Earth. This belief was still just as incorrect regardless how many people believed.

Something doesn't become more true because it is old.

This is a common misconception in the occult community. Some people consider old ideas to be more true than new ideas merely because they are old.

An idea might be true if it has been proven repeatedly and has withstood attempts to disprove it. In this case, an idea that happens to be old might in fact be more valid than a competing idea that is newer, but the difference is really a matter of testing and not of age.

Old ideas are frequently replaced with new ideas in science, as old ideas are refuted and new ideas prove true through testing. It is this replacement of old ideas with new more suitable ideas that accounts for advances in technology and medicine. If older were always better, then we would still be using slide rules for performing calculations, and these new-fangled computers would likely not exist. And there would be no such thing as faster, more capable computers becoming available to make older models pale in comparison.

There is an external reality that is independent of our perceptions of it.

Trees that fall in the forest still hit the ground regardless whether there are any humans around to observe or not. Birds that sing in the depths of the Amazon still produce sound, fish in the unexplored depths of the ocean still eat and reproduce and die, microbes still flourish regardless whether any humans realize they are there or not. There are an uncountable multitude of stars, solar systems, and galactic objects that orbit and spin in their cycles from before we came to be and will exist long after we are gone. Humans are just a small part of the universe. It is supremely arrogant for us to act as though everything exists on some human whim.

The more a claim conflicts with proven facts, the more reason to doubt the claim.

The process of learning involves building on what you already know, what has already proven to be a collection of reliable explanations which accurately predict phenomena. When new claims appear to conflict with existing reliable explanations, there needs to be a good explanation for why this should be true. In many cases it turns out that the new claim involves a phenomenon that is not accurately understood, and the proposed explanation is misleading rather than illuminating.

Proving the validity of a claim through rigorous testing is the only way to truly prove or disprove a claim.

Just because someone is an expert in one field does not mean they are an expert in another.

People who are experts in one field sometimes succumb to an over inflated sense of self-importance, and act as though their expertise extends to topics they haven't studied. This sort of arrogance has a tendency to make the expert appear like a fool, and sometimes tarnishes their reputation even in their area of expertise.

One historical example of this is Margaret Murray's post-retirement books on witchcraft in Europe and the United Kingdom. Murray was (and still is) considered to have made valuable contributions in her area of expertise, Egyptology. Unfortunately she made a lot of rather remarkable claims about European history regarding witchcraft that have been refuted quite soundly by people who are actual experts in this field. While her witchcraft theories were largely discredited her Egyptology work is still considered authoritative.

Look at disproving as well as confirming evidence when evaluating a claim.

People who have a specific agenda or claim to promote are often accused of selective presentation of the evidence. It's easy to impress others with a claim when only supportive evidence is presented. A more honest approach is to present a truly representative sample of the evidence which includes both supportive and discrediting material. Allowing people to make up their own minds is always wiser than trying to force a particular conclusion.

A claim is scientific only if it is testable.

Some claims just can't be tested because of the nature of the claim. For example, I could claim that in the year 1037 for thirteen days there was a colony of extraterrestrials who lived on the surface of our Sun, protected from the harsh environment by special ice houses which slowly melted. Since we do not have any method available to us currently that would either confirm or deny this claim, it cannot be considered scientific. A claim must be testable and the test must be designed to produce either a clear positive or negative outcome if it is to be considered scientific.

The best hypothesis is one that makes the most accurate predictions.

Occultism is not just about exploring the mysterious but is also about finding practical methods to help us live more fully. Mystical or magickal theories are entertaining but need to have practical uses to make them last. If an explanation enables accurate results to be obtained then that explanation is more valuable than one that is strictly theoretical and untestable.

The best hypothesis is the simplest one that explains the widest range of observations.

Scientific study has shown that in many cases the simplest explanation turns out to be the most trustworthy, the explanation that is most useful in accurately predicting phenomena. When examining two competing explanations simplicity and elegance tends to win out through testing.

A hypothesis, no matter how extraordinary, should be accepted if no ordinary one would suffice.

The whole point of an explanation is to accurately describe what is being observed and possibly also show how the phenomenon is produced. If an explanation proves reliable for predicting the phenomena and withstands tests to disprove it then it is likely the explanation is valid. This is true even though the explanation might appear to be extraordinary. Sometimes skeptics go too far in doubting and disbelieve an explanation even after it has been clearly proven.

Anecdotal evidence does not substitute for tests to prove a claim.

Anecdotal evidence is one popular way to mislead towards a desired conclusion by only presenting supportive evidence. No matter what the claim there are always at least one or two people who are willing to come forward with amazing stories to support the claim. It doesn't matter there are thousands of instances where the claim is disproved as those will of course be carefully omitted.

Carefully constructed tests with obvious positive or negative possible results, which are repeatable and verifiable, are the only real way to confirm a claim. If a claim is to stand up it must be able to withstand possible negative evidence and show how it is true in spite of apparently disproving evidence.

An idea can be true even though its source is questionable.

It does help when examining a claim to look at the character of the person making the claim, to suggest possible motives and methods that this claim could prove to be deceptive. Despite the character of the messenger, however, a claim must still stand on its own merits and withstand appropriate tests. Just because the person making a claim might have been a liar in the past doesn't mean that they are necessarily telling a lie right now. Be skeptical but examine the evidence and then determine if the claim is true or not.

In the occult community, it happens that people will allow prejudices to influence them towards discounting information. For example, due to the image of the Ouija board in the media and pop culture many practicing occultists refuse to accept there might be any validity to its use. Messages or phenomena that come through the channel of the Ouija board are discounted out of hand as frivolous, while the same information or phenomena produced through other methods such as a pendulum, tarot reading, scrying, or dream work is considered valid. The message should be examined on its own merit regardless of opinions about the messenger that brought it forward.

Insulting the messenger does not make their message untrue.

When engaging in discussion about a particular claim some participants resort to insulting their opponent rather than addressing the issue. This tactic, called an ad hominem attack, does not invalidate a claim made by an opponent. If anything, it just makes the one flinging personal insults to appear incapable of supporting their own position. People with the facts to back them up don't need to resort to distraction to try and win the favour of onlookers.

An idea is not made more or less true by our emotions or desires.

Unfortunately we sometimes invest a lot of emotion into particular claims being true. Perhaps we really like someone who made the claim and are trying to strengthen a personal relationship with them so we take their side in believing a claim. Perhaps we have invested a lot of energy in examining a particular claim and would feel a loss of face if the claim were disproved. Perhaps the claim is one that we worked hard in crafting ourselves through our own personal observations and feel that an attack on our claim is an attack on our person.

In all these cases the strength of one's emotional involvement in a claim has no bearing on whether the claim is valid or not. We fight against having our emotions hurt, which is a natural reaction. It is a mistake, though, to assume that a belief must be more true if we have strong emotions about one particular explanation or claim.

Generalizations that are insufficiently tested should not be assumed to be true.

The validity of a claim is dependent upon its ability to pass tests designed to confirm or disprove the claim. It is often tempting to make a generalization based on observations of specific cases that have passed tests. While generalizations can be helpful they must withstand testing of their own to be considered valid. Just because a specific case has proven true does not mean a generalization based on the specific case is also true.

Just because one thing happens after another does not mean that the first caused the second.

Humans tend to perceive things in a linear fashion where one thing follows another in a chain of events. Sometimes two events follow one another in such a dramatic fashion that we automatically assume they are connected. If they are truly connected events then it is a natural assumption to believe that the first event caused the second to happen.

While it is true that everything is connected in some fashion, it does not mean that two sequential events are necessarily a cause-and-effect pair.

For example, if I were to start feeling ill immediately after shaking hands with a specific person I might assume that I had caught the influenza virus from that person. Unfortunately, it often takes at least a day after exposure to the flu before symptoms start to appear. This means that when I start feeling ill it is more likely that the person I shook hands with a day or more ago was the one who transmitted the virus to me. The cause of an effect does happen first, but it's sometimes deceptive because there is a lag between the cause and its effect showing up.

Putting Critical Skepticism In Practice: Tips For Critiquing An Occult Book

Don't judge a book based on findings that came out after the book was published. Do judge a book based on the material that is presented. Note the worthwhile information while acknowledging other sources of newer or more accurate material.

If you don't agree with an author's preferences it doesn't mean the author is stupid. We all have our own preferences; it is hypocritical to condemn others for theirs if we expect our own to be respected.

Don't judge a book harshly based on things you think should have been included. Judge a book based on what it does contain. If you are looking for history, then by all means pick up a book on history. Don't complain that the cookbook you are reading doesn't have information on history, or that a spell book doesn't go into deep theological discussions.

Is it fair to judge a book harshly because the book offers criticisms of other ideas or groups? Forbidding criticisms of other religious groups or ideas is a form of political correctness and stifles critical discussion. Offering criticisms is not necessarily being patronizing towards other ideas or groups. If you disagree with the criticism provide your reasons; condemning the act of criticism puts your own criticisms into question.

If you disagree with a statement you should state so but don't go the extra step of insulting the author or calling the statement stupid just because you disagree. If you feel so strongly that it is wrong then it should be easy for you to prove your stance. Explain why you disagree and let your readers decide for themselves. Leave the insults out of it; they have no place in a mature discussion or critique.

If you have your own particular grammar or spelling affectations be wary of criticizing someone else for their writing style. It makes you look hypocritical and puts your objectivity into question. It's OK to explain why you don't like a particular style so long as you acknowledge openly this is your own preference.

Comments about grammar don't really indicate anything about the quality of the information in the book. Do the ideas make sense? Are the ideas useful? Are the ideas accurate? Are the ideas important? Some of the most valuable books are difficult to read because the writing style is challenging. It does help if the grammar is clear but unless it is so overwhelmingly distracting it should be noted but not necessarily held as an indication of quality regarding the actual content. Good books do tend to be straightforward in their manner of presentation but a book can also be important despite confusing grammar or style.

Saying that your friends or family agree with you doesn't necessarily mean your statements are therefore correct. If you are correct you should be able to prove it. Saying that a book is bad "because everyone says so" does not prove anything other than what the current fashion trends are.

Definitions of terms, especially in a field that has its own specific terminology and usage, are often an important part of a book. It allows the author to explain how they will use specific terms so that the reader can better understand when those words are used later in the book. The terms as defined might be different from your own usage, and might differ from generic dictionary meanings. This is actually quite common and is the reason why many scholarly works take great pains to define terms up front. Language, like life, is rarely a tidy set of ironclad categories and meanings. We must be flexible in order to learn from shades and variations in meaning.

If you disagree with an author's definitions it does not mean the author is wrong. It does not mean they are stupid. It does not mean they are dense and incapable of understanding basic terms. On the contrary, it means they are being honest about how they will be using these specific terms later in their book. It is unfair to judge an author as inferior by criticizing their usage of a term if the author uses that term correctly according to the definitions they have provided.

Don't judge a book because of what you perceive to be inappropriate motives or based on value judgments about the life or personality of the author. A book critique should discuss the importance, value, and clarity of a book based on its own merits. If you would judge a book differently because you didn't know whom the author was then you might want to reevaluate whether you are being objective. On the other hand, it is acceptable to describe the context of a book by comparing it to other works by the same author or by comparing it with other similar books. Be careful to not let an overall opinion about an author taint your objectivity in examining the book you are critiquing, though. Sometimes we are overly generous in a book review because we like the author personally or condemn a good book because we don't like the author.

Critiquing is a process of evaluating a book in order to provide a recommendation to others. It is only fair to be open and honest about the reasons why we are critical or favorable of a particular book. We must be truthful about our motives for our statements so that our recommendation actually holds weight.

Chapter 5:
Wiccan Philosophy and Ethics

A Wiccan Mystical Philosophy

All Is Connected

Science has proven that everything is connected, even if only in remote ways through intervening connections. The air that we breathe, the water that we drink, are the same air and water molecules that have been recycling through the Earth's ecosystem since the time of our parents, our grandparents, our great grandparents, and back through all human history. It is the same air and water that prehistoric humans breathed and drank, the same air and water from the time of the dinosaurs, all the way back to when the Earth first formed from stellar gases and dust. The matter that makes up our world, the component chemicals and compounds, came from the same swirling pool of matter in space from which the Sun and the other planets of our solar system formed. And the matter that constitutes our solar system is from the same pool of matter from which the rest of our galaxy evolved.

As Aleister Crowley poetically summarized, "Every man and woman is a Star." We are truly made of the same stuff as stars if you think about it.

The study of ecology has also proven that life exists in a complex web of interdependence. In the food chain predators near the top of the chain rely on herbivores for their food and herbivores rely on plant life for their food. Plants rely on the soil being fertile which is the result of the excreted wastes and decomposing flesh of animals and plants. Insects, bacteria, fungi, and other scavengers facilitate the decomposition and enrichment of the soil through their consumption and excretion of rotting materials. If one part of the chain is disrupted or eliminated it affects other parts of the chain. Ecosystems are a constantly adjusting process of balance.

The Whole Is Infinitely Complex

In occult terms, the complexity of the universe is often described in terms of a microcosm or infinitely complex universe at the level of the very small. The microcosm is usually discussed in conjunction with the macrocosm, which is the infinitely complex universe at the scale of the massively huge. By juxtaposing the microcosm and the macrocosm we are able to see that there is a balance – things are equally complex at the large scale as they are at the small scale. By examining one or the other we are able to learn about both.

As you learn more about a subject it is common to discover that there is really a lot that we don't know. When we think we've covered all there is to know on a subject, it's usually a good indication that we've really just scratched the surface but haven't gotten deep enough to realize how much there is to learn. Experts who have studied specific topics for their whole lives frequently comment that there is still a lot they haven't discovered yet, whole areas of their topic that they haven't explored. It is only the foolish that think they know everything there is to know on a topic.

We Are Part of the Whole

Everything exists in a larger context, as part of a greater whole or system. Nothing is truly isolated or independent. If one thing is affected, it will have a ripple effect that touches on other things, which then touch on other things that are farther away. One rather poetic way of describing this web of connections is the claim that if a butterfly flaps its wings here, it can result in a hurricane on the other side of the world. It all depends on how the ripple effect spreads out, what other ripples interfere or amplify things, which determine larger effects from small initial causes.

Biologists study the interconnection between living things and call it an ecosystem. They study the delicate balance that exists, and observe how even slight alterations to one part of the web of life affects all the rest as it is forced to compensate. Physicists, chemists, and astronomers study interactions at the atomic or stellar and even galactic level and observe how each part affects the whole. Understanding how these complex balances work allows scientists to send tiny ships into the vastness of space and accurately direct them to massively remote targets. Physicists have used the knowledge of atomic level interactions to produce nuclear power plants, and on the destructive side, nuclear bombs. Chemists use their understanding of atomic bonds and interactions between elements to formulate new materials and substances such as plastics and even medicines. In each of these examples, knowledge of the interactions and balance between parts of the whole leads to understanding how to direct the balance to achieve specific goals.

Deity Is Immanent As Well As Transcendent

Many Wiccans consider deity to be immanent or present within creation. It is often described as deity being omnipresent; deity is seen to exist in everything, whether it is an animal, a plant, a person, rocks, water, the sky, the sun and moon, planets, everything. The idea that deity is present in everything in the physical realm is also called pantheism. *Pan* means *everything*, and *theism* refers *to the presence of deity or philosophy of deity.*

Many Wiccans believe in the existence of a nonphysical realm, a spiritual dimension that exists as well. Some theorize this nonphysical realm is connected to the physical or even combined with the physical to a point where it is impossible to really consider one separate from the other. There are some, though, who consider the nonphysical realm to be quite separate and distinct from they physical. The term transcendent is often used to refer to the idea that deity dwells in a separate nonphysical realm.

It is common for Wiccans to describe deity as being simultaneously immanent and transcendent, present both within the physical world and also in a nonphysical realm. This philosophical outlook is often called panentheism. Where pantheists consider deity to be present in the physical realm, panentheists consider deity be present in the physical realm and also in a transcendent realm.

There is no central authority for all Wiccans that specifies we must all adhere to just one of these philosophies of deity. Various Wiccan sects or traditions teach their own philosophies of deity. Some traditions don't require adherents to follow a common philosophy of deity and instead encourage individuals to decide for themselves. Scientists and philosophers constantly rework theories that explain the universe as new information is uncovered and old ideas are disproved. It's not unusual for spiritual communities like ours, or even individual Wiccans, to change their philosophy of deity as they learn more.

Magick Is A Way To Unite Spiritual Forces With Mundane Existence

Magick is a way to tap into and connect with forces that are greater than ourselves. Many Wiccans, for instance, practice magick as a way to attune to the forces of nature, the forces of the Divine. Magick is a way to bring the sacred into our daily lives. It helps us to recognize the miraculous wonders that exist around us all the time, to actively participate in the divine act of creation.

Many Wiccans are pantheists or panentheists, recognizing that the Divine exists in everything including us. Many who hold this viewpoint attempt to recognize and honor the Divine in all of its manifestations no matter how insignificant or obscure. While acknowledging and paying due respect to base instincts and forces of discord and destruction, we seek to encourage and exalt the nobler forces such as love, creativity, and peace. We do not see rejection of the material realm or of base forces as healthy as this would involve rejecting part of the Divine.

The Great Work Is To Seek Communion Or Oneness With the Divine

One of the unfortunate side effects of turning our attention to the mundane requirements of survival is that we tend to narrow our attention down to just the things that are in our immediate surroundings. We miss out on the beauty that surrounds us, and develop an inherent sense of isolation from others around us and the larger world in which we live. It's easy to get lost in the details of daily life and miss out on the beauty of a sunrise or sunset, the laugh of a child, the gentle touch of a lover's caress.

Some religions try to explain this sense of separation from the rest of existence as a "fall from Divine grace" or an alienation from the Divine presence. This makes sense if you consider the Divine to be divorced from the mundane world, if the Divine exists solely in another realm separate from the physical.

Pantheists and panentheists, however, see the Divine as being omnipresent in everything around and within us. The problem is not that we are divorced from the Divine presence but that we get so wrapped up we fail to notice the Divine is always there. We take the Divine for granted so we just don't sense it in our routine lives.

In philosophies that are based on the idea that the Divine is solely present in a nonphysical realm separate from the physical, the physical realm often gets classified as a distraction, as harmful in our proper goal of seeking reconciliation with the Divine. In philosophies that include the concept that the Divine is omnipresent, even in the physical realm, rejecting the physical realm for the nonphysical is to reject part of the Divine. The problem is seen more as one of training, where we need to relearn how to perceive, learn how to sense the Divine presence that is all around us.

A Wiccan Mystic's Ethical Path

All Is Connected & Cause And Effect: The Foundation of Our Ethics

People who practice magick strive to gain an understanding of the interconnections between things and use that information to bend circumstances to help them achieve their goals. They know that this interconnection carries with it a grave responsibility too. We are able to obtain results because we have influence; our influence affects others so we must act wisely. Our actions, and the actions of others, will affect us too even if we don't understand where the consequences are coming from.

Many Wiccans summarize the idea of interconnection as the Threefold Law: What you send out will come back to you three times. It's not necessarily something that can be quantized literally, but we can be sure that our actions and decisions (and also decisions to not act) will have consequences that will affect us and everything else.

Things Are Rarely Absolutes

Humans are insecure creatures. We crave stability, a feeling that we know how things work and have control over our lives. As a result we tend to try and gain control over things by labeling them. We think that by attaching a name to something we have identified its essence and have some control over it. We think that by gaining some knowledge of a thing we can command it.

In magick this attempt to understand things, to gain control, is clearly a large part of what we do. We run into danger, though, when we start to believe that the labels we invent and the things we know are all there is to know about a thing. When we get arrogant and assume that we have truly pinned down something with a label we are in for a nasty surprise.

Labels are absolutes that we impose on things. They make us think things are simple. If we get lazy and act like our labels really are the essence of things we miss out on noticing the subtle variations in the things we have labeled. We might think we know something when in fact all we've observed is the surface.

Thinking in terms of absolutes encourages us to think in oversimplified ways and make terrible mistakes. For instance, we might think of plants, animals, and minerals only in terms of how they are useful to us. This misses completely the fact that humans are but one species in the ecosystem that is the Earth and no single species is inherently greater in importance than any other. The natural world doesn't exist for our consumption. Absolutist thinking has allowed us to forget our place in the natural world.

Let's look at how we consider virii as another example of how absolute thinking can be detrimental. It's common thought that virii are bad for people, since they by their very nature infect our bodies and cause illness. If we allowed the absolute label of virus=bad to limit our thinking, then scientists wouldn't have thought about how we can use the way a virus works to distribute medicine to the areas where it's needed in an ill body, or perhaps deliver corrected gene sequences and provide new ways to treat genetic disorders.

Thankfully there are individuals whose awareness is flexible enough to recognize when labels and absolute thinking hinders more than helps and challenge the common assumptions to bring about change. Freethinkers in the past have challenged absolute assumptions about women and won them the vote and ever-increasing equality with men. People who refused to accept absolute statements have challenged racism, homophobia, and other discriminatory practices. It is never easy to challenge absolute labels especially when the majority holds them as common knowledge. As practitioners of magick we must seek out, identify, and challenge our own assumptions to trigger growth and positive change.

Choice

There are choices in every situation, if only a choice to act or to refrain from acting. Most of the time there are more than just two choices available to us. Our responsibility as thinking creatures is to weigh the options available to us, to make a choice, and to accept responsibility for our choices.

The Wiccan Rede, "An it harm none, do what you will" is a guideline that is based on choice. We are directed to try and choose that which will result in the least harm. We are also instructed that it is up to us to decide what we will do.

To fully embrace this ethic of choice we attempt to broaden our awareness of the choices that are available to us in any given situation. When we see a choice it's easy to notice the obvious options. A wise person learns to pause and think for a moment to try and discern the more subtle options that are also available. Perhaps one of the more subtle choices is more appropriate, resulting in less harm than the obvious choices, and resulting in greater success as well.

The practice of divination is one way that many magickal religions attempt to encourage awareness of choice. Some people see divination as a way to see the future. Some who study divinatory methods frequently insist that it is more of a tool for contemplating possibilities; it's a way of uncovering subtle choices. Divination provides us with a method of introducing a random element into our examination of a situation and allows us to see things in new ways. Divination in this way is not at all about identifying an unchangeable fate but rather a way to anticipate choices that we might miss.

We can also reflect on past choices and consider how the consequences arose from our decisions. We can learn from the past and try to make better choices in the future. As we examine the past we can also anticipate choices that could allow us to change our present and redirect our future to correct past mistakes.

Acknowledging and accepting our choices is a way of taking control of our lives. We are no longer drifting aimlessly in the ocean of events, but able to purposefully move in the direction we want.

Responsibility

An important part of becoming a mature adult is learning to accept responsibility for one's own life and the consequences of one's choices. Children need adults to be responsible for them, to make choices on their behalf in order to protect them and provide them with a safe environment to grow. As a child grows up they become more independent, relying less and less on the adults around them, and in the process take on responsibility for themselves.

Some religious systems use responsibility as a mechanism to control others. When a hierarchy of authority is established those who are higher up have the responsibility to make decisions for those beneath them. Sometimes these decisions are handed down in order to keep the group functioning in a healthy way or to keep the group on target. Other times though control is exerted in a repressive way to enforce conformity or impose arbitrary taboos. What one person or part of a group considers a good thing can be destructive and counterproductive for others in the same group. Unfortunately there is a tendency for those who have the position of power to try and hold on to that power which often results in the health of the group suffering. People who are in positions of power need to constantly examine why they are supporting specific stances: are they really acting in the best interest of the whole group or are they merely trying to exercise control or advance a selfish agenda? When we acknowledge authority as something outside ourselves, whether it is a person, a group of people, or a book we are granting them at least part of our inherent and very valuable decision-making responsibility. Healthy groups include some sort of mechanism for those in power to be challenged and decisions overturned should they prove inappropriate.

Accepting our own responsibility and handing over our own responsibility to others we recognize as authorities is a balancing act that we do in order to live together. Communities are nothing more than groups of people who have decided to share responsibility in some way. They have decided at some level that the benefits of working together outweigh the loss of some individual responsibility. In many cases there is a tradeoff of responsibilities: while one gives up a measure of personal autonomous responsibility, one takes on other responsibilities for others. Couples often come together to have children and share the responsibilities as well as joys of parenthood. Wiccans who come together in covens sacrifice some of their freedom in order to work with others in community.

Being responsible means that we acknowledge our role in making decisions, regardless whether those choices are made after long contemplation or on the spur of the moment. We accept the consequences of our choices and learn to live with them.

Dogma is accumulated decisions or ideas that until now have proven worthwhile. There is a tendency in spiritual groups to treat dogma as sacred; it gets written down and then is considered to be scripture or sometimes even elevated to the status of Divine Law. Dogma can be a good thing as it provides structure for the group and a tangible link to those who have come before. Dogma is tradition. There is always a danger though in accepting dogma without critical evaluation. Decisions that were appropriate in the past are not always right because circumstances do change. If a valid reason can't be given to justify a particular decision then perhaps the decision needs to be reworked and made fresh. Dogma that is not open to the introduction of new ideas is dogma that is fossilized and in danger of becoming completely irrelevant to the current and future community.

Wicca is a religion of autonomy and personal responsibility. We do not have any central authority or universal scripture that holds the responsibility of making decisions for us. Many groups do establish their own internal authorities in the form of a degree system, leaders and followers, and even scriptures in the form of a group Book of Shadows. There is an acknowledgement though that the rules that have been established in one group do not necessarily apply to other groups or to those who practice as solitaries. Indeed, the closest thing that Wiccans have to a central authority is the eight words of the Wiccan Rede. And even with this not all Wiccans acknowledge the Rede as important to their Wiccan philosophy. The Rede is also considered to be advice at best and not a commandment. It is open to interpretation by each group and each practitioner.

As they say, great freedom comes only with great responsibility. Autonomy does not come without an acceptance of responsibility for one's choices. Being in a position of authority includes being open to challenge regarding decisions and being accountable to the whole group.

Chapter 6:
Magickal Theory

Theories of Magick

here are a number of theories about how magick might work, some of them contradictory. These theories are an attempt to describe a magickal worldview. They offer concrete suggestions for ways to work towards manifesting desired change. They can serve as roadmaps suggesting how to build a direct connection with the Divine. They provide a sense of logic to magick and if they are carefully and intelligently used as the basis for practice can enable greater success.

The Pyramid Of Manifestation

In ceremonial magick one of the foundations of magickal practice is known as the Powers of the Sphinx, the Magician's Pyramid, the Pyramid of Manifestation, or alternatively as the Witches' Pyramid. Regardless of the name it involves four basic concepts:

1. To Know.
2. To Will.
3. To Dare.
4. To Keep Silent.

All four need to be actively practiced in order for magick to be effective. If any one of them is neglected the magick is at risk of failing.

At the most basic level, "To Know" means the practitioner needs to know what needs to be done in order to achieve the specific goal. It also means that the practitioner must strive to understand the influences and conditions that affect the particular situation that is the focus of the magickal working.

It involves external forces, such as physical environment, time of day, seasonal effects. It's also important to account for the influences of other people if at all possible. Perhaps the most important influence to examine, though, is the magicians themselves. Often the biggest obstacles to achieving a goal are the contrary impulses the practitioner has suppressed.

"To Will" is the driving force powering the magick. It is the engine of emotional, intellectual, and psychic energy brought to an unstoppable force and then directed at the desired target. Many modern practitioners also draw from Aleister Crowley's philosophy of the Will, which identifies one's "true Will" as one's proper place in the grand scheme of the universe. From this vantage, to do your own magickal Will involves understanding your place in the universe and not attempting to fight the natural order of things through your magickal and mundane practice. When you work for your goals by going with the flow of the universe, your spells have not only your own innate energy but also the energy of the universe behind them.

"To Dare" is the courage to attempt the magick in the first place, the courage to carry through to reach the goal. In everyday life we often allow a lack of courage to hold us back from attempting things we would like to do. It's always easier to follow the comfortable, well-worn path than to strike out into unknown territory. The magician, however, realizes that usually growth and change requires breaking away from old habits. Daring to perform a magickal act requires a lot of courage. Like most things, the more you engage in courageous acts, the easier you will find they become.

"To Keep Silent" is often interpreted to mean that magickal work is an involved process for those who engage in it and needs to be carefully nurtured and protected in order to grow strong and thrive. Exposing one's magickal projects to external criticism, especially early in their life, can be deadly. Bragging about one's spellwork, rushing to tell your neighbors and friends about some magickal experiment you just performed opens those workings up to external forces which can undermine them. By keeping silent about your magickal projects except among those who are involved you minimize the influences that can cause the working to fail. This does not apply, though, to explaining how spells are performed or discussing spells you have done in the past. Openly discussing magick after the work is over and the results have been achieved (or failed to materialize) can help us to evaluate our work and learn ways to improve. Just be sure that your motives for discussing magick openly do not include self-aggrandizement, as an over-inflated ego is one of the surest ways to ensure your magick won't work in the future.

Laws Of Magick

In magick there are some generally accepted rules or laws which most spells follow in order to achieve their goals. Modern science recognizes some of these rules in more sophisticated forms. Most of the laws of magick merely provide a pattern to follow without an understanding of why they might work as they do. Perhaps science can some day provide an understanding of why the laws work or appear to work. For magicians the main concern is that they do work.

Some of these laws are variations or restatements of the same ideas encapsulated in the Pyramid of Manifestation. In many ways the Pyramid is a top-four listing of the rules that tend to be most important in magickal work.

The following list provides the basics for most of the major laws of magick but does not necessarily give all of the laws. Perhaps the first law should be that there is always more to learn!

Law of Cause and Effect

For every action there is a consequence. This is an important law to remember. If you do a spell you must be willing to accept the outcome. Cause and effect is the reasoning behind magickal correspondences and associations between apparently disparate things. Through observation and testing magicians come to recognize that affecting certain things in specific ways produces expected results. Effective magick is the result of real consequences produced by real causes.

Law of Knowledge

In order to be effective you must understand the circumstances that lead to success or failure for your spell. Knowing the requirements for success allows you to perform the required steps and reach the goal more easily. A mundane example is knowing the magick of the computer's on button is not going to work unless all the components are connected properly and plugged into the correct type of power source. Similarly, performing a spell with an arbitrary collection of herbs, candles, and incense without an understanding of why specific components are used will likely result in failure.

Law of Self-Knowledge

Know Thyself! If you are subconsciously opposed to the goal you are consciously trying to achieve you will likely fail. Your inner and outer goals, your mind and heart, must work together for magick to succeed. You must also have sufficient self-knowledge to be honest about whether a particular goal is realistic for you. If I have no talent for singing, for instance, it would not make much sense for me to set a goal to be a star performer singing with a famous opera company. When you honestly evaluate your own strengths and weaknesses it is easier to set realistic goals.

Law of Association

If something that has a quality you want is made close to you, you can acquire the quality as if by absorption. For example, eating strong, hearty food is often assumed to make one naturally healthier. Many people today still automatically associate eating red meat with somehow acquiring the strength and health of the robust animal it came from, even though dieticians warn us that red meat is good for us only in moderation.

Law of Names

This is related to the Law of Association; if you know a person or thing's name, then you can have some influence over it even though it might not be physically present. In some cultures, this belief results in people using public names and secret names, so that evil magick can't be done against a person when only their public name is known. Some witches today take on secret names that they use only in magick rituals and with their magickal working partners as a way to build and preserve their power.

Law of Similarity

This is related to the Law of Association; it is thought that if a thing is similar to the thing you want to affect, then it can act as a proxy or stand-in for the actual target. For example in healing spells it is common for a photo or poppet of the patient to be used if they can't be physically present.

Law of Contagion

In magick it is often assumed that you can affect the whole by working on a part. This is why healing spells often require a lock of hair or personal possession of the patient if they can't be present physically. Physically linking with a part is believed to allow us to affect the whole.

Another way that the law of contagion is thought to work is through the assumption that you can catch qualities from something the way you catch an illness. If you hang around with powerful people then you might catch their attitude or aura of power. If you are physically close to healthy people you might catch their robust constitution.

Law of Identification

If you are able to produce a strong identification with a role model you want to emulate then you will acquire the same qualities and success as the role model. Children and teenagers often do this by trying to dress, talk, and act like the famous people whose lives they admire. This is similar to the Law of Contagion; if you are able to associate yourself with a role model closely enough then you might share in their success.

Law of Synthesis

If you are able to bring two opposing forces together their union can produce a stronger product that the mere sum of the two. The Great Work of alchemists is an attempt to produce a grand synthesis between matter and spirit, uniting the seeker with their Holy Guardian Angel to produce something greater. The most ordinary ingredients when mixed together in the right way can produce the most amazing results.

Law of Polarity

This law is related to the Law of Synthesis. Polarity is the idea that most things can be reduced to one of two classifications: male and female, yin and yang, positive and negative. It is also assumed that there is usually a bit of the opposite force in each, that each man has some feminine qualities, and each woman has a few masculine qualities. Wicca uses the Law of Polarity as a core element for many of its rituals and magick.

Law of Balance

In order to be successful the best approach is to attempt to attain a balance in all things. When casting a magickal circle in which to perform spells a balance between the four elements is usually sought in order to power the spells most effectively. Similarly, a person who has dominant leanings towards some elements is often seen as unbalanced and therefore not whole. Wiccans seek to attain spiritual balance by respecting all parts of nature both light and dark, creative and destructive, as they are two sides of the whole. An exclusively female Divine is just as unbalanced and incomplete as an exclusively male Divine.

Upperworld, Middleworld, Lowerworld

In many shamanic spiritual paths the world is described as being composed of three parts: an Upperworld, a Middleworld, and a Lowerworld. Working major magick in these systems often involves the shaman traveling from the Middleworld to either the Upperworld or Lowerworld in order to find answers or to perform specific tasks that will bring about changes in the Middleworld.

The Upperworld is the realm of the stars, sky deities, and airy spirits. The Lowerworld is the realm of earth spirits and deities, and in many systems is considered to be the home of the dead. In Christian mythology the Upperworld is Heaven, and the Lowerworld is Hell. Pagan mythology rarely ascribes exclusively good or evil qualities to one or the other. In Greek mythology for instance the Olympian (Upperworld) deities are just as likely to be mischievous towards humans as are the inhabitants of Hades (the Lowerworld.)

In psychological models the Upperworld would describe one's "higher self," and the Lowerworld one's more primitive and primal essence, sometimes called the "shadow." Exploring and integrating these with your everyday self, your Middleworld persona, results in a healthy whole. Attempting to ignore or repress one of these components in favor of others frequently results in those parts building strength until the point when they act out and erupt in uncontrolled and usually very uncomfortable ways. Some believe that many illnesses, particularly illnesses triggered by stress, are the result of suppressed Upperworld or more often Lowerworld components of ourselves.

Frater U. ∴.D. ∴'s Magickal Models [5]

Magick can be also explained through five basic theories, summarized and paraphrased here from an article by Frater U.∴.D.∴. of Germany. These theories sometimes conflict within the fifth one which attempts to combine them all into a single unit. Modern practitioners of magick have not come to a universal agreement which of these theories, if any, is correct.

The Spirit Model

This model is based on the idea that there is an invisible realm populated by intelligent entities that can interact with us on the physical realm. Deities are actual distinct entities with their own personalities, motives, and desires that might or might not have anything to do with humans. Societies of the pre-modern eras often exhibited strong belief in spirit models, where all illness was attributed to invisible entities like demons and devils, and all good things were attributed to the active participation of deities or invisible helpers like angels and the spirits of ancestors.

The Energy Model

What humans perceive as invisible realms are really just energy systems that are currently unknown to science. Energy is neutral and does not have any intelligence of its own but can be used by humans. Magickal systems based primarily on working with chakras, chi, ki, mana, or orgone energies are examples of this system. The energy model is essentially a scientific one where everything is reducible to things and forces that can be identified, measured, and proven. Science has yet to prove the existence of any form of spiritual energy however.

The Psychological Model

The invisible realm is really just the human subconscious and does not necessarily have an external existence or reality. There is a possibility that the subconscious realm is a medium where physical humans can interact with each other at a noncorporeal level. Jungian psychology is probably the best example of the psychological model. Jung postulated the existence of a "collective unconscious" which individuals share. It could be essentially the hard-wired unconscious structure that we inherit from our ancestors or it could be a realm of archetypes that exists in community with other humans.

The Information Model

Consciousness is really just a byproduct of what is essentially an advanced computer system. Magick is a process of programming the human computer. By consciously editing our mental programming we are able to achieve all sorts of effects. Systems such as Neuro-Linguistic Programming are based on an information model. They see difficulties or psychological obstacles as bugs in our software that can be routed around with new programming or eliminated by careful editing.

The Meta-Model

No single model is necessarily the absolute truth; all models have their own validity and use. This is similar to the models of light used by physicists: sometimes it is helpful to consider light to be a wave, and other times a particle. Use what works in the particular situation but don't become trapped into thinking that only one model is correct all the time. Physicists insist that light is both a particle and a wave; we who study magick can also operate under the assumption that multiple theories of magick can be simultaneously correct.

Keys to Mystical Magick

Having an idea about how magick might work is an important part of a magickal mystical path. The next step is to put that knowledge into practice. Knowledge remains strictly theoretical until you can put it to use.

How can a Wiccan seeking mystical experience incorporate magick into their lives in a meaningful way? Is it just a matter of following any of the many magickal how-to books available on the market? What things transform mere spell-work into mystical celebration of a relationship with the Divine?

Three things are key in mystical expression: inspiration, creativity, and a sense of continuity usually found through ritual. Inspiration is the electric jump-start we get from the Divine. Creativity is how we manifest that Divine gift. And finally, ritual provides a structure or overall context that weaves it all into a larger pattern of existence.

Inspiration

Definition: Breathing New Life Into Something

A literal definition of *inspiration* is to breathe life into something. This
particular definition is very open. It doesn't say there are limits on what is
an acceptable trigger to bring life into something. It's more about energy,
perhaps the quality of motion and enthusiasm that is introduced. Indeed,
the word *enthusiasm* translates from the original Greek as "god within"
so to be enthusiastic is to be filled with the Divine presence. The idea of
breathing life into something also hearkens back to the creation myths told
in many cultures. Since breath and air are so clearly connected to new ideas
and new enthusiasm it makes perfect sense that occult philosophies should
attribute the element air with those qualities.

Immersing Yourself Into An Activity

Far too often we go through our daily life as if we were sleepwalking. We
get up in the morning, prepare for the day, go to work, come home, relax a
bit, and then go to bed to start the whole cycle over again. We do things out
of habit and without really thinking about what we are doing. One day we
might wake up and discover that a large portion of our lives has passed us
by and we feel we have accomplished little, or what little we have achieved
feels to have been done by someone else.

Being inspired means doing things with vigor and attention, so that the
activity is suffused with energy. Top athletes describe a good session as
being "in the zone" where they are fully immersed in their sport, and they
are attuned to their activity to such a degree that they become their actions.
This is different from doing things by routine and without thought. The
difference is that someone who is inspired is putting their all into the effort,
their full attention. Someone who is sleepwalking on the contrary is really
just doing the bare minimum with little mental engagement in what they are
doing.

Experiencing Routine Things In New Ways

We often take the things around us for granted. When we do the same
things over and over again our tendency is to tune out what we are doing
and let it just happen automatically. This can be a method for meditating if
you approach it for that purpose and actively work to calm your mind and

let the rhythm of your activity soothe you to a state of peace. Usually we don't use routine as a meditative technique but instead allow boredom to set in, or use the time we are doing routine things to let our minds drift to irrelevant details or mind-numbing trivialities.

Instead of focusing on the soothing aspects of our routine activities we can choose to push our minds to clarity and pay extra attention to what we are doing. Observe what you are doing; how does your body feel, how do you move, how does your body react? What objects are around you, what ones are you interacting with? How do you sense those objects: through sight, smell, touch, taste, or sound? Can you sense the objects through senses that you wouldn't normally use? How do the objects interact with the environment, with other objects around them?

What if you were doing this activity for the very first time? How would you feel, what would you pay attention to? How would you explain what you are doing to a child?

If you were to close your eyes could you do this activity still without difficulty? Can you imagine what you normally would see? How clear can you make that mental image and still do the activity? Can you imagine doing the activity without physically doing anything at all? Can you imagine doing the activity and change your routine, do it differently? Perhaps change the objects in your mental image and see where that takes you.

Open your senses and see if there are elements to your routine activity that you normally miss. What secrets are hidden there in plain sight? Can you see beyond the activity, see how it fits into the larger pattern of things? Where do you fit?

Mindfulness and conscious action is not restricted to things we do in a ritual setting. Bring it into your daily life and you vastly increase your connection to your spiritual center. Teach yourself to see the spiritual in everything no matter how ordinary and you will touch on the sacredness that is everywhere.

Opening To The Wonder That Is Always Around Us

In the Charge of the Goddess, there is a line that says: "And thou who thinkest to seek for Me, know thy seeking and yearning shall avail thee not, unless thou knowest the Mystery: that if that which thou seekest thou findest not within thee, thou wilt never find it without thee." The holy is with us all the time, without and within, whether we can perceive it or not. Those who follow a mystical path seek to open their awareness to that omnipresent holiness. We learn that spiritual wonder is not just for that once-a-week meeting, or restricted to full moon ceremonies or sabbat celebrations. It is all around us, in the trees, in the wind, in the sunshine and the darkness of night, in the touch of a friend or lover. It's in the laugh of a child. It's in a giggle over a stupid joke or sit-com pratfall. It's in the tear of the distraught. It's in love, and hate, and stillness, and roaring tumult.

It's within us as well as without. We go within to seek that which is without. In the microcosm we discover the macrocosm.

It's easy to talk but very difficult to listen. Our most challenging task is to learn to listen. Listen to the symphony all around us. Hearken to the still quiet sounds within. When we learn to listen and truly start to hear we can discover that the song of joy and existence was always there with us. We are never alone as we are all together in a vast web of existence, a dance of transformation that has no beginning and has no end. Listen to the music and let your soul dance!

Creativity

Creativity As A Primary Expression Of Life

The root of creativity is, obviously, to create. Bringing new things into the world allows us to express our ideas, to make the abstract concrete, to pass on to others part of our internal solitary lives. By externalizing our insights, by putting them into a form that can be shared with others, we confirm the validity of those insights and provide them with an opportunity to survive beyond our own personal lifespan. Insights that are not shared, that are not expressed externally in some form, die with us in the physical realm when we breathe our last.

One of the primary ideas in the Cabbalistic tree of life map of reality is that the Divine, abstracted as the topmost sephiroth Kether, is expressed through existence in various essential qualities or spheres until finally reaching the lowest sephiroth where it is expressed as physical reality, known as Malkuth. Some occult traditions describe this progression of manifestations as the Divine's descent from the highest vibratory level to the lowest resulting in the creation of the physical world. Expressing abstract ideas in some physical form allows us to partake of the process of manifesting the Divine.

Examples Of Creativity

Procreation

Bearing and raising children is the most biologically primal form of creativity. The adult participants engage in some form of genetic exchange, a child is conceived and brought forth to express qualities from both genetic donors. By raising a child the parent passes on ideas, values, and traditions and often invents new ones, or modifies old ideas and presents them to the child in new ways. The parent lives on through their genetic and cultural heritage in their child to become expressed in subsequent generations and therefore attains a form of immortality.

Parents also express creativity in developing ways to teach their children ways to cope in the ever-changing world. Methods that previous generations used to raise children are helpful as a foundation for future generations but must always be modified to fit current conditions. Raising kids isn't as easy as following a set of directions; parents are constantly challenged to find better ways to do things.

The Arts

Drawing, painting, sculpting, writing, and performing music are all creative acts. The artist takes ideas and shares them with the world in a form that others can perceive. For many artists a large part of the process is discovering ways to express the idea in ways that also demonstrate the personality of the artist, or present the idea that puts it in a new way.

Physical Crafts

Physical crafts such as knitting, sewing, decorating items for use around the home, beadwork, scrapbooking, and other things like this are also highly creative ways of expressing yourself and your spiritual ideas. Cooking a really good meal is highly creative, as is putting together an outfit or decorating a home. All of these things can involve learning about how they were done in the past, drawing on the wisdom and inspiration of others. They can also involve bold new methods that you make yourself. With enough work perhaps you could become one of the leaders in your particular craft.

Athletic Expression

Athletes, too, are creative. Training for a particular sport involves long hours and a fierce dedication to achieving goals. Creativity comes into a training regimen in the form of selecting innovative ways to strengthen and refine one's skills. For example, cross-training in gymnastics or dance is one way football players can bring new elements into their game. Dancers might take up weightlifting as a way to build strength. Golfers sometimes take up Tai Chi or yoga to increase their flexibility, stamina, and ability to relax and concentrate. Intense training for a particular sport often involves stepping outside the boundaries of that sport to achieve that elusive edge over competitors.

Problem Solving

If creativity in all its forms is an expression of unity with the Divine as the ultimate Creative Force then solving problems can be seen as a spiritual or mystical act.

Following someone else's pattern blindly, repeating old mistakes over and over again because that's the way it was done in the past does not involve any creativity or indeed much in the way of independent thought. Looking at how things are done and seeking out better or at least different ways of doing them involves creativity. It forces us to look at things in new ways. Solving problems encourages us to grow and change. Creativity is inherently progressive rather than conservative. We give ourselves opportunities to evolve all the time but only those who actively try to solve the problems, whether they are successful or not, are the ones who learn and grow.

Teaching

Imparting information and skills to another often involves problem solving on the part of the teacher. Each student is unique, and will learn things at a different rate, and in different ways, from every other student. The challenge for teachers is to discover how best to adapt the curriculum to the learning styles of the student and maximize knowledge transfer.

Teaching also can involve forcing the teacher to confront their own assumptions and come up with justifications to explain them. Often we get comfortable in our own ideas and ways of thinking, and don't examine them too closely until we are in a position of having to explain them to someone else. Teaching others the basics of our spiritual path can help us to clarify what those basics actually are, what is important, what is extraneous, what makes sense and what doesn't make sense.

Ritual: Milestones in Life

In Wicca we often speak about the sabbats, the cycle of annual religious celebrations, as the Wheel of the Year. Each of the eight sabbats represents a spoke of a wheel whose motion represents Divine intention in action. Wiccans celebrate the sabbats as a way to connect with and honor the Divine intention. Active participation in the cycle of life through ritual action keeps us grounded. It helps us to recognize and celebrate our relationship with the Divine.

Ritual As A Formal Recognition Of An Act, Event, Or Change

Rituals can be a formalized marker for things that we consider significant. We hold ritualized events to mark birthdays, anniversaries, and deaths. When public buildings are constructed there is often a groundbreaking ceremony to mark the start of the construction, and then a grand opening when the building is done. Newly constructed ships are launched with ceremonies where champagne is splashed over the bow of the boat. Fireworks are set off to mark special days like the start of a new year and also at national holidays.

Rituals can be simple or complex but tend to have repetitive elements to them. At birthdays, for instance, it is common for people to sing a special song to the one who is being honored. Cakes bedecked with lit candles are rarely used for other occasions but are common at birthdays. There is frequently an element of luck involved with the birthday person urged to make a wish on their special day.

Ritual To Invite Change

Ritual times are most often threshold times when we are at a point where change is likely and often encouraged. Options are open, old ways can be abandoned, new ways adopted. It is a time of choice and possibility where participants have special opportunities to decide.

Some rituals are performed to indicate the start of new undertakings as a way to try and invite good luck and success. In some cases the rituals are conducted to try and induce a threshold moment. For example, a community working through difficult times will sometimes hold a special event or ritual such as an organized religious ceremony or charitable event to try and turn things around. Attempting to bring the community together, focusing the community attention on the problem and possibly on things that can make things better, can turn out to be the threshold moment the community needed.

Rituals involving spell-work are another common example of a ritual done specifically to invite change. The whole point of a spell is to produce change. If circumstances do not change after a spell then the spell is assumed to have failed. Rituals for change can be very powerful and effective, though, if they are carefully worked with strong intentions and are done in accord with the Divine will. Rituals can be the dramatic trigger needed to instigate required change.

Ritual To Celebrate Change

Some rituals are performed at the height of active change as a way to celebrate. Formal dinners during a gathering are one common example; people get together to share food following common patterns of interaction knowing that this is just one part of an overall interaction with those present. Sometimes these sorts of rituals are working sessions where important information is exchanged or decisions are made by the group, but they might also be opportunities for celebration and camaraderie.

Rituals performed at sabbats are often celebrations that are part of the larger sabbat season. Some sabbats, in particular ones like Lammas, are usually marking the high points of particular seasons rather than transition times.

Ritual To Provide Closure To Change

Some rituals are clearly about recognizing an end. Funeral rituals, for instance, allow participants to formally acknowledge the end of a life and provide a sacred space to reflect on the deceased's accomplishments. Coming-of-age rituals mark the end of childhood and the start of adulthood. Graduation rituals mark the end of formal training and set the candidates apart as successful. These types of rituals provide emotional, intellectual, or spiritual closure for those involved. They frequently involve a community formally recognizing that a particular role is no longer

114 - The Wiccan Mystic

appropriate for the ones who are the center of the ritual. In some cases, such as ordination into a religious organization, the ritual marks the end of the person's status as a normal citizen. It can also be an initiation into a new role such as one having special knowledge.

Regardless what the specific purposes might be for a ritual, when it is conducted as part of a larger ritual framework it links participants into the Divine pattern of existence. Rituals can include re-enactments of Divine mythology, illustrate specific concepts, or provide an opportunity for participants to interact directly with deity. Connecting our personal lives to the Divine through ritual provides a larger context and spiritual meaning for the things we experience.

Chapter 7:
Wiccan Mystics In Community

Solitary Work

A Spiritual Path Is Essentially A Solitary Path

ach of us perceives and interacts with the universe in our own very individual ways. No one else in the world has exactly the same background as you, the same past experiences. Remember the parable of the six blind men and the elephant? Each one "saw" a different aspect of the animal. None was necessarily incorrect in his perception, but all were incomplete! We do know though that what we have learned growing up colours our outlook. The things we have lived through give each of us a unique perspective on life, our place in the universe, and how we interact with others. If we cultivate an awareness of our personal filters we can attempt to compensate for our limitations or at least acknowledge that they exist.

When a group of people go through an experience together each person senses the event and remembers it in a different way. Experiments that scientists have done to compare how witnesses to an event remember details show that no two people ever remember things exactly the same. If a roomful of people witnesses an event each person will remember things slightly differently; it's actually quite normal for people who saw the exact same event to disagree on the details of what they saw.

Mystical experiences are among the most subjective of things because they really do take place primarily in our inner worlds. Outside events or conditions might trigger the experience, but the sense of union, the expansion of awareness beyond the normal realms, is not something that bystanders can sense unless we describe it to them as it happens. We can try and describe a mystical experience to others but we can't pull them in to ours so that they feel them along with us. They must make the connections themselves, attain that "aha!" moment themselves, in order to feel the emotions and have the experience.

Gurus and teachers are people who are trying to guide others along a spiritual path that they themselves have followed. They are attempting to induce in their students those same insights and the same conditions that can result in enlightenment. They can't do the actual work for the student though. They can't guarantee that following the same path will result in the same experience. What works for one person, or even for a hundred or a thousand people, might still not work for you. We each have our own strengths to build on and our own weaknesses that hold us back. The best guru or teacher can try and help you along the way but there is no magick they can perform which will fix everything for you and guarantee a mystical experience.

Mystical experience, that union with the Divine, is about you and the Divine. All we can really do is work towards making ourselves worthy of this experience and then learn patience and acceptance. When the Divine feels we are ready for the experience it will come.

Spirituality Is About Personal Growth, Which Means Personal Work

We expect a ten-year-old child to be different from a five-year-old child. We expect a teenager to be different from an infant. Once we become adults our growth does not stop. We might slow down in physical changes but intellectually and emotionally we continue to grow throughout our lives. We should expect growth to be a constant throughout our spiritual lives as well.

Intellectual maturation requires years of training and hard work to bring us from childhood to functional adulthood. Once we've reached early adulthood many of us go on to take further specialized training so that we can start careers in particular fields. Just because we can read, write, and do basic arithmetic doesn't mean we are prepared to perform brain surgery or program computers. Just because we can sing "Happy Birthday" doesn't mean we are ready to sing an aria at the Vienna Opera House.

Preparing for a mystical experience involves building spiritual strength, clear perceptions, and a solid foundation or balance. A fortunate few are naturally gifted in one or more of these and might find mysticism comes naturally to them. For many of us, though, we need to work hard to develop the skills needed.

Spiritual strength is an ability to endure possible hardship. It's having the stamina to train long and hard for a possible future reward. People who are not prepared for the intense nature of a mystical experience can find themselves burned out. Having spiritual strength prepares and conditions us so that an intense mystical experience or the training that leads up to it does not destroy us in a physical, intellectual, or emotional way.

Clarity of perception doesn't mean you have to have twenty-twenty vision or perfect hearing but refers to being clear-headed enough to recognize when we might be fooling ourselves instead of having an accurate understanding of what we are sensing. Spiritual experience is highly subjective. What we perceive is filtered through our past experiences and existing world-view. Other people with different backgrounds will see things differently. It's not a matter of right or wrong, but a matter of perspective. When we have clarity of perception we are able to recognize that our view is not necessarily the only view. We are also able to determine whether what we perceive has an objective component to it and what part of our experience is objectively real. We can train ourselves to recognize self-deception and illusion. We can shift our attention to other points of view and gain a wider view.

When we have a strong spiritual foundation or balance we feel confident in ourselves so that we are not devastated when assumptions are proven false. Facing the unknown does not frighten a person who is balanced and secure. An unhealthy form of this is expressed as arrogance that one's spiritual foundation is the only correct one. A person with an unhealthy foundation is inflexible, ignores evidence that does not support their understanding, and will be in danger of finding their foundation crumble beneath them should they ever be confronted with contrary evidence that can not be ignored, or when faced with the unknown and nowhere to turn.

Know Yourself

When we embark on a career of spiritual growth we have to start somewhere. The logical place, although perhaps one of the most challenging, is to start with you.

Everything we experience is perceived through our own particular filters. Our background, our physical makeup and abilities, our state of mind, our emotions have a huge impact on how we interpret external stimuli. If we are to seek something like spiritual truth we must learn to recognize how our own perceptions and biases influence what we absorb and think we know.

Some mystics describe the process of seeking enlightenment as a stripping away of illusion. To seek knowledge of the macrocosm we must turn inward to the microcosm. By studying ourselves we can learn surprising things about the universe.

Self-deception, false assumptions, bad habits are all obstacles that hold us back from gaining spiritual insight. Self-evaluation is a form of purification that brings us closer to the Divine. As we cleanse our perceptions we are more able to embrace the pure light that is the Divine.

Experts are not people who know everything there is about a particular topic, but those who know enough about a topic to realize the breadth and depth of how little they really know. They are wise who have recognized their own limitations, as knowing the limits allow them to see where they can be stretched and expanded.

Conscious Action

Working effective magick requires determination. It's something that requires constant attention and discipline. Magick is something that is in your life twenty-four hours a day, seven days a week even if you don't work consciously at it through all that time. A lot of magickal work involves subconscious or unconscious effort that is just as challenging as conscious effort. When you are a witch or magician who works magick, you discover that it is a lot of hard work. It's not something you can be good at if you try to just pick it up on weekends.

Magick involves honing your awareness to the subtle influences around us. Recognizing cycles and understanding laws of nature allow magicians to know how and when to act. Magickal actions without a grasp of these concepts are nothing more than random flailing. It is theoretically possible that a thousand monkeys at a thousand typewriters could produce the works of Shakespeare. Isn't it more effective, though, to learn the rules of the game and then work intelligently and methodically to achieve a goal?

Some magicians suggest that those who want to work magick must always tell the truth. If your word is always true in mundane things it adds a compelling level of strength to magickal pronouncements as well. "So mote it be" is more than just a phrase to finish off an incantation. When spoken by one who has strengthened and proven their authority by always telling the truth, "so mote it be" is a commandment. Always speaking the truth also serves to build spiritual and magickal discipline. It hones the will to a razor-sharpness that can achieve precise and effective things. Establishing your authority as a truth-speaker clears the way on many levels and makes magick far more effective.

Being aware of the influences around a goal is only part of the process in effective magick. Conscious action is the other, more active, component. A magician learns by observation of influences what can be done at what moment in order to tip things towards their goal. Magick is not just hopeful wishing that things will go your way.

Some magicians extend this manipulation to include their own personalities. The theory is that the persona we adopt for a circumstance affects how others perceive us and affects how events unfold. By consciously selecting and adopting masks or external personalities according to the circumstance, magicians gain another level of control. We all take on different roles for different circumstances: we are quite different in our relationships with our parents or family members than we are with our work mates or friends. For one who practices magick, learning to recognize the different roles we take and then consciously tailoring them and assuming roles with determination can further our goals.

One of the side benefits of practicing magick as a conscious discipline is that we find our health improving both physically and mentally. When we pay attention to the things we can actually control in our lives and do something to make things better for ourselves then good things tend to result. We exist as whole beings, spiritual entities inhabiting a temple of flesh. If we are diligent in keeping our bodies, our most intimate temple, in shape and healthy then it's much easier to maintain a strong and healthy spirit. It's amazing sometimes how even the smallest changes done consciously and deliberately can snowball into wonderful results. Not eating that extra helping of dessert every day or doing a walk around the block three or four times a week, for instance, can make a noticeable difference in one's weight and overall health. Working in similar ways on one's mental health can have similar results. And manipulating to produce change is a lot of what magick is all about.

Building Spiritual Discipline

Spiritual discipline provides a number of purposes. It helps us to confirm our convictions and carry through on promises we have made to ourselves and to the Divine. It helps us to carve out a clear and predictable space into which the Divine can manifest more directly in our lives. It exercises our spiritual senses and attunes us to subtle influences. In some cultures people who have taken on outward expressions as part of their spiritual discipline receive more overt reinforcement of their dedication from others, and end up with a positive reinforcement loop to encourage their discipline.

When we decide to follow a particular spiritual discipline, we are making an oath to ourselves and to the Divine to engage in a particular practice as a sign of our devotion. The practice itself might be a routine process of tending an altar, lighting candles and incense, perhaps laying out small offerings of drink or food. It might involve praying at the same time every day. Perhaps it involves a program of meditation practiced in a standard routine. Regardless what the actual activity involves, it is something that is done in honor of the Divine and is made a regular part of the devotee's routine. Practicing routine acts of devotion confirms our spiritual choices by putting our ideas into regular action.

Christians often speak of letting Jesus into their hearts. This idea is not frivolous but is central to mystical experience. In order to be able to get a glimpse of the Divine, those forces and intelligences that are greater than the sum of all creation, we must make room in our crowded mundane lives. If we want to perceive the Divine we must learn to see past the noisy demands on our attention that are a routine part of everyday life. When we allow ourselves time to be quiet, time to truly listen to what is there inside and outside ourselves, then we begin to notice the steady presence of the

Divine. It's hard to hear when you're shouting, and hard to see when there is nothing but shiny objects in view. The Divine is always there but we can't perceive it until we make some space in our lives to allow us to slow down, to quiet down, and really listen and see.

In our daily lives we often don't perceive the things that are all around us because we're too focused on the things we think are important. If we stop and take the time to really look around us, to listen to the sounds that are there, those little details can become apparent. When you are walking somewhere outside how often do you notice the sounds of birds chirping, or planes overhead, or cars driving by? Do you hear people talking nearby, a cell phone ringing, maybe the sound of a door opening or closing? Do you hear your own clothes rustling as you move? Do you hear your own breath? Do you smell your own deodorant or cologne or perfume? Do you notice the warmth of the sunshine, or the smell of filtered air in your workplace or home? Can you smell the distinct odors of the season, whether they are the smell of leaves in the autumn, mud in the spring, the sharp crispness of winter, the heady smells of summer? We are immersed in all these things but fail to notice them until we stop for a moment and take the time to pay attention to our senses. We fail to notice the omnipresence of the Divine, the manifestations of the multitude of Goddesses and Gods, until we learn to make room for them, until we allow our senses to open up and notice what is already there.

In some cultural settings there is public reinforcement for those who practice spiritual discipline. In some settings taking on a life of spiritual discipline involves adopting specific clothing as an outward sign of one's devotion. Wearing the garb of a priest in a society that respects the role allows the dedicant to stand apart from their neighbors, and to be an object of respect for those neighbors. When there is regular use of respectful spiritual titles when being addressed it is easy to feel supported in one's spiritual career. In some cultures, such as in India, people who dedicate themselves to spiritual pursuits and who choose to adopt the outward disciplines of the yogi including poverty and the practice of harsh physical challenges are treated as living saints. The more obvious that a yogi has been practicing their devotions for a long time, such as through their appearance or their ability to demonstrate difficult physical feats done clearly for love of the Divine, the more reverence they are given. When it is outwardly obvious that a person has dedication to spiritual pursuits, it is easier for others who understand the ideas behind that spiritual path to offer their support.

Group Work

Mysticism is first and foremost a private and individual pursuit. It's about a personal relationship and experience of Divine communion which requires only you and the universe. No one can do the work for you. No one else can establish the link and just hand over the experience to you. Despite the inherently solitary nature of mysticism it can be very rewarding to join with others to work with in spiritual matters.

Community

Working with others provides a sense of community that we miss out on when we work strictly on our own. Community provides a feedback system, a network of support, which can encourage us in pursuing our goals.

Wiccan groups tend to be structured around small groups called covens, which usually are no larger than thirteen members. In such small groups it is easy to really get to know the others you are working with. Coven members who see each other regularly, who share themselves and their lives with the same group of people over time, grow to become like a family. When the chemistry is right life-long friends are made. Covens that are close laugh together, cry together, celebrating all that life has to offer. They know that they have a safe place to come for support that will always be there for them.

Differing Points Of View

Group work provides us with new perspectives on our insights as we struggle to explain ourselves, and as we hear what others have to say about things. Challenging our viewpoints opens us up to a larger perspective. We are encouraged to grow, to challenge opinions, and perhaps to abandon ideas that are no longer working for us. We learn that the things we take for granted might be just one way of looking at things, and that other viewpoints might provide more information than we thought existed.

Encountering new outlooks can force us to shift our own ingrained perspective and trigger new ideas. Breaking out of our habitual perceptions of ourselves, our lives, and our environment is a large part of the mystical experience. Cocooning ourselves away from life and new ideas is one way to try and avoid a mystical experience.

Combining Efforts

Each of us has our own particular talents, strengths and weaknesses. By joining with others in community we are able to combine our strengths and be more effective. Mysticism for many Wiccans is not just about sitting motionless in silence, waiting to hear the voice of the Divine. Wiccans who believe that the Divine exists in everything seek to show reverence by attempting to make the world a better place. When the Divine really is in everything we show disrespect to the Divine when we reject any part of the holy creation.

Many Wiccans work on environmental efforts to improve the health of the ecosystem, do charity work to help the disadvantaged, or focus on healing those who are ill. Others show reverence for the Divine by teaching others, by sharing knowledge, or by creating artistic expressions in honor of the Divine. But in all of these instances working in concert with others will always produce more substantial results than could be achieved when working alone. When we work with others towards a common goal the task is shared and the resulting effort is that much greater.

In magickal work some believe that our effectiveness is an exponential progression when we work with others. For instance, working alone might produce results on the scale of ten to the power of one. Working in a pair produces results of ten to the power of two. Three people, ten to the power of three (or ten cubed.) Each additional person who joins in the magickal working has a huge impact on the results.

One of the consequences of the impact of scale when working with others is that things can go wrong at a larger scale when others are involved too. It becomes very important, especially for groups wishing to do magickal work, that all participants are harmonious and comfortable with all other members in the group. One note of discord can knock the whole off balance. Groups that are most effective are usually the ones that grow slowly and deliberately.

Guidance From Others Farther On the Path

We are each on individual paths. When we work in groups it is inevitable that different people will have dealt with different issues in their own ways and in their own time. It is actually quite rare for everyone in a group to be at exactly the same point in their spiritual maturation, the same level of knowledge, the same background and opinions.

The differences can be a good reason to seek out others. When we have someone else to talk with about what we are going through, we increase the chance of having outside opinions and experiences to compare with our own. There are billions of people who have lived before us. Each of these people has their own story to tell, their own insights, their own revelations. While no other will have exactly the same experience as ours, hearing their accounts can shed light on our own. Every person we encounter knows something that can help us learn. We just have to be open to perceiving these lessons in personal encounters, through words, through visual expression, or through example and observation of action.

When we join with others who are of like mind, following similar spiritual paths to our own, we gain valuable opportunities to learn how others deal with issues we are likely to face ourselves. It's easier to relate to people who are closer to our own viewpoints.

Sometimes there aren't opportunities to join up with people who share our particular spiritual outlook. This doesn't mean that you are unable to join up with others exploring spirituality. Perhaps there are other groups in your area that focus on other spiritual paths that could still provide you with a sense of community. It will certainly be harder as you will need to interpret the ideas expressed in relation to your own path. It might also prove more challenging to maintain your independence regarding your own spiritual path; it is a common desire to want to change ourselves to fit in with the group. Learn what you can, ignore what is clearly not relevant for you, and decide for yourself. The final judges regarding whether you are following your own path are you and the Divine. Don't let other people try to dictate what your spiritual path should be.

Group Work Shouldn't Be A Replacement For Solitary Work

Group work is appealing because there is immediate feedback from others. We gain a sense of community, a sense of belonging, an identity within something larger than ourselves. It's easy to forget that our spiritual journeys are inherently solitary when friends and supporters surround us.

There is a danger in thinking that our spiritual path is all about fitting in with a particular community. It's easy to relax our critical faculties and just agree with what others are saying or doing. It's seductive to let others do the hard work and present us with simple answers. Learning to relax, to trust, and to allow others to have control for a change are valuable lessons but like many things they can also produce problems. When we give up the responsibility for making our own decisions we are giving away our freedom. The Divine didn't endow us with the precious gifts of intelligence and autonomy for us to casually throw them away.

Working with others can and should be a part of one's spiritual path but not at the expense of the real work: one's own individual spiritual growth. If working with a particular group is not helping you in your individual growth then it's time to question whether this group is worthwhile for you. Perhaps you have learned the lessons this group has to teach you and it's time to move on.

Group work should challenge you to grow, to question assumptions, to listen and learn from sources outside us. When they become dictatorial or restrictive, suppressing your individual spiritual growth, it is time to learn how to overcome these imposed barriers. In some cases it might mean learning to transform the group itself into a more healthy society, while in other cases it might mean learning how to leave a comfortable rut and move on.

Group work should complement and encourage your solitary work. It is not a substitute for solitary work. No one can do the work for you that is required to bring about greater spiritual maturation and wisdom.

Tutelary Deities

It is common for Wiccans to refer to deity as simply the Lord and Lady, and indeed to worship a wide range of deities drawn from a variety of cultures. It is also common for specific Wiccan traditions, covens, and even individuals to find they are drawn to one or two specific deities as the focus for their worship. These specific deities are often referred to as Patron or Matron deities. In some cases the specific deity names are carefully guarded as secret. In other cases the individuals or groups decide to openly declare themselves as being devotees of their specific deity or deities. There is no single way that is required of all Wiccans so there is some variety in the way Wiccans relate to the concept of Deity.

Muses, Or Patron/Matron Deities

Sometimes a particular deity or even a small group of deities will make Themselves known to an individual or group. Practitioners who are involved in creative endeavors such as writing, graphic arts, or music often speak of these greater-than-human entities as their Muses, their personal sources of inspiration. Sometimes the deity will come to the worshipper in dreams, speak through divinatory tools, or will appear frequently in other ways in daily life.

Other practitioners find that the stories and personality of a particular deity appeals to them far more than any other god or goddess. Giving this particular deity preference in worship seems more natural than it does for other deities.

Sometimes the worshipper tries to ignore the clear messages that are coming from the specific deity, perhaps because they don't feel they know the deity well enough, or perhaps because it seems incompatible with other goals at least on the surface.

Deities Are Not Stereotypes

Many occult and Pagan books describe deities in terms of attributes and correspondences. The Greek god Apollo, for instance, is associated with healing, prophecy, light (especially sunlight), and music. Athena is usually depicted wearing some form of armor, carrying a shield and spear, with a helmet on her head. Perhaps some of the standard myths are told about Them as well. Is this enough on which to base worship?

All of these details about specific gods and goddesses are like reading dating-service ads. They do provide some insight into the individuals but you really have to meet Them and interact with Them to get to know who They are. We would laugh at someone who insisted that they knew all about a person just from reading a dating-service ad. Likewise, reading descriptions and lists of details associated with a particular deity gives us nothing more than a glimpse of what that deity is like.

Treat deities like they are real people, no matter what your personal philosophy is about the nature of the Divine. If you want to get to know a deity then you need to make contact with Them. Talk to Them and be sure to listen to Their answers. Talk to others about Them, asking for insight and stories they may have heard. Look for the deity's signature in the things around you. Watch carefully to see if you can spot Them peeking out from different hiding places. Sing to Them, show Them respect and deference. Welcome Them into your home, your spiritual life, your mundane existence. As you tune into Their voices you'll discover They were often talking to you all along and you just didn't notice.

Seek Them out in visions, in omens, in the activities that are known to be Their favorites. Look for Them in odd places too. They are often right there where you least expect Them.

Deities are not stereotypes that are easy to define and label. Deities are greater than humans, and we bristle at attempts to label and limit us. Why should we think They would be any easier to box away all neat and tidy?

Ancestral Spirits

Many ancient Pagan cultures included reverence for ancestral figures as part, or the central element, of worship. In ancient Rome most households included small shrines to family or clan guardian deities known collectively as *lares*. Some ancient deities are believed to have started out as ancestral spirits whose worship grew and spread. It is rather fitting that modern Pagans might choose to continue this tradition of honoring their own ancestors.

One of the easiest ways to honor ancestors is to put photos of them in a place of honor in your home. The photos could be put in nice frames and put somewhere that you will see them regularly so it's easy to include them in your life. Don't hide them away in a corner – keep them out where you will see them, and they can see you, as you go about your normal routine. Let them know you see them there, and feel free to talk with them. Perhaps you can light a candle for them at special times like holidays and anniversaries. Put little bits of their favorite foods and drinks on little plates or in a small glass placed near their photo. Let them know they are not forgotten, that they are still loved.

Other ways to honor ancestral spirits is to research your family history. Draw up a family tree showing your ancestors and how they are connected to you. The tree can include people who aren't linked to you by blood or marriage, too – some ancestors have a profound impact on us even though they are not officially part of our family trees through genetic connections or through marriage. Did you have a special aunt or uncle who wasn't really related to you? How about family friends who were as close as blood relatives? Sometimes neighbors and friends are closer to us and more influential on us than our genetic relatives. All of these ancestors, though, contributed in their own ways to make us who we are today. They are all worthy of honor and respect.

Geographical Spirits

The theory of ley lines postulates a network of energy streams pulsing over and through the earth. It is believed that many holy spots are located at places where two or more of these veins of energy meet. Dowsers and psychic sensitives often speak about places having their own particular energies. In some cases these energies seem to manifest as intelligences or spirits that are attached to that particular place. Perhaps the energy itself manifests these entities or maybe the abundance of energies attracts them. In any case these psychic hotspots tend to be congregating points for nonphysical intelligences.

All over the world there are local deities and spirits that are associated with specific geographical features. Rivers, lakes, streams, and springs or wells are often believed to be homes of particular spirits or deities. The Irish goddess Boann, for instance, is said to dwell in the river Boyne. Ayer's Rock in Australia is a holy site with its own particular spirits and is sacred to the aborigines. In British folklore many hills were said to be the homes of faeries. It's also quite common for particular trees to be identified as harboring specific spiritual entities.

Many Wiccans consider their spiritual path to be one of Earth reverence, where the planet itself is considered to be Divine. What better way to honor that Divinity than to attune with the local geographical spirits?

The key is always to follow your instinct and seek out whatever moves you personally. For some it might be a particular body of water where they can walk its shores or perhaps swim or boat about. For others a local conservation area or park might be particularly peaceful and spiritually inspiring. It might be a rocky outcropping that speaks to you, or a particular tree or grove. Maybe it's the open fields, the top of a hill, or a stretch of sand dunes. The important thing is that it feels special to you.

Take some time to get to know your particular spot. Try to visit it over the course of a year, making a point to visit it in different weather conditions and in different seasons if possible. Take photos, draw sketches. Think up little rhymes that remind you of the place. When you are at your special place say hello to it silently. Open your eyes, your ears, your heart and your mind to this place and embrace it.

Leave little offerings to the place. A small bit of ground corn meal sprinkled around is one traditional and very eco-friendly offering. Perhaps a bit of bottled water, raised in a toast to the place, can be poured out and then a portion drunk yourself. Whatever you decide to leave as an offering try to keep it environmentally friendly and unobtrusive. Carving something into a holy tree, for instance, is not the most eco-friendly way to show respect and is more likely to injure and possibly kill the tree.

If you can, try to take some time to meditate in your special place. Sit or lie quietly, breathe deeply and evenly, and calm your mind. Listen, wait, and see what you can perceive. Open your mind, heart, and spirit for the messages that this place has to teach you. It has a voice that we can hear if we just open up to it and really try to hear.

On a more intellectual level it often helps to research the history of your area to discover how local deities or spirits have been identified and revered. In some cases, the name of the place identifies the local spirits. In other cases it might be harder to find out the name of local spirits. That doesn't mean they don't exist – it merely means you'll have to try and find out how the spirit wishes to be addressed in other ways. Divination methods such as pendulums, the Ouija board, scrying, runes, and tarot can all be of great help in attuning with and communicating with specific spirits.

Archetypal Spirits

Some of the most influential modern occultists have based their spiritual work on a blend of magickal practice and psychological or broader scientific theory. Dion Fortune, for instance, integrated a lot of psychological theory into her work in the Society of the Inner Light. Spiritual paths, including mysticism and occultism, can be integrated with scientific understandings if we approach both systems with open minds and a balanced outlook.

Psychology tends to encourage looking at nonphysical entities, whether spirits or deities, as archetypes. Archetypes are expressions of specific forces, ideas, or qualities. From an archetypal viewpoint, the Greek goddess Aphrodite embodies the concepts of love, sexual attraction, beauty and artistic creativity. It is no coincidence that Hephaestus, the god of metalworking, was Venus' husband; it reminded mortals that Beauty and Craft were married. The god Bacchus represents revelry, intoxication, the fermented fruits of the vine. Archetypes are considered anthropomorphized ways to try and understand and approach complex concepts.

Whether we see deities and nonphysical entities as projections of our own attempts to understand the world, as thoughtforms that have become independent through frequent attention, or whether we see them as independent beings in their own right, there are lessons we can learn from thinking in terms of archetypes. Archetypes allow us to identify, externalize, and personify abstract ideas. We can also discover how these forces or ideas manifest in ourselves, and as a result can encourage them to develop and integrate in productive ways. Archetypes help us to gain a better understanding of the parts of ourselves that we might be suppressing and learn how to deal with them in a healthy way. We develop balance by identifying and honoring the different forces that affect us externally as well as internally.

We can decide to pay more attention to a specific deity as a way to manifest that deity's influence in our own lives. For instance a person in the healing professions might decide to honor the Greek god Asclepius in order to attune with the energies of healing. It doesn't matter if the god is seen as a literal entity or as the mystical embodiment of an idea. Paying attention and showing reverence for the deity will encourage it to manifest in your life.

Getting To Know Your Deity: An Outline For Building Connection

The best way to attune with a particular deity is to spend time with your deity, to think about your deity, and to do things that will connect you with your deity. One very useful list of suggestions carried out over the course of a calendar year is called "A Walk With Your Goddess," produced by the talented women of the Amber Raven coven in Phoenix, Arizona. Following is my own variation of this program expanded and modified a bit to be useful for any sort of deity, spirit, force, or concept you wish to study. For maximum impact you should focus on just one deity or entity for a year-long investigation. Carefully select which deity or entity you want to focus on as you will be spending quite a bit of time and energy in this process.

Walking With Your God/dess

Inward Focus
Research and Study

Resource List
- Internet Sites (sites that are dedicated to your God/dess, locations of useful information, pictures, etc.)
- Books (material that is directly or indirectly about your God/dess)
- Songs and Music (historical or contemporary, instrumental, folk, or other forms)
- Sculptures, Paintings, etc. (artists, names of pieces, where they are located)

About the God/dess
- Representations
- Correspondences
- Powers and Domains
- Manifestations
- Symbols
- Aspects
- Festivals and Celebrations
- Scholarly History
- Mythology

Crafting and Creating
- Write a dedication ritual; if you are moved to do so, perform it for yourself
- Journal your progression of study and experiences (daily, weekly, monthly, seasonal insights)
- Create evolving altar dedicated to God/dess

- Daily offerings (research and perform historical or contemporary offerings, and develop your own)
- Weekly offerings
- Meditations (daily, weekly, etc.)
- Formal invocations for rituals (research historical and contemporary ones written by others, and write your own)
- Consultations, conversations, and "tea with your God/dess"
- Create a wall calendar representing the God/dess' year
- Create a "photo album" showing your God/dess and their family and friends
- Craft representations of the God/dess for every room in the home (these could be obvious, or subtle!)
- Craft representations of the God/dess for outside (yard)
- Divination
    - *o* Create a Major Arcana-style card for your God/dess. This could expand to a complete Major Arcana set, or even a whole deck using appropriate God/dess symbolism.
    - *o* Research any divinatory systems specific to your God/dess.
    - *o* Create a divinatory system (or modify an existing one) for your God/dess.
- Create invocatory movements for your God/dess
- Create a God/dess drum rhythm
- Write poetry for your God/dess
- Write chants or songs for your God/dess
- Research and recreate traditional dress, ornamentation for priest/ess of your God/dess
- Create purification materials associated with your God/dess
    - *o* Incense
    - *o* Oils
    - *o* Bath herbs
    - *o* Soaps
- Research or invent other craft projects associated with God/dess

Outward Focus
Sharing Knowledge

- Present both informational and practical material you have identified about your God/dess to your coven, or if you are solitary compile this into a written report, presentation, or website

  o Identify as much as possible which elements are historically accurate as traditional and contemporary or nontraditional
  o Identify role and interaction within God/dess' native pantheon
  o Identify role and interaction with other pantheons, psychological models
  o Share other information on God/dess, such as stories, correspondences, songs, foods, etc.

Ritual and Celebration
- Write moon phase or astrologically/astronomically associated rituals for your God/dess for solitary and/or group use
- Write spells employing God/dess' specific magickal strengths
- Write guided deep meditation (pathworking) to journey to God/dess
- Create children's activities to introduce God/dess and possibly God/dess' native culture/pantheon
- Write a festival celebration ritual for solitary or group use (i.e. Wheel of the Year sabbat)
- Celebrate at least the God/dess' most important festival

Helpers (Familiars, Spirits, Tools)

A spiritual journey is essentially a solitary journey, but it doesn't mean we have to isolate ourselves from others. Often we find our spiritual journey becomes more productive when we find others of like mind to share with. Our paths might not be identical, but by working in community we can gain valuable insights into our individual paths.

Friends

Friends provide flesh-and-blood feedback. They might not be on spiritual paths that are even close to our own, but if they are real friends that doesn't matter. They can provide a shoulder to cry on when you're struggling, alternate points of view, and suggestions for things you might never have thought of on your own. The best friends are those that are supportive but not patronizing. They respect your choices while providing challenges to encourage growth. They help you celebrate your accomplishments. They provide moral support when you are feeling down.

Some of the best friends turn out to be family members or loved ones. They are the people who often truly have your best interests at heart.

Seek out friends who are following similar spiritual paths too. Even though you might never do rituals with them, you will often find that having people who speak the same spiritual language as you provides a special form of support. It's not uncommon for members of a coven to describe their coven-mates as "closer than family." In a spiritual sense they often are. How many Wiccans grew up in Christian families that simply refuse to recognize them as anything other than black sheep? Sharing one's spiritual growth with a small group of regular confidants keeps us on an even keel. Just be selective in deciding who those special confidants should be and keep yourself safe.

Familiars

Many valuable lessons in life and spiritual growth are not taught to us in human language. Some of the most enduring lessons we can learn are those that our nonhuman family and friends teach us. Loyalty, dependence and independence, birth and life and death are all things we experience in our relationships with our familiars, whether they are animal, vegetable, or even mineral.

Animal companions in particular teach us what it is to love unconditionally. They demonstrate the interconnected web of life for us every day and keep us grounded in physical reality. They are also not as constrained by verbal language and the arbitrary rules for communication we humans have developed for ourselves. Cats and dogs, for instance, communicate with their people using a variety of methods including body language as well as audibly. They can't be bothered to lie or obfuscate when talking with us because getting the message is the important thing! Some people believe that animals are also more likely to pick up on telepathic levels than we humans and are more aware of nonphysical realms.

Spirits

Some witches work closely with all sorts of spirits. They might use scrying or other divination methods to contact and communicate with noncorporeal beings. Some believe that they speak with spirits during dreams or meditation. Others use methods such as pendulums or the Ouija board to try and make contact.

Many Wiccans believe in the existence of invisible realms whether described as an astral plane or some other system of spiritual levels. In attempting to establish a sense of balance it makes sense to learn to perceive and commune with these other realms the same way we try to commune with the physical realm. If we can befriend physical people, animals, and plants then why not do the same with invisible entities?

There is often an assumption that invisible entities are somehow superior or at least more knowledgeable than those of us in the physical realm. In some cases this might be true but we should be careful to not assume that it is so. In the physical realm we learn to protect ourselves from dangerous people. We should also be careful when venturing into nonphysical realms to ensure we are dealing with the types of entities that will actually help us to grow rather than exploit us.

In the mundane world parents are encouraged to "street proof" their children. In the occult community, we encourage practitioners to learn and use basic protective skills. Different people call these skills different things: shielding, warding, using protective charms, cleansing and strengthening one's aura or chakras. Ceremonial magicians often use a basic ritual called the Lesser Banishing Ritual of the Pentagram (abbreviated as LBRP) and Wiccans use a version of this in casting the circle. Regardless what it is called or what the specific method is, wise occultists will routinely perform protective rituals or spells to ensure their own safety.

Doing regular protective rituals is like doing regular exercise. The more you do it, the easier it becomes, and the more effective it will be for you. With strong protective magick in place only those types of spirits you want to work with and draw to you will be able to come close.

Elementals

Elementals are spirits that are essentially nonhuman and composed of the essence of air, fire, water, or earth. In Celtic culture these types of beings are often called faeries, while in others they might be called devas, or identified as spirits of specific places and objects like lakes or holy stones.

In European magickal practice elementals are often classified as follows:
Earth elementals are gnomes

> Air elementals are sylphs
> Fire elementals are salamanders
> Water elementals are nymphs.

There are variations to these, of course. Water elementals, for instance, are frequently shown as classical mermaids with a human upper body and a fish lower body. Earth elementals are sometimes called dwarves or kobolds or goblins rather than gnomes. The distinctions are really just human attempts to classify and understand what in reality can be very changeable. The only real constant appears to be that elementals are not human, are changeable, and have their own purposes, needs, and desires which might have nothing to do with what we humans would like. We can make contact with them, communicate with them, and in some cases even befriend them. We should never presume to treat them as servants or lesser humans though as their anger can be easy to arouse and difficult to assuage.

Tools

Magickal tools are symbols in physical form. They represent energies, concepts, or theories we attempt to manipulate in our magickal work. Skilled magicians really need only their own minds in order to work magick. Many of us though find that it is easier to focus our thoughts and energies when we use physical objects to represent abstract concepts.

Magickal working is often more effective when we are able to consciously handle physical components that stimulate multiple senses. Much of magick involves tapping into our deep minds, the vast resources of energy within us in our subconscious. Sometimes just one method of trying to reach the deep mind isn't effective. It makes a lot of sense to try and send the message we are trying to communicate to our deep mind using as many methods as we can. Something is more likely to get through that way, and if the message is received more than once perhaps the deep mind will pay closer attention and work a little bit harder.

Sight

While it is possible to do magick anywhere in any situation, it's often easier to concentrate when we practice in a setting where we are visually encouraged to think and feel in a direction we want to go. It's easier for many of us to get into the right magickal frame of mind when we are in a darkened room, lit only by candles, than in a place lit up by fluorescent bulbs. Better yet is a natural and peaceful setting such as a windswept hilltop, a forest clearing, or isolated seashore. Places that visually remind us of our connection to the environment and ultimately help us feel a link to the Divine are ideal.

Many witches choose their magickal tools based on how they look. Just as with the location for their magickal work it's easier to get in the right frame of mind when your props are convincing. Use things that you feel are right. Deity pictures, statuettes, or symbols are also helpful. Use what works for you.

Sound

When you close your eyes what do you hear? Do the sounds help or hinder your spiritual work? If you are trying to relax and find stillness, do you have soothing peaceful sounds to listen to? If you are trying to build up a sensual energy do you have suitable sounds that encourage those sorts of thoughts? How about energetic, active sounds or music for those stirring energy building times? Different sounds and music can have a profound impact on your magickal workings. Carefully select sounds that will help you to achieve your goals.

Many of us have experienced becoming immersed in music, essentially "tripping out" or being emotionally moved while listening to particular songs or performances. Teenagers know this and will often play the same song or album over and over again sometimes without any break. The experience found in "raves," long sessions of dancing to loud music in darkened environments, is frequently described as a trance even among those who do not supplement the experience with recreational drugs. These ways of using music and sound are awfully similar to more overtly religious examples such as the ecstatic trance dances of Voudou.

Some witches find that a specific sound such as a bell ringing is helpful in their magickal work to identify different phases of a ceremony. If you use the same sound consistently for the same things it builds up a pattern your deep mind will recognize and you will find your deep mind will come more readily to those signals. Specific sounds can be used as triggers to your deep mind and to spiritual work.

Smell

The sense of smell appears to be one of the strongest triggers for memory. Think about how you think of your mother, or an aunt, or a grandmother when you smell a particular perfume that they frequently wear. There is a reason why the perfume industry is so well established. Manufacturers have also realized that their products sell better when they have particular attractive scents that their competitors lack. Car manufacturers even have a carefully formulated "new car smell" that they spray in vehicles to help sell them.

Just as with sounds and sights, smells can induce a variety of emotional and intellectual states in us. These triggers can vary from person to person. If you have a bad experience that you associate with a particular smell, then it's hard to not feel some of that emotional echo when you encounter that smell again. It doesn't matter if the smell is pleasant for most people; if you have a negative association with it then it will be difficult to overcome.

Witches use the sense of smell in magickal work mostly through the use of incense, herbs, and potions. Specific herbal blends are burned for the scented smoke they produce and the magickal influences they can encourage. As with anything, though, it's often a matter of repetition. As you build specific associations with particular scents, it is easier and easier to use those scents as triggers for those associations. Build the associations that are most useful for you, and you can consciously use them in future workings.

Taste

A Jewish tradition often done with children is to reward them after a first lesson with a spoonful of honey so they come to associate learning with sweetness. In Wiccan rituals the sense of taste is generally used to trigger grounding or to "bring us back from the astral" through the cakes and ale sequence towards the end of a working. On a basic level eating or drinking provides fuel to our bodies to replenish us after exertion whether physical, mental, emotional, or spiritual. Taste and smell are closely intertwined, though, so we actually do use taste throughout our working although usually in a lesser way. Smells are strong triggers for memory so it makes sense to also use taste this way. When we have a bit to eat and drink, stimulating our taste buds, it tends to bring our attention back to our bodies, back to the physical realm and away from intellectual and spiritual contemplation.

Eating and drinking brings us back to the mundane world in a safe and quick way.

The sense of taste can be used though as the dominant sense for a spiritual ceremony. An altered state of consciousness can be achieved during ritual consumption of a meal where the ingestion of drink and food is slow, deliberate, and special attention is given to the tastes and smells. Eating as a purposeful celebration of sharing can result in a very real form of Divine communion. In Japan this type of spiritual practice exists in the tea ceremony. In Native American traditions this exists in the example of the peace pipe ceremony. In Christianity, it is represented in the last supper Jesus shared with his disciples. In the Jewish tradition, the Passover feast is a good example. In Wicca the "dumb supper" sometimes conducted at Samhain can be a deeply moving ritual when done with loving respect and a spiritual attitude.

Touch

Like all other senses, the sense of touch can be used to manipulate consciousness for magickal purposes. Many Wiccans do this by having special clothing that they wear only for ritual purposes. The sensation of those particular clothes on their bodies helps to put them in the appropriate state of mind. For some Wiccans, feeling the air on their naked skin as they practice skyclad fulfills this purpose.

Another way that the sense of touch is stimulated for magickal or spiritual purposes is through the use of specific bodily postures or gestures. People who meditate often have a specific pose they assume for their work. Ritual magicians frequently employ a set of ritual gestures as part of their ceremonies. Others might make use of mudras or ritual hand postures and gestures as a way of encouraging spiritual states.

Eclectic witches can invent or borrow gestures or postures that they choose to associate with specific concepts in ritual practice. Gestures can be used to indicate all sorts of activities and can be useful triggers.

Touch is also involved in some rather harsh and potentially dangerous methods used by some to achieve altered states of consciousness. Pain inflicted in specific ways such as through flagellation, for instance, is found in a variety of religious traditions including some Christian sects and also in Gardnerian Wicca. There is a question though whether the altered state of consciousness is really the result of the tactile sensory overload, the production of natural painkillers such as endorphins and adrenalines, or whether it is something else altogether or perhaps a combination of effects.

The sense of touch can be an important component in ritual or magickal work just as are the other senses. Effective work will include careful manipulation of all sensory input in order to achieve the desired goals.

Use all of your senses with intention in your spiritual practice and you will find your rituals, spells, and devotions gain a whole new level of depth that they might have lacked before.

Chapter 8:
Wiccan Mystical Ritual

Inducing a Mystical Experience

Trance and Magick

A lot of magickal work centers on attempting to reach an altered state of consciousness in order to achieve our goals. In traditional shamanic work, the shaman goes on a spirit journey to obtain information or effect spiritual healing. Spiritualist mediums set up an environment of quiet and safety with dim lights so that they can slip into trance and contact the spirit world. Those who meditate work to bring their awareness to a point of one-ness or even no-thought in order to touch Nirvana. Ceremonial magicians perform complex rituals in order to attain the knowledge and conversation with their Holy Guardian Angel, Higher Self, or the Divine. On a more mundane level, a lot of modern New Age magickal practice centers on quieting the conscious everyday mind in order to contact the unconscious mind, whether that unconscious mind is personal or collective. Urban primitives, that subculture in western society that embraces practices such as extensive tattooing, piercing, and other body modifications, and could also be considered to encompass "club culture" with their all-night dance sessions, speak about the personal spiritual significance of their sometimes extreme forms of hedonism. Altered states of consciousness or trances are an inherent part of magickal work.

Many practitioners define trance as a state of one-pointed concentration, where one focuses on a single thing or idea to the exclusion of all else, or alternatively as a state of "no-mind," where you empty your mind and relax to a point where you are totally receptive with the active daily chatter of the mind diminished to the point of silence. Both methods are of use in magickal practice. Focusing on one thing is effective in performing spell-work since the goal of spell-work is attempting to achieve a particular result. Emptying one's mind and becoming receptive is useful for communing with deity or one's Higher Self, as the quieting of the mundane mind allows space for inspiration to take center stage in one's awareness.

In his book "Trance Zero," psychotherapist Adam Crabtree presents his theory that we are always in a trance and that different trances vary only in their degree. According to this theory what we consider to be waking consciousness is merely one form of trance. He also extrapolates that the cultural paradigms we tend to take for granted are a form of collective trance; when we visit a culture that is unknown to us, we often have the feeling of "waking up" from our cultural assumptions and point of view. Crabtree's theory describes trance as a spectrum of consciousness including normal awareness instead of a single specific mental state.

Seeing trance as a normal function of consciousness and awareness frees us from the misunderstanding that magickal trance is something unique and rare, something difficult to attain. If Crabtree's theory is accurate in describing consciousness and trance we are all adepts at slipping from one mode of awareness to another. It is quite common to experience a focusing of awareness to the exclusion of outside stimuli when watching an engrossing television show, movie, or reading a really good book. Driving or riding in a car along a routine path often lulls us into a sense that the trip slipped by unnoticed. If we can shift from razor-sharp focused awareness to receptive listening so easily it should be just a matter of practice for us to reach the same states at will.

In his Book of Shadows, Gerald Gardner lists eight methods to work magick, all of which could also be interpreted as methods to achieve trance:

1. Meditation or concentration.
2. Chants, Spells, Invocations. Invoking the Goddess, etc.
3. Projection of the Astral Body.
4. Incense, Drugs, Wine, etc. Any potion that aids to release the Spirit.
5. Dancing.
6. Blood control. Use of the Cords.
7. The Scourge.
8. The Great Rite.

The methods listed all employ two primary ways of achieving trance: electrochemical stresses, and focus on pattern. Understanding the paths to spontaneous shifting of consciousness can allow us to more easily achieve purposeful trance states.

Electrochemical stresses include stresses on the physical body and consequently on the mind and consciousness such as through pain, injury, or changes in blood flow which tend to induce the release of endorphins and the body's autonomous reactions to these situations. Athletes engaging in tests of their endurance often describe being in "the zone" where they have pushed their body to extremes, and a mental and emotional state strikingly similar to the classic trance state is achieved. Individuals who undergo painful invasions or alterations of their bodies (during surgery without anesthetic, during an injury or illness, or during some forms of body piercing or tattooing) similarly speak about "going beyond the pain" to a state of emotional and mental focus sometimes described as bliss. These stresses can be very harsh on the physical body, however, so care and very conscious consideration of the consequences must be part of following these paths to induced trance states. Harsh methods should never be embarked on without the supervision of a guide with appropriate experience. It's too easy when one is "beyond the pain" to overdo it and end up needing medical or even psychiatric attention. A helper who has done these things themselves and is properly trained to guide others should always be present to monitor, assist, and ensure that all participants are kept safe.

Taking substances orally such as food, drink, or oral drugs is one way to achieve the same or similar effects on the brain and body as can be achieved through purely physical stresses. Inhaled substances such as incense smoke, perfume scents, and tobacco or other smoked substances also affect the chemical balance of the body to lesser or greater degrees. Affecting and controlling the chemical balance of the body in this way can and does change one's consciousness. It is wise to limit experimentation of altering consciousness by the use of ingested materials to only those things that are mild and safe such as most foods or the controlled use of alcohol. Changing one's body chemistry with controlled substances, refined drugs, or potent herbs carries the very real danger of causing lasting damage.

While electrochemical methods of inducing altered states can be quite effective with rapid results it can be quite dangerous and produce long-term health problems depending on the particular method used and severity of the electrochemical stress that is induced. A more gentle and just as effective method to achieving altered states of consciousness is through the use of pattern and mental focus.

While electrochemical stresses on the body are a quick way to altered states, mental focus and the use of pattern is a slower method requiring greater discipline and effort. The benefits of learning and practicing the gentle mental methods far outweigh those achieved through electrochemical stress. Regular mental focus exercises are known to sharpen one's senses, increase mental agility, reduce stress levels, and improve one's general health and happiness. Once you get the knack of using disciplined mental focus it becomes quite easy to alter one's state of consciousness unobtrusively and without requiring much preparation either. While the quick harsh ways can produce long-term problems, practicing the more gentle disciplined methods produce long-term benefits.

Mental methods include the use of pattern to help distract the mind from external stimuli, and act as an anchor to draw focus towards a sharpened level of consciousness. Techniques include meditation in all its forms, such as sitting in silence with eyes closed and focusing on one's breathing, or repeating a mantra or chant over and over, or reciting long and repetitive invocations and prayers. Reciting long counting-prayers like the Rosary or its variants is another method that works well for many. Visual stimuli can be used too, such as gazing at mandalas and yantras, images of deities, or indeed any form of visual art, particularly images that have repeating patterns. Simple visual triggers can be used as focal points too: sitting in a darkened room and staring at the flame of a candle for instance. For those who are more physical in their nature, long repetitive physical motions such as chopping wood, digging in a garden, knitting, rocking gently in a rocking chair, or other repetitive physical activity can be effective methods to achieve altered states of consciousness. Fancy rituals are very nice but are not really necessary. The simplest techniques will work just as well and require far less preparation to use.

The key for making the gentle methods effective is to practice them frequently, preferably in a regular routine so that a discipline of practice is established. The more regular the routine, the more skilled the practitioner becomes in the method, the more likely altered states of consciousness can be attained and maintained. Many find that establishing regular times and places where these meditation methods are practiced with minimal distractions makes success easy.

Effective magickal rituals often use a judiciously considered combination of methods to induce a shift of consciousness. For long-term practice gentle methods such as meditation and the use of repetitive invocations are most effective, but it is also common for some of the less harmful electrochemical stress methods to be included. Followers of Voudou, for instance, are famous for their lengthy and exhausting drumming and dancing sessions where practitioners are able to shift consciousness and tap into the power of the loa. Wiccans frequently employ dance as well, but just as often focus more on the use of specific incenses, limited ingestion of alcohol during ritual, chanting, and repetitive invocations as methods to achieving a magickal state of mind. Gerald Gardner's Wiccan tradition made some use of the ritual scourge and light bondage to stimulate blood flow and endorphin production. Ideally, the methods chosen for a ritual or an extended series of workings should be symbolic of the magickal goals. If one is working magick in order to encourage peace and tranquility, for instance, it would make more sense to focus on the gentler methods of inducing trance rather than some of the more stressful methods which are inherently painful or even violent.

One of the most common methods used by Wiccans to achieve trance, which is also perhaps an unacknowledged part of other more physical techniques, is to perform conscious breathing. Most of the time we breathe spontaneously, without thinking about the fact that we are taking air into our lungs and expelling it in a regular pattern. By paying attention to our breathing pattern, and then consciously breathing in and out in a measured and controlled way, the mind is quieted and outside distractions become less obvious. By breathing in deeply, focusing on the pauses between each inhalation and exhalation as well as the breaths themselves, the mind tends to relax. The most common breathing pattern used for this is called the four-fold breath. It involves breathing in for a mental count of four, pausing for another count of four, breathing out for a count of four, and then pausing again for another count of four before repeating the cycle. It also helps to inhale through the nose and exhale through the mouth.

The four-fold breath and other breathing techniques work to induce altered states of consciousness for two main reasons. First, breathing in and out deeply in a consciously controlled manner tends to bring more oxygen into the bloodstream than normal breathing patterns when one is at rest. Increasing the oxygen in the bloodstream has a very noticeable effect on the brain in particular, reducing stress levels and increasing mental clarity and a general sense of well-being. Second, focusing one's awareness on a specific repetitive task such as breathing and repeated counting patterns encourages one to turn attention away from external stimuli. This way both electrochemical and mental focus and pattern awareness techniques are being exploited.

Gentle Trance Methods

There are a number of gentle methods employed to induce trance states. Following are a few that are known to be quite effective and safe.

Meditation

Meditation involves setting aside some time to turn one's awareness away from external stimuli and turning inward, focusing on a particular task or idea to the exclusion of everything else. Like most activities, the more you practice meditation in a regular routine the easier it becomes and the more effective the results.

Focus and Attention

One of the simplest forms of meditation is to sit quietly in a place where distractions are at a minimum, and turn one's attention towards a single point of focus. Some use a word or phrase repeated over and over either out loud or silently in one's head as their object of focus. Some use a visual focus such as a candle flame, a simple symbol drawn on paper, or a holy object observed in dim light. The key is always to try and ignore all other stimuli and focus one's attention exclusively on the chosen target. When you focus on a single item it's as though the target is all that exists in the world.

Pathworking

Pathworking, sometimes called guided meditation, involves directing focus and attention away from external stimuli towards internal environments that are sometimes described as being on other planes of existence such as the Astral or Etheric realms. The technique involves what is essentially a form of hypnosis, whether guided by someone else or self-directed, where attention is directed at building up and exploring complex scenarios in the imagination. The participant is encouraged to experience the imaginary world in a vivid way, with all of the senses engaged. Some pathworking sessions are highly structured and directed, but they can also be designed to provide the basic foundation for participants to experience these other realms but also discover their own unique components through exploration.

Breath work

One common way to encourage single-minded focus in meditation is to direct one's attention towards patterns of breathing instead of focusing on words, ideas, or external objects. Perhaps the most basic breathing pattern described as a focus for meditation is the four-fold breath pattern. In this sequence, the participant breathes in for a mental count of four, pauses and holds that breath for a count of four, exhales for a count of four, and then pauses for another count of four before repeating it all again. When done slowly and deliberately it can quickly encourage the participant to relax and slip into a meditative state.

It is common for breath work to be used as one of the initial techniques for more complex meditation techniques such as pathworking. Breath work can be the sole technique used for meditation though and is quite effective all on its own.

Meditation forms focusing on physical movement such as Tai Chi and Yoga use breath work as one of the foundations upon which the movements rely. There is a school of Yoga known as Pranayama that has developed an elaborate system of meditation focusing exclusively on breath work.

Movement and Dance

Meditative techniques involving physical activity, such as Tai Chi and Yoga, are effective forms of meditation but are not the only ways of practicing focused attention. Any form of physical activity, especially if it involves repetitive and continuous motion, can be used as a way to achieve single-pointed awareness. Sufi mystics, for instance, are known for practicing a form of physical meditation that involves standing upright and spinning around and around. Dance, whether freeform or highly structured, is also used in a variety of cultures as a form of meditation or a doorway to altered states of consciousness. Devotees of Voudou, Santeria, and other Afro-Caribbean magickal religions in particular are noted for their use of ritual dance.

Dance is one of the easiest physically active forms of meditation because it usually involves repetitive movement and rhythmic music. Some mystical scholars and teachers, such as G. I. Gurdjief, explored meditation in the form of physical activity which isn't usually classified as dance. He found that repetitive and involved physical activity, whether working in a field or chopping wood, could be used as well as a form of meditation and spiritual discipline. Repetition and drawing one's attention to a single focus was the key regardless of the manner of physical activity that was used.

Prayer

Prayer, when practiced as a routine of repeating a standard wording, can be a powerful form of meditation. It has many of the key elements found in other forms of meditation: stepping outside of one's daily activities to seek a moment of quiet introspection, repetition of a formula, attempting to turn one's attention away from external stimuli towards a focus. It doesn't matter whether the prayer used is a traditional wording handed down intact for generations or whether the prayer is one you have invented yourself. It is also possible for a prayer that is spontaneous, never repeated exactly the same way, to act as a deep meditative experience if one is able to turn attention exclusively towards the act of praying and slip into an altered state of consciousness.

Ritual magicians often use the trick of reciting long repetitive prayers or invocations as a way to enter into trance states in which magick will be practiced. Some use what they call "barbarous language," long streams of words that are gibberish and have no actual meaning, as vocalized forms of meditation. Charismatic Christian groups that practice "speaking in tongues" are achieving trance states through essentially the same technique.

Chanting

Chanting is really just a simplified form of prayer when looked at as a meditative technique. Words are spoken, either out loud or mentally, in a pattern that repeats over and over again. Where a prayer tends to be longer a chant tends to be short and to the point, focusing more on repetition to achieve the goals. The act of repeating the same word or phrase over and over again draws the attention away from the outside world and allows one to focus on a single point or activity.

Rosaries (Repetitive Prayer)

Buddhists, Roman Catholics, Hindus, and other religious groups have long known about the usefulness of using repetitive prayers recited a specific number of times as a meditative technique. To free the mind from having to worry about the specific count in repeating the prayers a string of beads or a knotted cord is held, with one bead or knot shifted with the fingers for each prayer recited. Adding this tactile feedback helps to focus the mind and bring one into a prayerful attitude. Picking up the beads or knotted string helps set the mood for subsequent meditation or prayer sessions.

The simplest way to perform a rosary-style repetitive prayer is to choose a prayer that is meaningful, one that you look forward to committing to memory. It's OK to read the prayer off a written sheet or out of a book as you start. Hold the string of beads in one or both hands, with your fingers focused on a logical starting place in the beads, perhaps by a clasp or a specific bead that stands out. Take a deep breath and then begin repeating the prayer slowly and with deliberation. The goal is not to rush through the prayer but to really speak the words, hear the words, and understand their meaning. Once you have finished the first recitation of the prayer shift one bead on your string, and start the next repetition.

It's often easiest to use a single prayer that you repeat over and over again once for each bead on the string. As you become more proficient you might decide to start using more than one prayer in the recitation, perhaps using specific prayers for specific types of bead in your string.

In her book "A Circle of Stones," Erynn Rowan Laurie details a Celtic Pagan variation of the rosary that she uses herself. Her string of beads is constructed of ten different kinds of beads, each type of bead representative of particular Celtic symbolism. She has a whole sequence of prayers and affirmations to recite for the different beads encompassing a whole mystical worldview based on Celtic mythology. Her prayers and affirmations are provided in both English and, for the historically-minded, Gaelic.

As with most spiritual practices, how complex or simple a method needs to be is really up to the particular practitioner. The important thing is to try a method, find what works for you, and then use it.

Music and Song

Music is a language of emotion that transcends limitations such as words. A song can deeply touch listeners even though there might not be any intelligible lyrics. Beat, rhythm, melody, tempo, layering can act as very direct emotional triggers.

Many in the Pagan community have rediscovered the ecstatic joys involved in immersing yourself in playing music particularly with percussive instruments. Today in most urban areas with any sort of Pagan presence there are regular "drumming circles" where participants gather to engage in impromptu music-making.

Many musicians find that they get into a mental and emotional state while performing where it seems like the music is playing through them, as though the music has an existence of its own and is using the musician as a channel to manifest. It doesn't matter if the musician is technically skilled or not, although competent performers often have an advantage of familiarity with their instruments which newcomers lack. The process of playing, of giving voice to sound and pattern, can trigger ecstatic states.

It's no coincidence that traditional shamanic rituals often focused on drumming and rattling, that traditions like Voudou employ long drumming sessions, as methods of attaining mystical awareness.

Listening to music, especially in situations where you are able to fully concentrate on the music, is another method for attaining altered states of consciousness that many find easy to use. The trick, like with most methods for attaining altered states of consciousness, is to minimize outside distractions and focus attention on one thing, in this case music.

It doesn't really matter much what the actual music is that you use. Different music has a tendency to induce different emotions, thoughts, and states of awareness in each of us. When preparing for a musical meditation session, try to choose pieces that makes sense together. It is likely going to be difficult to meditate to a series of songs that jump from one theme to another, that go from soothing to jarring to contemplative. Try to pick pieces to play in sequence that will provide the particular rhythm you are seeking to achieve in your meditation session.

For deep relaxation sessions some people find soft new-age style music or natural sounds are most effective. Others find that repetitive music such as drumming or other percussive instruments are best at slowing them down and relaxing. A lot of it depends on your personal preferences, the type of music you enjoy listening to, and the effects that particular types of music have on you. It pays to listen to a variety of types of music and decide for yourself what types produce the effects you are looking to induce in yourself.

It is also a matter of personal preference whether songs with lyrics help or hinder meditative states. Some people find that listening to familiar songs with lyrics they can follow does the trick for them in bringing them to the right state of mind, especially if the lyrics build on the themes or emotions being sought. Others find lyrics distracting and work better with purely instrumental music, or perhaps with music where the lyrics are in a language they don't know or are wordless chants.

One memorable meditative session I participated in happened in Phoenix, Arizona where I was fortunate to attend a ceremony in honor of the goddess/Buddha Tara performed by a group of visiting Tibetan monks. The ceremony involved the monks sitting on the floor, playing percussive instruments and horns at particular parts, but mostly singing and chanting long and complex songs. The ceremony went on for well over an hour and had a profound effect on the audience, who sat in rapt attention. It was very easy to just let the sound wash over me, feel it move through me, and slow my thoughts down and to that still, relaxed state of deep meditation. I will remember this particular event for a very long time.

Today it is easier than ever to listen to music in any sort of setting you like. Portable music players with effective and unobtrusive earphones are cheaply and readily available. With computers and new music technology it's easier than ever to put together custom mixes of your favourite music. Even those of us with absolutely no musical talent can put together sequences of moving songs and play them for personal enjoyment anywhere we want.

An easy way to get into a meditation routine is to put together a sequence of meditative songs, or choose a favourite meditative album, and then listen to it on a regular basis. Set aside time to just sit and listen to your music and let yourself relax and really get into the music. Perhaps you could do this in bed before you go to sleep, or sitting quietly on a park bench, or even sitting in a library with the volume discreetly low through your headphones. Make it a routine, and try to use the same music in the same sequence for at least a dozen sessions to give you a chance to build the routine. You will be amazed at the results if you give yourself a chance.

Arts and Crafts

Immersing yourself in a hobby or practice like arts and crafts is another way to produce circumstances where mystical insights can manifest. As with music, working with visual arts or producing craft objects engages our creative faculties and encourages us to engage in problem solving.

Concentrating on our fine motor skills, working with visual senses of balance, colour, texture, and weight can bring us out of our routine sleepwalking to a level of refined concentration. Honing our senses for a particular task has the added benefit of sharpening our awareness of other things including potential spiritual experiences.

It isn't a coincidence that performing magick is sometimes called spell-weaving. The act of drawing fibres together to make thread or yarn and then manipulating these to produce cloth has long been considered a miraculous art. The Three Fates of Greek myth were responsible for creating and manipulating mortal destinies by spinning, manipulating, and then severing our life-threads. Mythical witches weave magick out of the words, motions, and various ingredients of their spells to effect change. One fictional woman, Morgause in Marion Zimmer Bradley's novel "The Mists of Avalon," cast a death curse by concentrating on the ill she wished to bring about while she wove a garment on her loom. Weaving, though, like most crafts and arts is inherently a creative process so it is much better suited for productive magick or magick intended to strengthen and protect.

Sometimes the best trigger to mystical awareness is the novelty of engaging in an artistic activity. If you normally draw try sculpting for instance. If you normally do crafts try sketching a landscape! Try something that is very tactile like finger-painting or playing with clay or dough. Relax, get into the process, and just do. Don't worry about the result — sometimes we all need to do things badly and not care about the result in order to just have fun with the process.

Try, and do, and find joy in the activity of it all. Pay attention to how it makes you feel and explore your gut emotions. Express yourself! You'll find ideas are like a fountain; as you let the surface ones out all sorts of things come welling up from unknown depths.

Daily Living as a Meditative Practice

Any activity, no matter how mundane, can be made into a spiritual and mystical practice if it is approached with serenity, deliberation, and precision. Why not take advantage of the things we have to do anyway and include them in our spiritual practice?

Everything from simple household chores like cleaning, preparing meals, and tidying up can be done in a meditative manner. Are they done in a rush, thoughtlessly, with a sense of frustration? Or are they done with a feeling of dance and pattern? Daily chores are part of the rhythm of life. When we consider the Divine to be immanent and omnipresent, then why not honor the Divine in the everyday things around us? Touch the things around you with the same reverence you would objects in a holy shrine. Speak to your houseplants, your animal companions, your family and friends as you would to saints and deities in the flesh. Look for the spark of soul in them and honor it. Encourage their spark to shine forth by showing them love, and compassion, and respect. Give them a smile and a kiss.

If you are fortunate enough to have a garden spend time getting to really know your plants as individuals. Feel the soil where they are planted, smell it, look at it carefully. Listen to how the foliage moves against your hands and how it moves in the wind. Observe how they look in different kinds of light, by moonlight as well as sunlight and shade. If you can make the time to really listen and observe you will find there is a lot they have to teach us.

Animals, too, provide us with precious opportunities to learn by observation and by interacting. Get to know your animal friends as individuals. What are their likes and dislikes? How do their moods cycle? How do they smell, feel, and look? How can you show respect and love for them? How can you honor them as a manifestation of divinity?

Sex

Sex is one of those activities that is usually considered to be special and when we do engage in it we easily focus on what we are doing rather than allow ourselves to become distracted. As a result sex is easily used as a magickal technique for raising energy or for attaining altered states of consciousness. Mystical states are frequently described in terms that sound suspiciously sexual. Some magickal systems consider sexual techniques to be central to their philosophies.

On a symbolic level sex clearly represents the mystical goal of union with another. The act of sex with another involves exposing ourselves, revealing parts that we usually keep hidden from the world, and sometimes parts we even keep hidden from ourselves. We surrender our bodies to another, embracing them so close that our bodies become one. Physical sensations are stirred and raised to a peak where release is achieved. Emotions, thoughts, and feelings are whipped into a frenzy. People who have sex with specific partners usually feel deep connections with each other because of the intimate nature of what they have shared physically and emotionally.

Sexual magick, even when practiced as a solitary, encourages us to stretch the boundaries of our identities. It takes us out of our daily awareness and allows us to really pay attention to bodily sensations. If we approach sex as holy, a sacrament of celebration and joy, we open ourselves up to discovering the Divine spark in our lovers and ourselves and by extension in everyone else. Sex in a loving consensual setting allows our Divine spark to flare and shine like a beacon. If we let it sex can be a glorious celebration of life and creativity.

Other Sensory/Emotional Stimulation

Other types of sensory or emotional stimulation can be consciously used to induce altered states of awareness, and invite mystical experiences. Most of us have been so engrossed in a movie, a theatrical performance, a book we were reading, or music to the point that we have lost track of time or anything else that might have been happening around us. Many who read for pleasure tend to describe curling up with a good book as "escaping into a story." These instances are all perfect opportunities for us to build a spiritual discipline if we just learn to appreciate them.

One way to consciously build a spiritual discipline based on these methods would be to select books, movies, plays, or music with particular spiritual themes and then set aside special time to become engrossed in them. Perhaps it can be part of a daily routine, perhaps a few minutes each morning before you start your day or a few minutes at night just before you go to sleep. Or maybe you want to use these methods as the centerpiece of a spiritual retreat session for you, where you dedicate a solid block of a few hours, a whole day, a whole weekend, or perhaps longer to just that one thing with only breaks for eating, sleeping, and other bodily concerns.

Of course a whole ritual could be built up around reading a book or watching a movie. You can choose your location carefully, adjust the lighting, and perhaps use specific background music to complement the experience. Appropriate incense can be lit to add a scent reminder. Related food and drink could be researched, obtained, and prepared for the occasion. It can be as complex or as simple as you desire.

When the Divine touches you and moves you, go with it. Allow the emotions and the experience to flow over and through you. Pay attention to what you are experiencing and try to express it when you have time, through words, images, movement, or whatever methods make sense to you. Set the stage, make space in your life, and encourage the Divine. Whatever methods work best for you are the ones that you should use.

Harsh (And Potentially Dangerous) Trance Methods

Many of the most dramatic mystical experiences described in religious literature were triggered by extremely stressful conditions. While they are not encouraged as safe methods to employ in a spiritual exploration, they can shed light on how and why mystical experiences might happen.

The common feature that appears to be consistent is that mystical experiences slip into our lives in moments when our awareness is drawn away from the mundane sleepwalking of everyday life. Our daily routine is often so ingrained in us that we go through them without really paying attention to what we are doing. When we are put into novel situations where we are forced to pay attention, or when our attention is caught by something unusual, the Divine has an opportunity to reveal Itself.

Physical Stress

Physical stress is one way that we are "brought out of our heads" into a sharpened awareness of our bodies and sensory input. Stress can be induced through physical exertion or through more dangerous methods such as injury or imbalances.

It's no surprise that people who suffer from serious bodily injury or life-threatening situations report mystical experiences. The body's ingrained defense mechanisms kick in, sharpening the senses in anticipation of flight or fight. Pain makes us aware of our bodies in a very immediate way. In these sorts of circumstances we can sometimes discover that our daily obsessions are trivial and the real meaning of our lives becomes sharply clear to us. Sometimes the revelations are expansive, lifting the person out of their everyday awareness in a truly life-changing way.

Chemical Imbalances

Stress on the body can also take the form of chemical imbalances including fluctuations in blood sugar levels. Some notorious modern cults have used this technique to devastating effect; they starve their congregants when they want to induce feelings of guilt and shame, and then stuff them with sugary junk food when they want them to feel euphoria towards the group and cult leaders. It's a crude form of brainwashing but it is effective. These methods can be just as harmful to the body as injury and extreme physical stress as organs can break down in ways that are difficult or impossible to heal. Chemicals frequently act directly on the brain as well and can cause the permanent impairment or loss of brain matter. Drugs can produce the effects they have by the very nature of what they are doing to the body: poisoning the system and inducing extreme responses from our autonomic systems. The long-term consequences of experimenting with drugs can be quite severe, canceling out any short-term benefits in spiritual experience.

Fasting

Blood glucose levels are a slightly less dangerous way of inducing stress on the body and therefore can be useful in opening to the possibility of altered states of awareness and mystical experiences. People who live with chronic metabolic disorders such as diabetes know very well how blood sugar levels can affect their ability to think and function. Those who are in any way susceptible to diabetes or other metabolic imbalances should follow their doctors' recommendations and should avoid playing with their blood sugar levels unless given the go-ahead under the supervision of their medical advisors.

Healthy people, though, go through normal cycles of highs and lows with blood sugar levels. In healthy people techniques such as fasting can be an effective method to seek spiritual experiences as part of a mystical or religious system. Fasting and its opposite, feasting, have a long history of use within spiritual traditions. Blood sugars are allowed to reach a low through fasting, and then a ritual feast follows which floods the system with glucose. The rapid highs and lows can be as effective in shifting one's awareness as other more strenuous and more dangerous methods.

Recreational Drugs

Other common methods used in many spiritual traditions is the sharing of ritual alcohol, or in some traditions, ritual smoking. Worshippers of Dionysus in ancient Greece routinely drank wine, the blood of the God of the Vine, to excess as part of their religious festivals. Christians use wine in the communion ceremony as do many other religions. Wiccans, too, often share wine during ritual as an act of celebration and thanksgiving.

There are many substances that we ingest routinely in our food and drink that are just as potent as any substance normally identified as a drug. Caffeine, for instance, is a powerful stimulant. It's found in many soft drinks, in coffee, in many teas, and in chocolate. Chocolate is another interesting food regardless whether it's taken as a food or a drink – it contains many substances that are known to have rather interesting effects on the system, particularly the brain. Some researchers[6] have claimed that the effects chocolate produces in the brain are similar in many ways to being in love.

It is highly advisable to focus any experimentation with recreational drugs on legal and commonly available foods and drinks rather than resorting to illegal substances. Legal foods and drinks have the advantage of widespread quality controls and more in depth research into their benefits and problems. Illegal substances are not as likely to be well understood or subject to quality guarantees. People who take illegal recreational drugs are really gambling with their lives for short-term reasons.

Restriction of blood or oxygen

It is well known that increasing blood and oxygen flow in the body can produce dramatic changes in awareness and trigger mystical experiences. Spiritual disciplines such as yoga, both in the form of physical exercises and in breath control, are clear examples. The reverse is also true though: through calming or restricting blood flow and the regulation of oxygen we can experience changes in awareness. At the most extreme level people who suffer from restricted blood flow or a lack of oxygen will lose consciousness. At more precarious levels the results can mimic intoxication or what might appear to be a sharpening of awareness, very likely caused by the body going into a fight-or-flight response to perceived danger.

During the Victorian era women who wore the tight corsets that were the fashion at the time were frequently known to suffer fainting spells. Modern sexual fetishists[7] who experiment with corsets or other extremely tight or restrictive clothing, or who engage in bondage, often describe how these practices alter or heighten their sensual and sexual experiences. Lack of oxygen to the brain for extended periods of time can have very serious effects. Unfortunately it is easy to go too far with these types of things and end up with critical or even fatal consequences.

Moderation is preferable, and safer, than excess. Knowing how an excess or a deficit of oxygen in the system affects our perceptions, we can consciously focus on breath control as a reasonably gentle method to encourage new perceptions and spiritual experiences. Inducing these experiences through extreme methods is like using a hammer to crack the shell on a hard-boiled egg. It will certainly have an effect but the consequences overall are just too drastic especially knowing that we can use milder variations of the method to achieve the same effects more safely.

Wiccan Ritual Structure

What exactly is a Wiccan ritual, and what makes an effective one? How does a Wiccan ritual help a goal to manifest? How is ritual important in a mystical or spiritual path?

What Is Ritual?

Ritual in a Wiccan philosophy is a symbolic enactment of purposeful actions in order to achieve a specific goal. The goals can be quite varied although there are some that are common.

Many Wiccan rituals available in published books are primarily centered on worship; they strive to provide an opportunity to connect the participant with particular manifestations of the Divine. Many do this by recitation of invocations, evocations, prayers, or chants aimed at specific deities. Others, particularly sabbat rituals, might include dramatic enactments of mythology related to the deities.

Other rituals are designed to either celebrate change in a participant, or trigger that change. Initiation rituals are a good example of this. In many circumstances they are performed to formally acknowledge a change in a participant. In some circumstances the ritual is designed to try and trigger the desired change in the participant, although this change might or might not occur depending on what the change is. These types of rituals are often seen as milestones in one's life.

Some rituals, often the ones Wiccans consider to be spell work, are performed specifically to bring about a desired change. These are the ones where it is most important to have clear goals, clear understanding of the symbolism being used, and strength of purpose. Energy is raised, built to a peak, and then directed to the goal. This type of ritual is just one step in the process of working towards a goal. There is always follow-up work to be done, usually including mundane steps that need to be taken, and sometimes follow-up rituals that are performed to further clarify and strengthen the purpose towards achieving the goal.

It is important the participants use symbolism that they understand and agree with regardless the type of ritual. In the southern hemisphere, for instance, the winter solstice is in June and not December, so performing a winter ritual with all its associated symbolism during the summer months is not as likely to be effective. That doesn't mean that Yule has to be held in June in Australia though. It just means that south of the equator (and anywhere in the world, in fact) it is important for people doing spiritual or magickal rituals to adapt the material to suit the symbolism that corresponds with where they are, who they are, and what makes most sense to them. Using symbolism that doesn't make sense for the particular circumstance is just adding another layer of confusion when we are trying to strip away the difficulties and obstacles between us and our goals.

Basic Structure

Most Wiccan rituals follow a general structure:

- Set the scene (choose the location for the ritual, gather props, set things up.)
- Purification.
- Consecration (includes "calling the quarters" or "setting up the watchtowers," as well as invitations to spirits and deities to be present.)
- The middle part, which can be spellwork, divination, enactment or sharing of mythology, or something as mundane as discussion. This is the portion where energy is raised and directed if appropriate.
- Celebration (usually the sharing of ritual drink and food, the "cakes and wine" part.) This helps to ground any excess energy that might have been raised.
- Thanks given to the deities, spirits, elementals etc. present for the ritual.
- The ritual is formally concluded. Props are put away and the site restored to its previous state.

Rituals can be very elaborate or very simple. Some practitioners enjoy highly scripted rituals with long incantations, specific ritual actions, and regular patterns of visualization. Others feel more moved by spontaneous activity and are inclined to perform rituals on the spur of the moment without a lot of planning or preparation. Even within a single coven there is a range within the types of rituals that tend to be performed.

Effective Rituals

Rituals are effective if they satisfy the needs of the participants and if they help achieve their goals. For instance, if the goal for a particular ritual is to build a sense of community among the participants involved, the ritual actions, words, and symbolism might not be as important as how the ritual is performed: are all the participants fully involved or are some merely observers?

Rituals designed to connect the participants with a particular energy or deity are much more likely to be successful if the participants have carefully researched the symbolism of the energy or deity. Have they included the scents, sounds, motions, food and drink favored by the deity? Are the props and setting evocative of the energy? Is the mood of the ritual suggestive of that particular god or goddess? Are the participants fully engaged through multiple senses towards the goal they are trying to reach?

Rituals are often most effective through repetition. Within a single ritual there is repetition of the ritual theme through the concerted direction of symbolism through various senses. For important work, though, it can be just as important to repeat a particular ritual or theme across multiple individual ceremonies. Pace and build your energies towards the goal. Exercise your determination, your will to achieve, and the forces of the universe are much more likely to shift in your favour.

Setting the Scene

Spiritual seekers, even within the Wiccan community alone, practice mystical and magickal spiritual paths in a wide variety of ways. Many Wiccans consider the Divine to be immanent or present in everything, and therefore strive to consider everywhere as being sacred space. It is quite common, though, for ritual space to be set aside and consecrated or cleansed and dedicated for the duration of the working.

Making Space

Many mainstream religions set aside permanent sacred space in the form of temples, churches, or other religious buildings or sites. Pre-Christian Pagan communities did this as well, although the sacred sites were just as likely to be a holy well or sacred mountaintop as a human-constructed building.

Modern Pagans, following the examples of ceremonial magicians who often practiced in secret, have adopted the practice of setting aside sacred space that is considered sacred for the duration of the particular ritual. The most common way of establishing this sacred space is by casting a circle, although other formulaic methods are also used based on the philosophy of the practitioner.

Purification

The first step is usually to cleanse the area, to make it fit for ritual and religious use. This involves physically tidying up the space and perhaps modifying things a bit to make it suitable. Purifying also involves attempting to set the stage for the type of working that will be done. Unnecessary distractions are kept to a minimum, and appropriate symbolism is introduced to remind the participants why they are there.

Purification usually involves symbolic cleansing using various substances associated with spiritual purity. For Wiccans, this usually involves elemental representations being taken around the space with the intention that they will drive away unwanted influences and attract desired influences. Often this is done through the use of incense (which can represent both fire and air), water with salt in it (which represents both water and earth), or alternately with salt or special herbs sprinkled around (representing earth), a candle flame (fire), or the use of magickal tools such as wand and athame.

Banishing is a method of accomplishing spiritual or mental purity by casting out unwanted influences. Some spells for protection of this type are described as guards or wards or shields. A cast circle is often visualized as a sphere of energy that keeps out unwanted energies and entities, while attracting the desired influences, and also helping to contain any energies that the participants raise inside so that they can be more condensed and easily directed.

Consecration

Consecration is a form of promising or binding something to a purpose. It involves attracting desired influences and attempting to forge a link, at least temporarily, with those influences. In the Wiccan process of casting the circle this is often present in the form of a statement of purpose, such as the saying aloud that the circle is a place between the worlds, in a time outside of time. It is a declaration that the space and participants are now in a special circumstance, a threshold moment where dramatic things can be accomplished. It is a promise to the Divine as well as to ourselves that what we are about to do is important and worth noticing.

Building Up the Layers

Magickal and spiritual work functions on a number of different levels: spiritual, mental, conscious and unconscious, and also on the physical realm. In music, an effect is achieved by working with a variety of components such as rhythm, tone, melody, not to mention the variety of instruments that can be used including the human voice. In magick we work with symbolic language at many levels: physical through motion and touch, texture, smell, sight, sound, and even taste. Our spiritual work touches us at many levels so we approach it through many ways. The more layers of meaning we can build up, the more we can direct our overall message to a single coherent goal, the more likely we are to manifest that goal.

Goals

Working magick or embarking on a spiritual career is just like starting up any important project. If you set clear goals for yourself, and attempt to reach those goals through consistent efforts and realistic methods, you have a much greater chance of succeeding. Goals that are vague, with no real plan in place to attain them, are much harder to reach. Working at clarifying your goals also helps you to identify your priorities and avoid wasting time on things that really don't matter much to you.

It often helps to re-evaluate goals on a regular basis. The Wiccan wheel of the year provides eight sabbats that make perfect opportunities for looking at your life, your goals both mundane and spiritual. How can the change in seasons affect your goals? Do you find that some of your goals are unrealistic, or are some perhaps more important than you originally thought? Are there any things that you could eliminate from your goals or from your life to make room for other things? Where do you want to be at the next sabbat with regard to your goals? Where do you want to be next year when this sabbat comes around again? Where do you want to be in five years, or ten?

If you consider the Divine to be present in everything you should consider all your goals, whether overtly spiritual or mundane, in terms of how they honour the Divine. How do your goals fit in with your ethical system such as the Wiccan Rede? Are you working towards minimizing harm and maximizing creativity? Are your objectives being worked for the good of all or at the expense of all? Who will benefit and who will suffer? Are there ways to change your methods to be more in tune with your ethics yet still work towards your goal? Will your goal contribute favorably to your personal relationship with the Divine?

General and Specific Goals

Some goals are general, such as wanting to learn more about occultism, or wanting to become physically healthier. It's good to identify some general goals to give you a broader picture of where you want to go.

General goals are not usually that effective on their own. To reach those goals, to make them manifest in your life, you need to set smaller and more specific goals that help you towards the larger goal. The more specific a goal is, the easier it tends to be when you plan out how to reach it, the easier it is to know when the goal has been reached.

Making A Goal Concise

It's commonly said that for magick to work best we need to have our target outcome clearly identified. It's easier to focus on something that is obvious rather than something that is nebulous. Make your target clear and you are well on the way to reaching it.

Breaking Down A Goal, Identifying Steps

Any task can be broken down into smaller steps that are easier to manage. It's an old cliché that even the longest journey begins with a single step. We get to our destinations by taking each of those steps, one after the other, purposefully working away until we get there. The overall journey might seem overwhelming. Focus on the smaller steps that you can see yourself completing. Keep working at it, and in the end you'll discover that your determination and patience pay off.

Mundane And Magickal Efforts

Reaching a goal through witchcraft or occult methods is not just a matter of saying an incantation or mixing some herbs and burning a candle. Magick is about producing results, knowing what the connections are between things and manipulating things to bring about the goal. It involves effort on many levels, from the psychic and spiritual to the mental, to the mundane and physical. For example, creating a cleansed space for ritual work can involve reciting a banishing incantation, burning a cleansing incense, but also sweeping or vacuuming the area and tidying up! All the incantations and incense in the world won't make my ritual space cleansed on all levels if I neglect the physical realm.

Goals that appear to be primarily mundane can have important mental or spiritual components to them. Professional athletes, for instance, often speak about their "mental game" which puts them ahead of their competitors. The opposite is also true: spiritual and mental goals often have physical components that we ignore at our peril. If I want to work at building a more healthy spirituality for myself then I need to be sure to include working on a healthy body too. A healthy and productive spirit needs a healthy mind and body to work at its best!

Divination

Many magickal traditions teach divination as a foundational practice. Today many magickal practitioners use divination as a prelude to spellwork, as a way to determine ways to fine-tune a spell and predict the outcome. Divination can form an essential practice for exploring your spiritual path even if you never intend to perform spells.

Why Use Divination?

Divination performs a number of functions for those who practice it. Along with meditation, divination can be one of the most useful and easily practiced disciplines in a magickal spiritual path.

One of the primary introspective purposes of divination is to provide other ways of looking at things. If you are puzzling over a problem, whether a mundane or spiritual issue, consulting a divinatory method can suggest new ways for you to look at the elements and influences of the situation in question. Sometimes the divination method puts the problem into perspective by pointing out a larger picture. Other times, it helps us to break down the problem into pieces that can be examined separately, recast into different patterns, and compared with others. We often get too close to a problem to really see it objectively, and evaluating a problem through divination techniques provides us with alternative angles.

Divination has a tendency to speak for our subconscious selves. Consciously we might believe a problem is all about one thing, when subconsciously we know it's really about something completely different. Performing a divination can help us to uncover and confront those subconscious influences.

Some believe that when they consult a divination method, they are speaking with the universe or a divine intelligence. Even if we consider the skeptical viewpoint that divination is nothing more than random messages, we can still consider it to be a way for the Divine to speak to us. These messages are from outside us, and regardless where we think they are coming from they can lead us to insight. Opportunities for us to learn come in all manner of guises including seemingly random events. The important thing is what we gain from this interaction.

Finally, some believe that divination allows us to predict the future. It is perhaps simplistic to believe divination is some sort of infallible way to identify future events. However, if we consider the fact that everything is connected in a web of interactions, and look at divination as a way to try and gain insight into the chain of consequences, then perhaps it does allow us to anticipate possibilities. We always have a choice in every situation and our decisions affect the outcome. Divination can help us to see where our paths are headed and provide us with opportunities to make different choices.

Structured

Some divination methods are based on systems of symbols, essentially a language by which messages are communicated to the practitioner. In these types of systems practitioners are encouraged to study the established symbol language and familiarize themselves with how it is usually interpreted. Once the practitioner has developed some facility at interpreting the symbols they usually find they can go deeper into the meanings and start to discover subtle connections and alternate meanings that make their readings more accurate. It really is like learning a language; the more you practice it, the more proficient you become.

Tarot

The tarot is one of the most popular structured divination systems. It is based on a deck of cards, usually with four suits (the Minor Arcana) representing the four magickal elements, and a fifth set of cards known as the Major Arcana representing larger forces such as love, death, the sun, and the moon. There are many different decks commercially available although many are just variations of the ever-popular Rider-Waite deck. The easiest way to do a reading is to draw a single card randomly and interpret the symbols. Other common reading patterns are the three-card spread (usually with one card representing the past, one for the present, and one for the future) or more elaborate spreads such as the Celtic Cross layout or ones based on the twelve astrological houses.

When learning the tarot it is often easiest to start with a standard deck like the Rider-Waite and one of the many beginner books on the market. Once you are familiar with the deck and the process of interpreting the cards, you can seek out a deck that uses symbols that speak more clearly to you to use instead.

Astrology

Astrology, the mathematical study of planetary and stellar positions in relation to the timing and location of events here on Earth, is a structured divination system that is quite widespread across different cultures. In astrology, the language is essentially a mathematical one, but where different planets and stellar objects are associated with particular meanings. Some argue that the heavenly objects are the source of the particular influences, but others argue that astrology is really just a mathematical way of identifying trends or cycles to try and make predictions. Astrology uses the symbolism of the stars and planets to explain the trends and cycles but those heavenly objects are not necessarily the cause.

To illustrate the cycle theory, consider how we often get hungry when the clock shows it's lunchtime. It's not the clock that makes us hungry; it just helps us predict when we usually do feel hungry and then get something to eat. Whether the actual positions of the stars and planets are correct using the old astrological calculations isn't really all that important. It matters more whether we find the astrological mathematical predictions are accurate or not, whether they are good at identifying the trends and cycles.

Numerology

Numerology is based on the idea that numbers have philosophical or spiritual meanings that are associated with them. By examining the numbers around us, such as the date and time, and manipulating those numbers in specific ways we can attempt to identify significant meanings.

Numerology also often takes words and evaluates those words by comparing each letter with specific number associations that have been built up. For instance, the number associations of the vowels in one's name can be added up, reduced to a specific range of numbers, and then evaluated for its meanings. This can be compared with the numerological evaluation of one's whole name to see how the inner significance of one's name matches up with the outer significance.

Runes

Runes are an alphabet system which have specific larger meanings associated with each letter. Most people think of the Norse alphabet system when they use the word runes, but there are other alphabet systems that are sometimes used in the same way as the Norse set in magickal practice.

Working with runes is very similar to numerology. Specific letters are given particular significance and their meanings interpreted, such as one's initials or the vowels or consonants in one's name.

Runes can be used for divination purposes by inscribing them on small stones or pieces of wood and then drawing them randomly for interpretation, or tossing them on a surface such as the ground or a table and observing the patterns that emerge in proximity and arrangement. Runes are also often used in spellcasting, where a specific rune is used as the focus for meditation, or drawn with magickal intention in order to attract the related meanings into manifestation.

I-Ching

The I-Ching is a Chinese divination system based on a binary philosophy: the concept of yin and yang. The method involves determining even or odd by random methods such as manipulating yarrow sticks or flipping coins, with one resulting in a solid line and the other resulting in a broken or dashed line. Three of these lines make up a trigram, and six of them (two trigrams) make up a hexagram.

Broken lines are yin lines, solid ones are yang. Yin is considered to be feminine and yang masculine. A theory of correspondences is used to identify the eight possible combinations of three lines, the trigrams, and their meanings. The eight trigrams can be combined to produce sixty-four possible hexagrams that make up the full complement of I-Ching outcomes.

In addition to the basic yin/yang lines, the trigrams and the hexagrams, there are ways to identify specific lines within the trigrams and hexagrams as "moving lines," lines that can change from one type to another in certain circumstances. This allows for even greater specificity in interpretation, narrowing down on particular elements of meaning for a trigram or hexagram reading.

Because the I-Ching can be a complex system, it is most often that practitioners will flip coins or manipulate yarrow sticks to determine the hexagram and moving lines then consult a textbook of interpretations in order to determine their meaning. Other divination systems such as the tarot rely more heavily on imagery within the cards themselves so skilled practitioners of other systems often find they don't need to consult the books after getting the basics internalized.

Unstructured

Not all divination systems rely on the practitioner learning an established language or symbol system. There are many unstructured divination systems that rely much more on the practitioner's inherent precognitive faculties, or at least their own interpretation of patterns recognized in seemingly random media.

Many find that it is much easier to do unstructured divination after they have first practiced extensively with a structured system such as the tarot. It doesn't mean that few of us are natural scryers but rather that many often find it difficult to begin with an unstructured system. Starting with a structured system helps us to stretch our divinatory faculties and perhaps more importantly it helps us to gain some confidence. Once we feel more comfortable with divination in general it usually becomes much easier to learn other forms that might require more mental flexibility.

Scrying

Scrying is essentially a vision experienced during a trance state. The term is sometimes used to refer to any form of divination where the practitioner tries to notice patterns or see visions in random sources. Scrying is usually considered to be a form of inner sight rather than mundane sight – a witness present who is not psychically inclined might not see anything at all when the diviner sees all sorts of things. In Celtic communities this inner vision is sometimes called the "second sight."

Sometimes people who are blind are thought to have the clearest "second sight" as they do not have mundane vision to distract them. Some witches find that closing or covering their physical eyes helps them to see better with their inner vision.

Magick Mirrors

Magick mirrors, crystal balls, polished gems, and even bowls of water or ink are all popular tools for focusing the mundane vision in order to allow the inner vision to come to the fore. For some, the mirror or crystal ball does not actually serve as the place where the vision manifests, but rather serves as a focus to help induce a trance state so the vision can come forward.

Divination using mirrors or other visual focus objects usually works best in low light conditions, such as in a dark room lit only by candles. It's also wise to perform divination experiments such as scrying while within a cast circle in order to ensure that the participants are balanced, grounded, and protected from outside distractions.

Dreams

Dreams are the most direct access that we have to the unconscious and to symbolic connections with the Divine. The trick with dreams is to acknowledge their importance, to pay attention to them, and to open ourselves up to learning the wisdom they have to teach us.

Some people find that they have difficulty remembering their dreams. One very helpful trick is to take a B-complex vitamin with your dinner or just before going to bed along with a healthy glass of water. The B vitamins seem to have a particularly strong impact on dreams. When I take B vitamins regularly I always find my dreams are more vivid, and they are much easier to remember when I wake up in the morning. And it's no wonder, really. Vitamin B is known to affect the brain and nervous system. Some believe it helps to alleviate depression and can do wonders with creativity, logical thinking, and memory as well. All of your nerve cells benefit from getting enough of it. Just be sure that if you choose to take supplements that you do not exceed the recommended dosage on the label and keep your medical doctor informed as everything you ingest can have an impact on other medications you might be taking.

Another key to remembering dreams is to train yourself to remember them more clearly by writing down the details as soon as you wake up. Keep a notepad and pen or pencil by your bed, and as soon as you wake up, before you get out of bed, write down anything you can remember about your dreams. If you wake up in the night, write down your dreams. They don't have to be complete scenes or even make any sense. Just write it down no matter what it is! No one needs to see this dream diary except you. As you build up the routine of writing down those dream images you will find that your dreams become much easier to remember. You'll also build up a valuable record of your dreams and will be able to evaluate them later to look for common themes, symbols, or clues to things your subconscious might be trying to tell you.

Seeing patterns

There are divination methods that are a step between full-fledged psychic visions and concrete symbol systems like the tarot. These ways involve the interpretation of symbols observed in random sources. They can serve as a good way for people who are not confident that they can produce visions to glimpse meaning without a lot of preparation or special tools like a tarot deck.

Any source of random patterns can be used. Cloud watching is one way that many children are familiar with – why not concentrate on a question and then look up to see what answers might be lurking there? If cloud watching does not work for you, or if it's not practical at the moment because of the timing or weather conditions, there are other ways to generate patterns.

One way to do this inside is to go to your sink, clear it out so there is nothing in it and it is reasonably dry, and then toss a handful of salt or flour and observe any patterns that appear. You can interpret the symbols based on their location in the sink too – perhaps they mean one thing if they are closer to you, or if they are closer to the drain. And when it's all over you just need to rinse out the sink to be done with it.

Tea leaves are another traditional way of divining through pattern recognition in random sources. Brew yourself a cup of tea and be sure to get a few bits of tea leaf in your cup; rip open the teabag if you have to! After you've drunk most of the tea away and have just a little bit left in the bottom, turn the cup upside down on your saucer and turn the cup at least once to distribute the leaves. Then tip the cup over and look inside to see what appears. Again, you can interpret the symbols by how close they are to the rim or the bottom of the cup, or how close they are to the handle of the cup. Decide ahead of time what these things mean, such as closer to the rim means closer to the present time and closer to the bottom could mean farther in the future. It's also helpful to consider what the combinations of symbols might mean and how they might modify each other depending on how close or far away they are from each other.

If you are lucky enough to have a wood-burning fireplace or are out camping and have a fire burning, you have a perfect opportunity to look for patterns in the dance of the flames and in the glowing embers. Some people find that asking questions, even just thinking them silently to themselves, and then watching the fire will bring answers. Listen to the voice of the fire too; the crackling, popping, and snapping can provide all sorts of clues.

Smoke provides another interesting medium for seeking out patterns and symbols. The next time you light up some incense, try sitting quietly and observe how the smoke roils and curls through the air. Does it move towards you or away from you? Does it shift around to point at particular things around you? Does it take on shapes or letters or numbers that might mean things? If you ask it a question does it give a response?

Water, particularly natural bodies of water like lakes, rivers, oceans, streams, or ponds, can provide a natural crystal ball for those who are inclined towards trance visions. They can also produce symbols in the play of light and shadow, in the movement of the ripples and waves across the surface. What do you see in the depths? If you ask the water a question how does it answer you?

Treat the methods you try with respect and they will answer many questions for you. Show them honor and humility and they will share their secrets with you.

Evocation and Invocation

Incantations or prayers to deities or forces you wish to invite to participate in spiritual or magickal working can take two basic forms: an evocation or an invocation. What is the difference between the two? Is there really a difference?

Inviting To Be Present Or Inviting To Express Within Yourself

According to most dictionaries there is really no difference between the words invocation and evocation. Both mean to invite or summon something to be present. Within the occult community, however, the two terms have come to mean slightly different things depending on where you want the manifestation to occur. Evocation is an invitation for the spirit, energy, or deity to be present with you in the ritual space. Invocation is an invitation for the spirit, energy, or deity to manifest within the body of at least one of the participants.

In a Christian example, one might evoke the spirit of Jesus to be present in your home, like a member of your family. Or a devout Christian might invoke Jesus to be present within their heart so that they might personally manifest Jesus' love and compassion.

Within Wiccan ritual, we often evoke elemental energies to be present to guard our ritual space and participate in our ceremonies. Invocation, which brings the energy directly into at least one of the participants, is best seen in the sequence known as drawing down the moon. In drawing down the moon, incantations are recited to invite a goddess to literally possess the body of a participant, usually a priestess, so that the goddess might interact with those present. There is also a corresponding invocation of the god known as drawing down the sun.

Religions like Voudou have ritual possession of participants as a central activity. In a Voudou ritual drumming and dance ceremony anyone present is capable of being "ridden by the Loa" or possessed by the spirits. When possessed, the participant takes on the mannerisms of the spirit in question and interacts with others who are present, giving advice, answering questions, performing healings or other magick. When the ritual is over the Loa departs, leaving the possessed one to return to normal awareness.

Many of the ritual magick ceremonies described in classic grimoires such as the Goetia are works of evocative magick. In these ceremonies spirits are summoned forth to interact with the participants, but the spirits are not permitted to go inside the participants. In many of the examples in these grimoires the spirits are constrained to appear inside magick mirrors, crystal balls, or in the smoke of burning incense or candle flames placed in magickal triangles carefully drawn and placed outside the protective magick circle where the participants remain. Evocative magick of this type often includes strong protective components performed before the evocation, and precise banishing formulae that are conducted after the working is done to ensure the spirit has really left the premises as requested.

When summoning spirits, energies, or deities it is important to be sure whether you are trying to invoke or evoke them, and perform the appropriate type of ritual.

Evocation

Evocation is the process of inviting a nonphysical entity to be present during a magickal or spiritual ritual. Examples include asking elemental guardians to protect the boundaries of your ritual space, or saying a prayer to a deity to ask them to be present. In fact, any attempt to welcome an invisible entity to be present is really an evocation, regardless how or when or where it is being done. Successful evocations do usually involve a few specific factors though.

One factor is a good understanding of the entity being invited: their name at the very least, and preferably an in-depth knowledge of the spirit's likes and dislikes, abilities, weaknesses, and any special etiquette required for communication. The more you know about what you are inviting, the more likely you will know what to say to make the entity feel at home. It's like doing an interview with someone who has gone out of their way to meet with you; they will be more friendly and cooperative if you've clearly done your homework about them and their background.

Another factor is a suitable environment established to welcome the entity. For instance, elementals are not going to have an easy time manifesting in circumstances that are contrary to their basic nature. It's hard for a water elemental to manifest in a bonfire or incense smoke when a bowl of water or better yet a natural body of water like a lake or pond is their natural abode. Similarly, deities are much more likely to manifest during rituals if you use incense that is associated with that god or goddess, and if you use words, music, motion, colour, and textures that They favour. Don't make it hard for Them to manifest and you'll have better success.

Another factor is the opening of an easy path for the entity to come through to manifest. In Wiccan rituals this might take the form of a skilled astral-worker opening some form of portal or establishing an astral link between the natural realm of the spirit and where that spirit is expected to manifest in this realm. It might be done through raising energy that is directed at the place where the spirit should manifest, in a way providing a psychic lure for the spirit to notice and follow.

This last part is often the trickiest part. It's wise to leave intense manifestations to those who are highly skilled, especially those proficient in protective magick and banishing, rather than taking risks to bring forth entities that turn out to be difficult to dismiss. In less intense evocations, such as inviting elementals to guard a ritual space, or inviting a deity to be present in a ritual, more overt manifestations are not usually required so participants usually rely on simpler methods such as visualization to accompany the incantations or prayers that are recited.

The triangle of evocation

Grimoires, the famous manuals of ritual magick, frequently describe the use of a triangle of evocation as a key part of summoning spirits to manifest. These triangles are usually not used in Wiccan rituals for inviting the elemental guardians or welcoming deities into the circle. Triangles are sometimes used (and are actually a very good idea) when the point of a ritual is to summon a specific entity in order to ask it questions or perform a task for you, or if the spirit is expected to manifest in some more difficult way than normal such as to visible appearance. The triangle is another magickal boost to try and limit the energies involved to a specific physical location, containing the magick so it is able to do its work without dissipating, keeping out external distracting energies, and also protect the enclosed spirit from the outside and protect the outside from the spirit that is enclosed in the triangle.

The triangle is usually physically drawn with a double line border, and between the two lines are inscribed powerful names of protective deities or spirits, or perhaps powerful binding or protective incantations. I've seen examples of the triangle on a piece of wood (usually plywood) three feet on each side, down to triangles printed out or drawn on regular writing paper and cut out into the triangle shape. In most operations the triangle is placed outside the ritual circle where the participants remain for the duration of the ceremony. This protects the participants from any danger that might be involved in bringing forth the spirit. I have seen some instances though where a triangle has been used inside the circle, usually one of the smaller ones on paper, which is placed underneath a crystal ball or small scrying mirror placed on the altar. I would not recommend using the triangle inside the circle unless you are summoning a deity or specific spirit that you are absolutely positive will be friendly and will do no harm to anyone present. If you're ever in doubt, the triangle should be placed outside the ritual circle to ensure the participants are safe.

Spirits that are being evoked to some sort of manifestation need to be given an easy way to do so. It's not enough to just have a magick triangle drawn, ritually purified and consecrated, and then charged. If the spirit is an air elemental they usually like having incense burning in the triangle so that they can use the smoke to manifest. A candle flame is perfect for a fire elemental. A goblet of water works for a water elemental, and a bowl of earth, or perhaps a special rock or crystal works well for an earth elemental.

Another more flexible way to provide a medium for the spirit to manifest is to place a scrying instrument in the triangle. Often a crystal ball works perfectly for this, or a scrying mirror. A bowl of dark water (water with black ink or food colouring in it) is also an effective scrying mirror. The drawback with using a crystal ball or scrying mirror is that while it's easier for the spirit to use, it requires the human participants to be skilled at using their astral vision. Participants who have difficulty with visualization or have no luck with scrying will likely not see much.

Invocation

Invocation is the process of inviting a nonphysical entity, whether a spirit or deity or energy, to be present within your physical body. It's a type of possession and can take a number of forms. It might be almost imperceptible to the human participant, where the entity is able to see and hear through their eyes, perhaps experiencing some event through the human's form. It might manifest as ideas that just pop into the participant's awareness. Or it could take more dramatic forms such as the human losing awareness of what is going on, and the spirit or deity speaking and acting through their body. In Voudou ceremonies, this most impressive form of

Divine possession is expected and welcomed, and is called being ridden by a Loa.

Assuming a godform

In many occult traditions, especially those with a strong mystical emphasis, participants are encouraged to identify with the Divine however it is being described and to invoke Their presence. Particularly in ritual magick lodges, ceremonies are conducted which actually require specific participants to successfully invoke particular deities and then play out specific parts in the ceremony as that deity. Within Wiccan ceremonies the most common form of this is drawing down the moon and drawing down the sun when the goddess and god are invoked into human representatives so that they might interact directly with the participants.

In ritual magick texts the process of invoking a deity is often described as assuming a godform. It doesn't matter if the ritual is in a magickal lodge, in a Wiccan circle, or in a Voudou drumming session; the general process is very similar. The participant who wishes to invoke must be a suitable vessel, often undergoing various purifications and preparatory tasks. They go into a calm, still state of mind often described as a trance. They open themselves up to something higher than themselves. They invite whatever deity has been encouraged to make contact through the symbolism inherent in the ritual up to this point. If the conditions are right and the Divine is willing, then there is an influx of energy into the participant and some sort of possession takes place. The participant might feel that there is little change if the possession is very light, but regardless they are able to complete the remainder of the ritual overshadowed by the Divine. If the possession is an intense one they might not know anything has happened until after the ritual comes to a conclusion and the Divine has ended the possession, when the other participants can share what they witnessed.

As with evocation, it is important to approach invocation seriously and choose carefully what energies you are willing to open yourself up to. You are literally giving your body over to them, after all, and you don't want to risk hurting yourself by making foolish choices.

Prayers to invite a deity into your heart are a mild form of invocation, although they are just as serious as full-blown possessions. Be sure that you really are willing to let that deity into your heart before you send out the invitation!

Dedications and Devotions

Dedications are promises or oaths that we make. They can be promises we make to ourselves, promises to others, or promises to the Divine. In a magickal life it's important to treat promises as iron-clad and deadly serious. Never make a promise that you can't keep. As you prove to yourself and to the Divine that your word really is law your magick will become more effective as your words will carry much more power. Every time you break a promise, no matter how small it might seem, you are undermining the power of your words and are weakening your magick. If you can't really guarantee something you should consider not promising that you will do it. There is honor in being honest about what you can and can't do, and being up front about when you might not be able to complete something.

When starting a new spiritual path it often helps to devise and enact a dedication ritual for yourself to indicate your promise to yourself and to the Divine that you will pursue this path. Give yourself time, though, to explore the path sufficiently before you decide to actually dedicate to it. It's OK to change your mind about something. You should be sure about the promise you are making before you do that formal dedication.

You can also perform dedications as a way to renew your promise at various times in your life when you feel the need. Refreshing your promises can bring a new spark to your life. It sometimes provides the extra boost you need to move ahead, and sometimes helps to open up new opportunities for you that you didn't notice before.

Formal initiations into groups are a form of dedication ritual in many ways. They involve participants promising that they will work with the group, and the group promises to work with the participant.

Devotions are one way to put spiritual promises into action. They usually take the form of routine, often daily, ritual attention paid to one's spiritual life. Usually it involves the participant paying their respects to a particular deity, although it can be something a bit different than that such as a regular meditation or prayer routine. Devotions can be small acts but it is the intention and the routine that makes them special. They can be as simple as lighting incense in front of a small statuette or picture or symbol, or lighting a candle each evening, or taking a moment before you go to sleep at night to look up at the sky and whisper "goodnight moon, goodnight stars." Devotions are small promises that we keep as a way to connect with our spiritual lives and the Divine.

Building An Other-Focused Daily Discipline

Devotions are inherently focused on something outside ourselves. We don't do them because we need something to fill up time. Nor do we do them because we have candles or incense to burn. Performing devotions are like those little things you do for a loved one. They're the little kindnesses we do as a way to show that we care.

Mystical yearning is a desire to make contact with the Divine. It's a deep and abiding love for that something greater than ourselves, however we define the Divine. It is selfish because it's about us trying to establish and strengthen a personal relationship. Yet it is also selfless, as it involves giving of ourselves to something that is outside us, above us, and beyond us.

Some people express this love for the Divine through acts of charity, allowing that love and devotion to overflow in their lives and touch others around them. In Sanskrit expressing spiritual devotion through acts of charity is known as Bhakti Yoga. This is perhaps one of the most beautiful manifestations of mysticism. It demonstrates in a concrete way how the power of Divine love can really change the world if only one small bit at a time.

As they say, smiles are contagious. Don't hide your love away or it will wither and perhaps even die out. Let it shine forth and it will grow ever stronger and light the way for others. Let your love be expressed in everything you do, in small ways as well as large. Love grows through action much more than through words. Words are cheap; it's the actions that make the significant difference.

Shrines and Altars

One way to build a relationship with a particular deity, spirit, or even abstract energy or idea is to build a shrine or altar to it. What items do you associate with the deity, for instance? What colours, foods, objects, scents, drinks? Pictures that remind you of the deity are also very appropriate – it doesn't matter how artistic or well done they are, so long as they remind you of the deity and have appropriate emotional connections for you. They might be crayon scribbles lovingly drawn by your child or snapshots from your vacations. They could be souvenirs or knickknacks you've picked up over the years. It doesn't really matter what the individual items are so long as they make sense to you and help to build that link to the specific deity. If you're unsure of any associations it's time to do some research to look for confirmation or more ideas. Research isn't the only way to find out either. Meditate and pray to the deity and ask for guidance. Watch your dreams carefully, do divinations, pay attention for omens and signs. Anything that sparks a connection or idea for you that you identify with the deity is appropriate for your shrine or altar.

The shrine or altar itself can be a permanent fixture in your home or garden or in some other special place where you can work in safety and privacy. It can also be a temporary thing, something that is easy to pack away and then bring out and set up again each time you want to work on it. There are some amazing portable shrines that creative Pagans have done over the years in the form of cloth or paper books or little boxes that open up or unfold. In the age of the Internet a shrine can take the form of a website or a single user's carefully arranged computer desktop with an appropriate background image and icons placed purposefully. Shrines and altars can be as simple or as complex as you desire. The goal is that connection with the Divine and whatever you feel in your gut works for you is the way to approach the task.

Ritual Actions

Many religions have developed sequences of ritual motion or ceremonial action that they incorporate into worship. Just like incense or candles and other props, careful selection of actions and physical motions can serve as reminders to help connect the participants with the Divine. They can be more than just reminders, too, and serve as powerful triggers to altered states of awareness. They can make visualization and spoken components more meaningful as well by adding a physical dimension.

One common ritual motion that is used around the world is putting one's palms together in front around chest level, fingertips up, as a gesture of prayer and worship. In the Catholic faith, worshippers often draw the sign of the cross on themselves by touching their forehead, their chest, and then their shoulders. Many religions also draw small crosses (a universal religious symbol, not exclusive to Christians) on their forehead with a fingertip, often dipped first in holy water or oil.

Hinduism and Buddhism have a complex system of hand positions and gestures, known as mudras, which are believed to assist in connecting with specific Divine forces. Many are familiar with the image of sitting cross-legged, the palms held up with a thumb touching the fingertip of a specific finger on each hand as a way to meditate. This is one simple form of mudra, perhaps the most common one in use.

As with any ritual component the important part is that the participant attaches specific meaning to the motion or gesture and uses it consciously. If we don't know what the significance of a motion is within our spiritual framework then we are not using it effectively. If we are performing a ritual gesture unknowingly how do we know that it is helping our work and not hindering it? Use what makes sense to you, what you understand, and not just because someone else says to do it. If you aren't sure about something then ask the Divine about it and use it only if you feel the answer you receive supports it and truly makes sense.

As with a lot of spiritual practices related to specific deities it always helps to research what has been done in the past to see how others related to this form of the Divine, how they interpreted the Divine's preferences. Evaluate the information for yourself and don't do things that you don't feel comfortable doing. And don't feel that you must slavishly follow some established method if something you've invented yourself helps you to feel more in tune with your particular deity. If something helps make your relationship with the deity stronger then use it. If it is just another level of unnecessary complexity then ask yourself if it's needed at all.

Prayers

In any relationship communication is important. If you don't communicate how do you know you even have a relationship established?

Prayer is really just talking to the Divine. We might think that prayer is a monologue but in fact it is a dynamic conversation where the Divine responds using Its own language which we sometimes have difficulty deciphering. The Divine is talking to us constantly if we just learn how to listen. The Divine voice can come to us in the small hours of the morning as we sleep, in the winds, in the crunch of snow under our feet. Divine words are written in the stars, in the clouds, in the stones. The messages are all around us, answering our questions, offering us comfort and hope. So long as we have at least one sense available to us we are open to those messages from outside. Even without external senses, we have internal ones, the vision of imagination, which can receive those communications. We have to learn to listen instead of always focusing on talking.

Building a mystical life means working hard at your relationship with the Divine. Talk to the Divine throughout the day and listen for the responses. It doesn't matter what you talk about with the Divine, just that you do it. Share your thoughts, your fears, your hopes. Share the details of your life and dreams. Share, and you'll find that sharing opens up your life to new possibilities. Sharing builds that link with the Divine and lets the love flow between you.

Offerings

Sacrifice is a scary word. It means giving something, which some people perceive as losing something. It is true that the most valuable sacrifices are those that are most difficult to give. But giving to another doesn't necessarily mean losing something and in fact can mean gaining far more than you have given.

When two people fall in love they sacrifice their private time to spend with the one they love. They give of themselves, their thoughts, their experiences, their emotions whether they are good or bad. And in exchange, this sacrifice brings companionship, friendship, and the most powerful gift we have: love. We lose some of our autonomy perhaps, and the ability to be completely selfish, but we gain so much more. Sacrifice is what we do when we interact with others and look outside ourselves.

Offerings or sacrifices to the Divine are gifts we give in Their honor, to further Their glory, to express our personal love and respect for Them. Offerings can be physical things like favourite food or drink, incense smoke or candlelight. Songs and artwork done in Their praise are also offerings that are best appreciated when they are shared. When done purposefully in Their honor everything we do can be an offering to Them. It is possible for us to live our lives, however mundane they might seem, as offerings to a deity. It just has to be a gift freely given for it to have any real meaning.

Making the Experience Concrete

Mystical experiences can be extremely moving and personal but are they really of any consequence if there are no effects on our lives? Spiritual insights and astral journeys need to be grounded in all the realms, including the mundane, if they are to be truly significant. We can talk the mystical talk, but until we walk the mystical walk in our daily lives it is all just daydreaming.

The Magickal Diary

One highly recommended way to ground your mystical and spiritual experiences is to put it onto physical or electronic paper. Write down what you are doing, what your thoughts are, describe the images that you saw or things you felt. Describe as much as you can remember. Draw if you are inclined to that even if you do not consider yourself an artist. No one else ever needs to see what you are expressing unless you choose to share it. Keeping a magickal diary such as this provides a way to solidify what you have experienced so that later on you can review it and remember. Sometimes the real insights come much later when you look back and notice the common threads that run through everything, or you have a chance to review something with later information now in your grasp.

Some draw on their magickal diaries, which are kept private, and use the material there to inspire them in writing or graphic arts. Really important ideas become more valuable as they are shared. Don't let them whither away unappreciated in your private journal when you know they should be allowed to grow in the larger community.

Inspiration Into Action

Mystical insights can move us to make changes in our lives and circumstances. When the Divine touches us, it is often hard to not change in some way. Feel the energy, learn to channel it, and use it to do good. Don't let it stagnate as that is probably one of the greatest ways to disrespect it. Energy is a gift from the Divine that we spurn at our peril.

Changing your life for the better

Perhaps the energy moves you to make changes in your own life to better yourself or your circumstances. Are you learning more, venturing into unknown territory? Are you stretching yourself and your abilities? Are you discovering parts of yourself that you thought were long gone, or didn't know you had in the first place? Are you finding ways to solve problems or eliminate obstacles you face? Are you uncovering ways that you can make a difference to help others, to make the world better?

Exploring new facets of your personality

One of the unfortunate consequences of the idea of an "immortal essence" is the assumption that this means our personalities are unchangeable. This might seem a comforting thought on one level but it also holds many of us back from exploring new things and expanding our awareness, our ability to love and experience, because we think those things are "not me."

We are very different people when we are ten years old, when we are seventeen years old, when we are twenty-two, and when we are forty. We can become quite different people when we hit fifty years old, or sixty, or seventy, or eighty. Things happen to us through our lives that trigger changes in our personalities. Certainly there are consistencies no matter where we are in our lives as change of this sort is rarely all-encompassing. Change is usually gradual but it does happen. It's unrealistic to expect our personalities to stay static.

If we acknowledge that our personalities can evolve then we have taken a huge step towards being able to notice the cycles we go through in our own behaviour. We can see our personalities and capabilities as something else we can manipulate through magick. Purposeful action can guide our selves to expand, to grow, and to become what we desire. We are not victims of our life circumstances unless we allow ourselves to be so. We have the potential to become as successful and as capable as our heroes.

Mystical experiences put us in touch with the primal forces of potentiality and creativity. When we experience communion with the Divine we are awakened to new possibilities within ourselves. Perceptual filters that we have built up over time are removed if only for a moment. We can bring this awareness into our daily lives and express new facets of our own personalities that had lain dormant. We can blossom like flowers into radiant inner beauty. We can discover that our "true selves" are really anything that we desire.

The challenge of growth: outgrowing some things, growing into new roles

When mystical experiences affect us we grow in some way. Growth involves changing and change can be uncomfortable. But all living things grow. They all change through their lives. It is unrealistic to expect that things will never change.

The challenge we are given then through mystical experience and through personal relationships with the Divine is to grow. It is up to each of us whether we grow according to the ethics we have accepted for our lives. It is up to us to decide whether we grow closer in our relationship with the Divine, whether we embrace our capacity to grow and make the world truly a Heaven or whether we make it a Hell. If the Divine is truly omnipresent then Heaven is right here right now, in all the realms, and not divorced from us in some other place. Do we choose to make the best of it and manifest that Heaven or do we transform it into something else? Do we grow in love and compassion and peace or do we grow in hate and discord? Do we express the Divine gift of creativity or do we suppress it and make everything grey and dull?

Sharing the Experience

Some educators believe that we haven't really learned something unless we can prove it by expressing it. Can you put your spiritual experiences into words, images, music, movement? Can you demonstrate your spiritual relationship with the Divine through action? Can you prove that your insight has meaning if you can't share it in some way?

Working with others of like mind

One common way to expand on mystical experience is to share it in discussion with others who are on the same spiritual path with you. In Wicca, many practitioners are members of covens where one of the primary purposes of the group is to enact rituals to express mystical insights and enable members to discuss experiences. Groups like this might decide on communal spiritual goals and work together to achieve them. This can be a wonderful resource for spiritual seekers to explore their spirituality in community.

Others take this sharing a step further and try to reach a larger community through publishing books or websites. Some are talented speakers and give public speeches on their chosen topics. Others might become involved in organizing community events around specific themes as a way to share and encourage others to explore. Spirituality does not have to be a lonely experience although at its heart it really is a solitary one.

Creative works

Expressing your mystical awareness doesn't have to mean being a reporter or a scientist and dissecting it with words. It can be expressed through the arts, through cooking, through creative expression that captures, at least for you, some of the emotion or meaning of the experience. Can you capture your experience in a gesture? A texture? A stroke of colour on a canvas? How about in an arrangement of notes? You will know you've succeeded when it feels right for you. And you then have at least an opportunity to reach out to others and share the experience. Others who understand where your motivation comes from might surprise you with their perceptiveness. Those who haven't experienced what you have might find the first glimmers of insight triggered by your expression.

Social and political action

Some of the best-known spiritual seekers choose to express their Divine experience through social or political action. The Catholic Church, for instance, is famous for its selfless devotees who often give their whole lives to minimize the suffering of others as a way of expressing Divine love. Mother Theresa, for instance, left her European homeland and went to India to live among the poorest of the poor and minister to the sick. The Dalai Lama of Tibet is another excellent example with his efforts to encourage interfaith communication and seeking real peace and love among all. History is filled with the stories of remarkable mystics who have worked to spread Divine love.

How can you help express Divine love through social action? It's all about doing what feels right for you, what challenges you to grow, what helps minimize harm and encourage happiness for the most possible. Try getting involved with local charities or nonprofit organizations and donate your time. If you don't have time to donate you can usually donate money or goods. If you can't do that perhaps you can help raise awareness by talking with others about the issues and encourage people to look at the options. There is always something you can do whether it is something big and noticeable or small but still very important.

Wiccans such as Starhawk have taken their spiritual dedication to bringing about change to lessen harm and focus largely on political activism. Starhawk's tradition, Reclaiming, is active in anti-war movements, environmental awareness, and seeking social change to liberalize society.

Other Wiccans such as the Farrars encourage our community to connect at an intense spiritual level with the lands where we live and do what we can to heal and protect Mother Earth. Attempting to minimize harm often means working overtly to make things better at many levels.

Transformation of society at large happens because people change. Work on yourself, and help others where you can, and changes will come about. Be observant of the cycles, the circumstances, the actions and consequences. Make decisions and act with purpose to make changes to move towards the goal. When you move with the tides of the universe you cannot do anything but succeed!

Conclusion:
Living a Mystical Wiccan Life

The Path Onward

Exploring mystical experiences is not just a hobby to take up for those moments when you've nothing better to do. Attaining the skills needed to have a mystical experience takes time and effort. And as with most disciplines the benefits of regular practice have a tendency to spill over into other areas of your life. When you make a commitment to yourself to begin a discipline, and then actually carry through on that commitment, you discover strengths in yourself that you didn't know were there. New ways of looking at things open up. Old problems seem to resolve themselves or don't seem to be nearly as troublesome as they once were.

Striving to do one's Great Work involves actively working towards a greater spiritual maturity. Things like formal membership in groups, degrees and titles are outward things that are meant to imply advancing spiritual maturity, but in the end they are just things that other people grant to us. What really counts is not whether one has a specific title but how one's spirituality manifests in daily life. We can have all the impressive degrees and titles in the world but if we don't put the ideals into practice, if we can't honestly demonstrate and live our spiritual maturity, then what have we accomplished?

Enlightenment is just an amusing diversion if it does not change our lives in some profound way. Spiritual initiation is nothing more than a distracting fantasy if we don't take our lessons to heart and act on them in daily life. Pagans who profess to believe that the earth and all that exists is a part of the Divine are showing dishonor to the Divine when they fail to bring back their otherworld lessons into the physical realm.

When we think we've reached the pinnacle of our spiritual development, when we think we know it all and are spiritual masters, we miss out on one of the most important lessons the Divine has to teach us. We are part of the Divine, and can experience oneness with the Divine, but we are still also living here in a physical world in finite bodies for a limited amount of time. There is always more maturity ahead of us no matter how advanced we think we are.

Wise people often say that true wisdom is being humble enough to acknowledge that we really know very little and have a lot of maturing to do. Only fools think they know it all and have no more growing to do.

Advanced Doesn't Have to Mean Complicated

Thankfully there are myriad techniques, old and new, for developing spiritual discipline and seeking mystical attainment. People are diverse and so it makes sense that diverse methods work. What works really well for one person might not work at all for someone else. And what a particular person learns and experiences through a particular spiritual technique is not guaranteed to be exactly the same for anyone else.

It's a commonly accepted myth that advanced means complicated. Advanced topics can be quite complicated but they don't have to be. For instance, an artist who has mastered the basic techniques doesn't necessarily have to abandon the fundamentals in exchange for obscure and difficult methods in order to be considered advanced. Sometimes becoming more advanced involves looking at the fundamentals and discovering how they can be simplified even more to reveal an essential core.

Advanced studies often involve selecting one particular idea or method from the fundamentals and then exploring it in more depth. Frequently this sort of study involves looking for this very idea in other incarnations. Looking for the particular idea in other spiritual systems, in science, in art, in music, and in the natural world can bring startling new insights. Ideas are not limited to where we happen to find them first. They have a tendency to appear again and again in different disguises all over the place.

Finding Your Calling

Being a witch or Wiccan can involve filling a wide range of magickal roles. Some specialize in teaching, leading ritual, organizing community events, herbalism, healing, creative arts. Even within some roles there can be a lot of specialization. Someone who feels drawn to teaching, for instance, might find their path focuses on putting their knowledge in written form while others might discover that they are best at teaching newcomers, and others focus more on public speaking and acting as a public face for their group or denomination.

It is wise to have a solid grounding in the basics of Wicca before deciding to specialize. Having a broad and solid base to build on helps our new branches become more secure. Knowing where we come from, what others have done in at least a general way, helps us to see what really needs to be done.

As we expand into our individual specialties it is important to put a lot of effort into researching our specialty, both within an explicitly Wiccan context and outside it. Get a solid grasp on what the topic covers, what has been done, what is already known. It's easier to see where the real work needs to be done when we understand what others have done. There's no reason why we should waste time reinventing what others have already done for us. Our creative efforts can be better spent in looking at ways to adapt existing material, combining it in new ways, drawing new insights from existing material, and ultimately building new material on top of what already exists.

Growing Towards Elderhood: Being a Role Model

In the Charge of the Goddess, She advises us: "Let there be beauty and strength, power and compassion, honor and humility, mirth and reverence within you." That covers a lot. If we try to follow the advice we can become much better people.

In discussions on the Internet there is often condescension displayed towards people who are clearly new to the Pagan scene. Some people state quite clearly that they feel it is their place to disrespect others merely for their choice of online or Pagan pseudonyms; and in many instances the basher is often someone whose own pseudonym is just as pretentious and ridiculous as the target being bashed. These petty bullies consider themselves to be elders or teachers and use this presumed status to justify their opinions. As elders or teachers, though, they set a very poor example for novices to follow.

If I were in the teachers' lounge in a school and witnessed another teacher badmouthing students they would be castigated for doing so. If students aren't "getting it," then it is the teacher's duty to be the mature one in the situation and try to help the student to overcome the problem. It's never the place of a teacher to purposefully humiliate or belittle a student.

If I had a child in a school where one of my child's teachers behaved publicly in this way I would work to have that teacher removed. Bashing is not teaching. Bashing is assault and should be treated as such.

People who want to be treated as elders or as teachers have obligations that go along with the status they seek to claim. Those obligations include behaving with dignity, compassion, and wisdom; setting an example worthy of emulation; modeling respect by showing respect for students as well as other teachers and elders. It's no wonder that new students are showing little respect for the teachers and elders of our community: they are learning their lessons, although the lessons are not the ones the elders and teachers think they are teaching.

People who want to be considered elders and teachers do our community an enormous disservice when they bash newbies or "fluffy bunnies" as they are often derogatorily labeled. Beautiful spiritual passages like the Charge of the Goddess ring terribly hollow when the elders and teachers of our community can't demonstrate in everyday interactions that they live the ideals. When behavior modeled by our leaders is nothing more than petty bickering and childish insult the lessons learned by newcomers will be ones of close-mindedness and immaturity.

Another problem that crops up from time to time in all spiritual communities is sometimes humorously called "High Priest/ess Disease." This is a situation where someone who considers themselves to be an elder or leader allows their assumed superior status to over-inflate their ego to ridiculous levels. They usually insist that they be addressed as "Lord," "Lady," or with some other honorific at all times. They speak to others in a condescending manner making it clear they consider themselves to be of higher status. When they speak their words are to be considered proven fact even when what they are presenting is opinion or conjecture. They might be actual experts in one particular field but this does not stop them from assuming that they can speak in other fields with the same authority. In many ways this is a continuation of the old myth of the divine right of royalty. People who feel they are of such obviously higher status often act as though they are justified in their actions by Divine authority.

Within Wicca one might think that this would be rare since one of the basic tenets many Wiccans espouse is that ours is a religion without the need for a middleman between the individual and the Divine. Many Wiccans were drawn to this religion in part because they despised the hierarchy of mainstream religions where the faithful are only permitted contact with the Divine through an established priesthood.

The reality is that as Wicca has grown various traditions or sects have become established with their own hierarchical authorities in order to provide some structure. Structure is not a bad thing in itself of course. There is certainly room within the diversity of Wicca for both hierarchical authoritarian sects as well as nonhierarchical egalitarian groups as well as a multitude of solitary practitioners. Unfortunately one of the side effects of establishing formal titles, degrees, and levels within Wiccan groups is that there will always be some who use these trappings as an ego trip. The deference, respect, and sometimes adulation that come with elder or leader status can be intoxicating. Without other elders to remind one to keep a balanced outlook, to maintain a healthy humility, it is easy for status to corrupt.

What are the examples we want to set for our community?

As a Wiccan, I base my spiritual practice on the thirteen Principles of Wiccan Belief, the Wiccan Rede, and inspirational passages such as the Charge of the Goddess. The ideals described in these texts are ones of community, hope, honor, compassion, and personal responsibility. As a Wiccan it is my duty to strive to live up to these ideals, to make my life worthy of Divine blessing. Showing disrespect to others, no matter how new to the community, is not the way to demonstrate my spiritual ideals. Playing superiority head-games with others is not part of a healthy spiritual life nor does it set a good example for others to follow. Let's focus on the positive and strive to live the spiritual life we seek. Demonstrate our love for the Divine in action as well as words. Make healthy spirituality an integral part of our lives and let its blessings fill us and overflow to touch everything around us.

And as the Goddess tells us at the end of The Charge:

"And thou who thinkest to seek Me, know that thy seeking and yearning shall avail

thee not unless thou know the mystery, that if that which thou seekest thou findest not within thee, thou wilt never find it without thee, for behold; I have been with thee from the beginning, and I am that which is attained at the end of desire."

Appendix I: Wiccan History

A Timeline Of Events⁸ Relevant To Wicca

1889   Charles G. Leland publishes "Aradia: The Gospel of the Witches." Scholars have since questioned the validity of the text: it is still debated whether Leland or his informant, Maddalena, were merely inventing material that would sell instead of presenting authentic folklore. Portions of "Aradia" were later used in Gerald Gardner's Book of Shadows, particularly in "The Charge of the Goddess."

1909   One speculated date given for the death of "Old George" Pickingill, the purported legendary English cunning man or male witch. Some believe the New Forest coven said to have initiated Gerald Gardner was associated with Pickingill.

1921   Margaret Murray, the famous Egyptologist, publishes her book "The Witch-Cult in Western Europe" as a project during her retirement. While her Egyptian work is still considered important, her European witchcraft theories have been largely debunked.

1931   Margaret Murray publishes her book "The God of the Witches." Gerald Gardner later cited Margaret Murray's books on witchcraft as proof that Wicca was a continuation of an intact pre-Christian Pagan faith. Few today believe that Gardner's claim was correct.

1939   Gerald Gardner's book "A Goddess Arrives" is published. It is a novel speculating on goddess worship in ancient Cyprus.

1939   Gerald Gardner is purportedly initiated into a Wiccan
               coven in the New Forest area with either Dorothy
               Clutterbuck or another woman in the coven acting as the
               high priestess.

1947   Gerald Gardner meets Aleister Crowley and acquires an
               official O.T.O. charter that permits Gardner to start up
               a group and grant the first three degrees. Crowley dies
               later that year. Gardner never does start an O.T.O. group,
               focusing instead on Wicca.

1949   Gerald Gardner publishes "High Magic's Aid" under the
               pseudonym Scire. It is a novel containing descriptions
               of magickal ceremonies including what is essentially a
               Wiccan first-degree initiation rite. Gardner claimed that
               the New Forest coven would only let him write about
               their ideas and rituals if they were presented as fiction.

1951   England repeals the anti-witchcraft laws.

1951   "Old Dorothy" Clutterbuck (a.k.a. Dorothy Fordham)
               dies. Gerald Gardner claimed "Old Dorothy" was the
               high priestess of the New Forest coven that initiated him
               into Wicca.

1953   Doreen Valiente initiated by Gerald Gardner. Doreen
               becomes Gerald's high priestess. Doreen also rewrites
               Gerald's book of shadows and is responsible for the
               commonly known versions of ritual invocations such
               as "The Charge of the Goddess," which many later
               consider traditional.

1954   Gerald Gardner's book "Witchcraft Today" is published.
               Gardner's promotion of Wicca kicks into high gear.
               He claims Wicca is a continuation of an ancient Pagan
               religion, the religion of British witchcraft.

1957	Doreen Valiente and a few others split from Gerald Gardner's coven over Gardner's publicity-seeking and his attempts to control dissent by the introduction of "The Ardanes" or Wiccan Laws which he claims are ancient.
1959	Gerald Gardner's book "The Meaning of Witchcraft" is published.
1960 (Jun. 6th)	Gerald Gardner initiates Patricia Crowther.
1961 (Oct. 11th)	Gerald Gardner gives Patricia Crowther her 2nd degree initiation. She starts her own coven shortly after.
1962	Patricia Crowther first appears on a television program to speak about witchcraft.
1962	Alex Sanders manages to get a copy of the Gardnerian Book of Shadows.[9]
1962	Alex Sanders meets Maxine Morris and initiates her (she was sixteen years old at the time, he was in his mid-thirties.)
1963	Monique Wilson (Gerald Gardner's high priestess at the time) initiates Raymond Buckland, who had corresponded with Gardner by mail and telephone for a year prior to initiation. Raymond Buckland is credited with being one of the first people to bring Gardnerian Wicca to the United States.
1964 (Oct. 3rd)	Doreen Valiente gives a speech[10] which includes "Eight words the Wiccan Rede fulfill: An it harm none, do what ye will." This phrasing of the "do what you will" idea catches on and becomes famous as the Wiccan Rede. It is subsequently quoted in various Pagan publications including the first issue of the magazine Pentagram, and comes to the forefront in Wiccan philosophy as an overall ethical guideline.

1965   Alex Sanders gives Maxine Morris her 3rd degree initiation, making her his high priestess. (Maxine was eighteen or nineteen years old at the time.)

1965   Alex Sanders claims in a press account that he has 1623 initiates in a total of 100 covens.

1966   Robert Cochrane (a.k.a. Roy Bowers) dies. He claimed to be an hereditary witch and like many who claimed an hereditary tradition he was unable to prove it. Cochrane is often credited with coining the label "Gardnerian," originally meant as an insult. Doreen Valiente worked with Cochrane's coven during the 1960s.

1967   Alex Sanders marries Maxine Morris (who was twenty-one years old at the time.)

1969   Raymond Buckland publishes his first book mentioning witchcraft, "A Pocket Guide to the Supernatural."

1969   June Johns publishes "King of the Witches," an unskeptical biography of Alex Sanders. It includes, for the first time in publication, "The Ardanes" or Wiccan Laws.

1970   Alex Sanders initiates Janet Owen and the same year Maxine Sanders initiates Stewart Farrar. Janet and Stewart strike up a working and romantic relationship through their involvement in the Sanders' coven. They receive their 2nd degree initiations later that year and set up their own coven.

1971	Lady Sheba (a.k.a. Jessie Wicker Bell) publishes "Lady Sheba's Book of Shadows." It is the first time a more-or-less complete Wiccan Book of Shadows is put into print. It was essentially a Gardnerian Book of Shadows with alterations and additions. Many Wiccans were outraged at this as it was felt that Lady Sheba was violating the oaths of secrecy that are part of most Wiccan first degree initiations. Lady Sheba asserted the Goddess directly instructed her to publish her Book of Shadows.
1972	Janet Owen and Stewart Farrar are legally married.
1973	Patricia Crowther publishes her first book on witchcraft, "Witchcraft in Yorkshire."
1973 (Sept. 20th – 23rd)	"Witchmeet" held in Minneapolis, Minnesota hosted by Llewellyn Publications.[11] At this meeting Lady Sheba attempted to have herself proclaimed the Queen of American Witches. She also wanted initiates to hand over their Books of Shadows to her so that they could be examined and then a single Book established as authoritative. She failed in both her goals.
	Also at the Witchmeet the Council of American Witches, a group of about 70 Wiccans from various traditions, was established and issued a document titled "Principles of Wiccan Belief." While the Council disbanded shortly after, many Wiccans now consider the Principles to be foundational.[12]
1974	Raymond Buckland publishes "The Tree: A Complete Book of Saxon Witchcraft" as an openly modern creation with fully published rituals. It was also controversial for permitting self-initiations into the new Seax-Wicca denomination.

1974   Selena Fox and Dr. Dennis Carpenter establish Circle Sanctuary as a Wiccan church and community resource. Their networking efforts, largely through their publications "Circle Guide to Pagan Groups" and "Circle Magazine," help to bring together many Pagans over the years. They are located in rural Mount Horeb, Wisconsin, where they hold regular events.

1975   Zsuzsanna Budapest publishes "A Feminist Book of Lights and Shadows" (republished in 1989 as "The Holy Book of Women's Mysteries.") Budapest was highly influential in the growth of feminist elements within Wicca.

1975   Lady Gwen (Gwynne) Thompson publishes "The Rede of the Wiccae" (also known incorrectly as the long version of the Wiccan Rede) in the Ostara 1975 issue of Green Egg magazine. Lady Gwen claimed her grandmother gave her the poem before her death in 1947, but this is doubtful.[13]

1975   The Covenant of the Goddess (COG) is founded and incorporated in California as a not-for-profit Wiccan and Witchcraft organization. The group helps to establish Wicca and Witchcraft as valid and legally-recognized religions within the United States.

1979   Starhawk's book "The Spiral Dance" is published. Starhawk's work helped spread the word about Wicca and Witchcraft as meaningful spiritual paths particularly among feminists and progressive liberal thinkers.

1979   Margot Adler's survey of Paganism in the United States, "Drawing Down the Moon," is published. It has been revised and updated through a number of editions, most recently in 2006, and is still valuable as a description of the diversity in the Pagan and Wiccan community.

1979   Pete "Pathfinder" Davis establishes the Aquarian
        Tabernacle Church. Like the Covenant of the Goddess,
        the Aquarian Tabernacle Church helps to establish
        Paganism as a valid and legally-recognized religious
        category in various countries.

1981   Janet and Stewart Farrar publish "Eight Sabbats for
        Witches." Many Wiccan groups with Gardnerian or
        Alexandrian leanings consider this book to be essential
        reading.

1982   Scott Cunningham's book "Magickal Herbalism" is
        published. It is the start of his influential career writing
        Wiccan instruction manuals.

1984   Janet and Stewart Farrar publish "The Witches Way"
        which is later combined with "Eight Sabbats for
        Witches" and published by Magickal Childe as "A
        Witches' Bible." "The Witches Way" fleshes out a lot of
        the philosophy of Wicca.

1986   Raymond Buckland publishes "Buckland's Complete
        Book of Witchcraft." (Many Wiccans affectionately
        refer to this book as "Uncle Bucky's big blue book.")
        This book is one of the standard texts frequently
        recommended to many beginners.

1987   The Unitarian Universalist Association establishes a
        charter for a subgroup, the Covenant of Unitarian
        Universalist Pagans (CUUPS.) Today there are CUUPS
        groups in many places around the world, providing
        publicly accessible rituals and worship services for
        anyone who wants to attend.

1988   Scott Cunningham's book "Wicca: A Guide for the
        Solitary Practitioner" is published. This book provides
        a solid argument justifying solitary practice; previously
        Wiccans were commonly expected to be members of
        covens.

1989   Doreen Valiente publishes "The Rebirth of Witchcraft,"
            exploring the history of Wicca including many
            interesting accounts of her role in its development and
            first-hand accounts of various incidents. In this book she
            helps clarify the connection between Alex Sanders and
            Gardnerian Wicca.

1991   Aidan Kelly's book "Crafting the Art of Magic" is
            published. Many Wiccans vilify Kelly and his book.
            Kelly's work casts doubt on the authenticity of the
            Gardnerian Book of Shadows and Gerald Gardner's
            claims that he was merely passing on things he was
            taught as an intact religious system. Many Wiccans up to
            this point believed Gardner's claims.

1999   Ronald Hutton publishes "The Triumph of the Moon,"
            a scholarly historical exploration of modern Witchcraft.
            He makes it very clear that there is little evidence to
            support the claim that Wicca existed as a coherent Pagan
            religious system prior to Gerald Gardner.

2000   Philip Heselton publishes "Wiccan Roots," an attempt
            to uncover historical evidence for Wicca prior to Gerald
            Gardner. The book provides an interesting account
            of the circumstances around the start of Gardner's
            involvement with Wicca and raises useful questions.
            Unfortunately it fails to provide conclusive proof that a
            religion such as Wicca existed prior to Gardner.

            Heselton continues this valuable research in his book
            "Gerald Gardner and the Cauldron of Inspiration"
            published by Capall Bann in 2003.

2001 and beyond	Witchcraft and Wicca are moving increasingly into the mainstream. Popular fictional television shows such as "Buffy the Vampire Slayer" and "Charmed" feature major characters that are openly witches and are not stereotypically evil. There is a boom in Pagan and specifically Wiccan publishing with hundreds of titles flooding the market. Some popular authors, such as Silver RavenWolf, write largely for the teen market. The growth of the internet provides another valuable and accessible source of information for those drawn to Wicca and the occult. With the rapid growth of information now freely available there are visible conflicts within the community between factions of "traditionalists" and "eclectics."

With growth comes increased diversity. Some segments of the Wiccan population work towards establishing hierarchies, rules, and dogma, while others stretch the boundaries of what is Wiccan by inventing and incorporating even more diverse material.

Appendix II: Guided Meditation or Pathworking

Basic Pathworking Structure: Beginning & Ending Scripts

o make it easier to establish a routine of meditative pathworking practice it's recommended that you try and use the same beginning or induction and the same ending or conclusion phrasing each time. The middle sections can be substituted as appropriate for different goals in each meditation. Feel free to use these as a guideline for writing your own or modify the scripts to suit your own preferred imagery. If you have dedicated yourself to a particular deity or mythological system it makes sense to modify the scripts to focus on your preferences.

Another good idea, especially for those who have trouble remembering written directions or who aren't comfortable meditating while reading a script, is to tape-record the pathworking and then play it back as needed. Once you have gone through a particular segment enough you will find you are familiar enough with the process that you can dispense with the recording.

The middle sections are listed in a logical order with introductory meditations first and then more advanced ones later on. Start with the ones in "Establishing a Safe Space" and once you are comfortable with working in meditation you can move on to other more specific goals. The workings provided include those that help establish and strengthen psychic skills as well and can be adapted to be done on the physical plane rather than exclusively in meditation.

Meditation is much easier to perform if you are comfortable and able to relax as fully as possible. Some people like lying down while others find they need to sit up, often leaning against something, to avoid falling asleep. Sitting cross-legged on a cushion on the floor and leaning against a wall with a pillow or rolled up blanket propped behind you works well for many people. Make sure you can breathe freely and that your clothes do not feel constraining. Some people, particularly if they are working alone in a private place, will meditate naked. It is best if you are comfortable though so make sure you are not going to be too hot or too cold and arrange your clothing or environment appropriately. And please turn off your phones and lock the door! There's nothing worse than being disturbed in a good meditation session by a ringing phone or someone walking into the room unannounced.

Meditation is like any skill; it gets better the more you do it. You will find that repeating a specific meditation over the course of a week will bring much better results than if you try it just once. Sometimes the first or even second attempts are like dress rehearsals rather than the real thing. Give yourself permission to not do things perfectly the first time. You can always repeat a meditation later to see if it works better the next time around.

Some people are naturally talented when it comes to visualization. Others find that they have trouble seeing pictures with their mind's eye. We have more senses than just sight though so feel free to focus more on the senses that do seem naturally attuned for you in these sorts of astral workings. If you don't see energies or entities but you can feel their presence then focus on that. We learn how to expand our senses in the astral, our hearing, our sense of smell, touch, or taste, and our ability to see by trying things out and working at it. If it doesn't work the way you expect on the first attempt it doesn't mean it will never work for you. Just keep trying. Keep a realistic pace to your attempts though. I would not recommend repeating a challenging meditation more than once every twenty-four hours unless you have purposefully built up to this and really do intend to complete a mental marathon.

You will find that as your senses become strengthened in the astral plane you can carry this over into the physical realm. The astral planes interpenetrate the physical. When we develop our sensitivity to the astral it sharpens our ability to perceive things we would otherwise miss in the physical. You might notice little details you normally overlook. Perhaps you'll start to notice subtle things on the astral levels even when you have your eyes wide open. One of the goals of pathworking and meditation is to cleanse our senses to allow us to grow in our awareness of the Divine presence. Learning to perceive past the surface of things lets us open ourselves to the Divine in a direct and very personal way.

Beginning (induction)

Make sure you are seated or lying down in a comfortable position. Feel free to loosen your clothing a bit so you don't feel constrained.

During the meditation session you will be in complete control of yourself, your body, your senses, and your experiences. If you feel any discomfort or become aware of any danger you will be able to handle it easily, or will immediately return to your normal level of awareness if required. You will remember everything that happens. When you come out of the meditative state you will feel relaxed, refreshed, and energized.

Start now by closing your eyes and focusing on my words. Take a deep breath, slowly, in through your nose for a count of four. Hold for a count of four, then slowly out through your mouth for a count of four. Hold for one, two, three, four, then in through your nose, two, three, four. Hold, two, three, four. Out through your mouth, two, three, four. Hold, two, three, four. In, two, three, four. Hold, two, three, four. Out, two, three, four. Hold, two, three, four. In, two, three, four. Hold, two, three, four. Out, two, three, four.

Continue the breathing pattern, in through your nose, hold, then out through your mouth, hold, then in again. Hold, then out through your mouth. Hold. In through your nose.

Feel the solid earth beneath your body, supporting you. It is very solid, very strong. The floor rests on beams and concrete that is cradled in solid rock and hard-packed soil, which is very dense and goes down, down, down for miles. The earth is huge, solid, and supports us. It is also very much alive and has a gentle energy we can tap into.

As you breathe, in through your nose and out through your mouth, feel the solid earth beneath you. Feel the subtle energy of the earth beneath you, supporting and sustaining you. That energy flows gently into you through the ground, through the floor, through your contact with the solid earth. Feel that energy, gentle, flowing like a quiet pulse. It ebbs, it flows; each breath in draws it up from the ground and into your body. Each breath out spreads the energy through your body, helping it to seep into your blood, your muscles, your sinews and fat, your bone. Each breath in draws more of the earth energy up into you, each breath out helps it spread through your body, healing, relaxing, filling you with refreshing energy.

Feel the energy flow in as you breathe, spreading through your body as you breathe out. In, and it seeps in, out, and it spreads through your body even more. In, and you fill with energy, out and the energy heals, and charges, and refreshes your body.

As your body becomes charged, as you body becomes energized, your inner senses become more acute. You start to realize that you are now in a safe place, a holy place, a place that is all your own. It is a place that is not a place, in a time that is not a time. It is a threshold place, a place of safety where you stand between worlds. Your body here is perfect, and strong, and energized. And this is your sacred, safe, protected space.

It is time now to honour the elements, to ask for their blessing on your astral temple. Move to the east side of your temple space and raise your hands. Take a deep breath and feel the energy flowing through you. Feel the air moving gently about you, then moving to blow softly in your face. A glowing pentagram flares into life on the wall of the eastern boundary of your temple. Hail and welcome, powers of East, powers of Air. Blessed be.

Move now to the south edge of your temple space and raise your hands. Take a deep breath and feel the energy flowing through you. Feel the heat of the sun, fires internal and external rising and crackling. The heat bathes and bakes you from the south. You see a glowing pentagram flare into life on the wall of the southern boundary of your temple. Hail and welcome, powers of South, powers of Fire. Blessed be.

Move now to the west edge of your temple space and raise your hands. Take a deep breath and feel the energy flowing though you. Feel a rising mist, watery depths, a surf rising and falling and gently calling your name. Feel the movement of the waters, the liquid essence inside and out, the salty and sweet waters that beckon. You see a glowing pentagram flare into life on the wall of the western boundary of your temple. Hail and welcome, powers of the West, powers of Water. Blessed be.

Move now to the north side of your temple space and raise your hands. Take a deep breath and feel the energy flowing through you. Feel the dust, the dark rich soil, the dense rocks. Sense the mountains, the expanse of desert sands, the solid body of mother Earth. You see a glowing pentagram flare into life on the northern boundary of your temple. Hail and welcome, powers of North, powers of Earth. Blessed be.

Move back to the center of your temple space and pause for a moment of quiet reflection. Feel the energy of the elements pulsing around you, filling the space with their holy presence. Feel the energies merging, mingling, and becoming something much greater than the sum of their parts. Raise your hands high above. Hail and welcome, powers of the Centre, powers of Spirit. Blessed be.

The energies pulse through your temple, through your body, relaxing, refreshing, and energizing. Breathe in through your nose, hold, breathe out through your mouth, hold, and bask in the holy energies that surround and permeate you. In, two, three, four. Hold, two, three, four. Out, two, three, four. Hold, two, three, four. In, two, three, four. Hold, two, three, four. Out, two, three, four.

Ending (resolution)

Every time you attempt to meditate like this, every time you go within like this, you will find that it is easier and easier to do. Your experiences will become more vivid, more real, each time you attempt to reach these states of awareness. You will find your awareness unfolding, new insights and abilities coming forward for you. You will also find that things will come more easily to you. You will be more in control. As the spirit realms become more familiar you will find yourself more relaxed, more empowered. And this strength and empowerment will remain with you no matter where you are or what you are doing, whether you are awake, or asleep, or in a meditative or spiritual state like you are now.

Breathe in the energy, feel it coursing through your body, healing and charging you with energy. You are being cleansed, softly, gently, made whole. You are at peace.

A mist gathers around you until you can see nothing but the gentle, moving whiteness. It caresses your body. It has a faint scent that brings back memories of feeling safe. The mist is warm, inviting, and healing. Everything is quiet and serene in the mist.

And then the mist dissolves and you find yourself coming back to your physical body, back into your physical senses. The mist dissipates and you can feel your body again. Feel your arms, your legs, the ground beneath you. Breathe deeply and feel energized as you return to your normal senses, your normal state of being. Move your fingers, then move your arms slowly, then shift and move your body and stretch when you're ready. And when you're completely back, open your eyes and sit up comfortably. You're safe, back in your body, at ease and rested and filled with energy and inspiration.

A Selection of Pathworking Journeys: "Middle" Scripts

You can do all manner of things in the middle portion of a guided meditation. If you have particular needs to address, for instance, you might want to use the middle portion to conduct a spell. It might be a time for rest and relaxation, or creative expression in a safe astral space. If you are using music it often works well to have some music play for the middle part that you feel is appropriate for the mood you want to work with and then let inspiration guide you.

There are specific things you can do in this middle part to help strengthen your safe space on the astral and at the same time strengthen your own abilities. The following scripted middles can be used in successive meditation sessions or can be used in whatever order would work best for you. It is recommended that you do start with at least the sequence for establishing the astral temple and furnishing the temple so that you have your safe space firmly created before moving on to other explorations.

Establishing a Safe Space

The Astral Temple

This astral place is your personal safe space, your temple. It will become more detailed and more solid each time you visit. Every time you think about it, whether you are in trance or not, you are directing energy to it and making it more real.

This is your astral temple. It is your space and yours alone. Anything you need or desire can be found here, and everything is yours in its most perfect form. It is just a matter of looking around for it, or calling out for it and it will be there for you.

Breathe deeply, drawing in energy, and as you breathe out direct the energy to you astral temple. The astral mists swirl and gather about the edges of your safe space, becoming more solid, revealing forms and shapes. Pay attention to the shape of your sacred space. How is the place constructed? You can see the edges of the space more clearly now, more distinctly. Notice the walls, the ceiling, how enclosed or open this space is. Perhaps you can see openings, windows or doorways, perhaps archways, and a faint landscape beyond. This is your place so it will appear however you want. Your sacred temple is exactly where you want it to be, with landscape that is both picturesque and placid. Your temple is in a very safe area, a place of great power, a place where your will is manifest.

Move about the perimeter of your sacred temple and reach out to touch the walls, the window or doorframes, the texture of the things that surround you. Breathe deeply, and notice the comforting smells. There is a deep, rich, satisfying smell to this place. It recalls memories of safety and security. It reminds you of times and places where you were completely relaxed, completely at ease. The smells are soothing, calming, yet also energizing. You feel completely aware, in control, at ease.

Notice the floor beneath your feet. It is solid, secure, supporting. You can walk here barefoot in perfect comfort if you wish. Reach down and touch it with your fingers, press your palm against it. It's that perfect temperature – cool enough to be refreshing, yet warm enough to be gentle.

You'll notice, too, that the flooring has a faint pattern in it. In the temple ritual space, the floor has very distinct markings to indicate the ritual space, and to indicate the four directions. As you look closely, you might notice that the markings shimmer and move gently of their own accord. They are magickal bands of energy, localized ley lines that are pulsing and streaming in ways that best suit your temple and magickal needs. Reach your hand out to one and notice how it shifts like it's alive, moving ever so gently like a cat reaching to feel the touch of your hand. You can direct the energy bands as you wish. Make a gesture at the bands, and notice how they shift to your bidding. You can direct them to stretch, contract, expand, or shift as you wish. You can use this energy to inscribe runes or symbols. And whether you focus on them or not, the energy bands are there, pulsing and flowing about your sacred temple, protecting your from outside forces and concentrating pure energies within for your direction.

This sacred space is truly your space. As you explore further, you'll find that it is decorated in precisely the perfect way for you now. As you think about it, it is so. If you wish this space to be bright with light colors, it is so. If you desire more subdued lighting, darker colors that are more suitable for quieter work, then it is so. This place is yours, a safe place that will always exist for you on the astral planes.

Furnishing the Temple

The altar

This is your astral temple. It is your space and yours alone. Anything you need or desire can be found here, and everything is yours in its most perfect form. It is just a matter of looking around for it, or calling out for it and it will be there for you.

Look around yourself and note what your temple looks like. You are protected, safe, secure. The space is open and comfortable, with lots of room for you to move around and dance if you wish. There is an altar here as well – go over to it and examine it. Take note of what it is made of, how high it is, how long and how wide. It is your altar, and is the perfect size for you. It is exactly as big as you need or desire.

Reach out your hand and touch the altar, feel its surface, the sides. Run your hands over it and feel it pulsing gently with the energy of the place, the energy of the elements and your own Spirit entwined.

There is a cabinet hidden under the altar as well, built in and hidden unless you know it's there. But you know it's there. Open the cabinet, and take out the ritual tools you would like to use. Take them out, one by one, and feel their energies. Wield them, and place them on the altar if you feel that is right. If this is not the time for a particular tool, then put it back in its special spot in the cabinet. It will be there should you need it later.

The altar has a symbol glowing gently on its surface, traced by mystical energies. The symbol means something to you – if you are not sure what it means then it represents something that you need to know. Focus on the symbol; remember what it looks like. When you return to mundane consciousness you will be able to remember this symbol clearly so that you may draw it on paper and research its meaning further.

The astral wand

This is your astral temple. It is your space and yours alone. Anything you need or desire can be found here, and everything is yours in its most perfect form. It is just a matter of looking around for it, or calling out for it and it will be there for you.

Go to your altar and open the cabinet hidden underneath. In one of the compartments you will find a magickal wand. Take out the wand and examine it. Get to know your wand, as it is yours and yours alone. It is perfectly proportioned for you, and designed exactly as you need a wand to be designed for your individual use. As you hold the wand in your hand you can feel energies pulsing, coursing. Your hand tingles slightly as you hold your wand. It tickles a little bit, but it is a very pleasant feeling. The weight of the wand in your hand, the energies are very familiar to you. Perhaps you felt this in a dream when you were a child.

The wand helps you extend and direct your will, directing magickal energies to do your bidding. You can see gleams of light around the tip of the wand, or perhaps they appear to be tiny sparks that hover and gather around the wand's tip. Take a deep breath in, and as you slowly breathe out hold up your wand. Feel the energy spreading through your body and down your arm, into your hand and into the wand. The wand's own energy increases dramatically, and the tiny sparkles and lights at the tip flare into life. There is a sphere of glowing, gentle, healing light pulsing gently at the end of your wand now.

As the wand pulses and hums, you notice there is a faint, pleasing smell of fresh spring air. As you move the wand slowly around in front of you tiny air currents shift and eddy around you, blowing and whispering around your face. It brushes your hair ever so gently, caressing your cheek. It's like there is the faintest, chaste kiss of air against your forehead.

Take another deep breath, and as you slowly breathe out extend your wand and move it in a grand sweeping motion. The tip glows brightly, and the gentle eddies and breezes pick up speed and become stronger, moving around your temple and blowing clean and fresh. Your hair and clothing is ruffled in the wind. As you experiment more with your wand you will find that the wind currents will move as you wish, picking up speed and strength or calming down to stillness as you desire. Explore your talents with the wand, feel the exhilaration as you exercise your magickal abilities.

When you are done using your wand, place it back in its special place in the cabinet below your altar.

The astral athame

This is your astral temple. It is your space and yours alone. Anything you need or desire can be found here, and everything is yours in its most perfect form. It is just a matter of looking around for it, or calling out for it and it will be there for you.

Go to your altar now and open the hidden cabinet beneath. In one of the compartments you will find an athame, a ritual knife. It is designed specifically for you, so will have the perfect structure, weight, and balance for you. It is the perfect length, the handle sized exactly to fit your hand. It is very sharp and has a pointed tip. As you turn and admire the blade in your hand, you notice that there is a faint glow emanating from the knife.

There is a faint crackling energy in the athame, too, that you can feel as you hold it. It is a warm energy, a hot energy, the energy of fire contained and tempered within the ritual knife. As you concentrate, the glow playing along the length of the blade grows brighter, springing to life as mystical flames that lick the blade and flicker up towards the tip. As you move the blade through the air the mystical fire stretches from the knife tip, trailing and lingering in the air to leave a visible line of flame. Take a deep breath, and as you breathe out move your athame and draw a circle in the air before you. Watch as the magickal flame issues from the tip of the athame blade, and remains in the air as you draw this flaming circle. Complete the circle so that it is one continuous band of fire glowing in the air before you.

Now take a deep breath, and as you slowly let the breath out trace the flaming circle with your athame again, but this time focus on drawing the flame into the blade. Notice how the fire is drawn into the blade and absorbed, almost like a vacuum draws in a line of dust. Move your athame around the flaming circle, drawing it in completely until it is all absorbed back into your athame.

By concentrating and practicing with your athame here in your astral temple, you will find that you can control the fire energy with your athame, to produce different colours and qualities of flame, different strengths, and flames that will purify or flames that will heal. The fire you can produce with your athame is limited only by your own imagination and will. You can do anything you can conceive.

When you are done working with your athame, place it back in its special place in the cabinet beneath your altar.

The astral cup

This is your astral temple. It is your space and yours alone. Anything you need or desire can be found here, and everything is yours in its most perfect form. It is just a matter of looking around for it, or calling out for it and it will be there for you.

Go to your altar now and open the hidden cabinet beneath. In one of the compartments you will find a goblet, a ritual cup. It is designed specifically for you, so will have the perfect shape, weight, and size for you. The bowl is the perfect capacity, the curvature of it fits comfortably cradled in your hand. As you turn and admire the cup in your hand, you notice that there is a faint glow emanating from it.

Take the cup in your hands, cradling it as you would an enormous egg. The cup represents fertility, possibility, generation and regeneration. Raise the cup in both hands, high above your head. Take a deep breath, and as you breathe out feel the energies of this place swirling and focusing on the cup in your upheld hands. You feel the cup vibrating with energy.

Lower the cup now to chest level, and you will discover there is now something in the cup. It is a liquid, a swirling brew of inspiration and healing, formulated just for you. It provides exactly what you need at this moment, exactly what your soul and body require. Breathe in the heady scent of this potion, feel its fumes caressing your face gently. And when you are ready, raise the cup to your lips and drink deeply.

The cup is your cup, a cauldron in miniature, a magickal receptacle to focus your inspiration and healing powers. As you use the cup more you will discover that it will always provide you with the perfect brew for the situation. All you need to do is hold it high in this sacred space, breathe deeply, and the mystical energies will oblige.

When you are done working with your cup, place it back in its special place in the cabinet beneath your altar.

The astral pentacle

This is your astral temple. It is your space and yours alone. Anything you need or desire can be found here, and everything is yours in its most perfect form. It is just a matter of looking around for it, or calling out for it and it will be there for you.

Go to your altar now and open the hidden cabinet beneath. In one of the compartments you will find a small platter with a pentacle design on it. It was created specifically for you, so will be the perfect size, weight, and symbolism for you. It is the perfect diameter, not too big for you to handle but large enough to be impressive. Turn the pentacle in your hands as you examine it and notice the colour, the material it is made from, the decoration and design. As you turn and admire the platter in your hands, you notice that there is a faint glow emanating from it.

The pentacle is helpful for a number of magickal tasks. By placing things on it they become blessed and magickally charged. You can hold it in your hands and use it as a focus to direct protective energies, acting as a magickal shield. If you find you are having difficulty directing magickal energy hold the pentacle towards the energy when you give it verbal commands and it will always work. The pentacle is perhaps the strongest of your magickal tools – while the elements of fire, water, and air might be fickle, the element of earth is always stable.

Hold the pentacle in your hands and hold it outward from you as a shield. Feel it hum and vibrate with energy. Take the pentacle around the perimeter of your working space and as you do so notice that the energies at the boundary grow strong and solid. Casting the circle using the pentacle will always produce a particularly strong and protective space for your workings.

When you are done experimenting with your pentacle, place it back on your altar or in its special place in the cabinet beneath your altar.

Expanding the Temple

The astral bonfire

This is your astral temple. It is your space and yours alone. Anything you need or desire can be found here, and everything is yours in its most perfect form. It is just a matter of looking around for it, or calling out for it and it will be there for you.

You notice that in the centre of your ritual space there is a circular groove in the floor, a few feet across. As you examine it you realize that it is an inlaid covering, thick and protective, over an opening in the floor.

As you stand back a bit from this central circle you notice that there is a faint colouring to the circle, traces of red and orange and yellow flickering and shifting faintly. You intuitively make a gesture and the solid circle vanishes, revealing a fire pit a step down in the floor.

As you look at this marvel, the pile of logs and kindling in the centre of the firepit flicker into flaming life. The smell of fragrant wood burning cheers you, a warmth emanating from the firepit. The smoke from the firepit rises up and dissipates invisibly. This is the ideal open fire for you: it has all the benefits, and no acrid smoke to get in your eyes or make breathing a challenge.

Spend some time enjoying the fire. Perhaps you want to sprawl out on the ground near the fire, comfortable on cushions you find nearby, or maybe you feel inspired to dance about the flames. The flames are friendly, and seem to speak to you in the crackles and pops. The flames lick and gesture in meaningful ways.

When you feel you have spent enough time with the firepit, you will find that it will put itself out magickally and the cover will reappear so the floor is again whole. All you need to do is thank the firepit when you are done.

The astral cauldron

This is your astral temple. It is your space and yours alone. Anything you need or desire can be found here, and everything is yours in its most perfect form. It is just a matter of looking around for it, or calling out for it and it will be there for you.

As you look around the temple space, you notice a niche or closet off to one side. You move closer to examine it and discover a collection of items that could be of use to you in various magickal workings. One item that is close by is a nice sized cauldron, and beside it a metal support which can be set up to hold the cauldron over an open fire.

You grab the metal support and cauldron and find they are surprisingly light, yet clearly sturdy and meant to be used. You take the cauldron and stand out into the center of the ritual space where the fire pit is located. You uncover the fire pit and set up the cauldron stand over the fire, and hang the cauldron on the suspended hook meant for that purpose.

You notice there are faintly glowing symbols inscribed on the cauldron, both outside and inside. As you look at them more closely, you realize what they mean. When you speak one of them, it will make the cauldron become larger in size, large enough that you could take a bath in it if you wanted. Another makes the cauldron shrink down to a smaller size, say if you wanted to brew some water for tea. Another symbol, when its name is spoken aloud, causes the cauldron to magickally fill with pure water ready to heat over the fire. Another symbol induces the cauldron contents to vanish so the cauldron is empty again.

Yet another symbol makes the cauldron cool down so that you can grasp it easily without burning yourself. There are magickal methods for all sorts of things you might want to do with the cauldron, and many you had never thought of. You'll discover that the cauldron anticipates your needs and a symbol will be present to match that need with a corresponding solution.

Take some time to explore the cauldron, and brew up something that you might need now if you like. Perhaps you desire a refreshing hot drink, something to soothe, something to heal, or something to promote inspiration. Whatever brews you need can be created with your cauldron.

When you are done with your cauldron, be sure to express your gratitude and thank the cauldron for its help. Use the magickal commands to empty the cauldron, cool it down, and make it a manageable size and then put it and the stand back in the storage area at the edge of your ritual space.

Thank the central fire pit, and restore the area to the way it was before you brought out the cauldron.

The tower

This is your astral temple. It is your space and yours alone. Anything you need or desire can be found here, and everything is yours in its most perfect form. It is just a matter of looking around for it, or calling out for it and it will be there for you.

Moving around your temple space, you discover a hidden door in the east that opens into a staircase that curves up and away along a rounded wall. The stairs are solid stone, perfectly set and massive, strong and enduring. There are handrails on both sides of the stairs that you can grasp. Each step is quite wide, although it does narrow a bit towards the curved inner wall. On the wall to your right just beside the lowest steps you notice a large pale-colored button, within easy reach. The button has a symbol on it: an arrow pointing up along the staircase.

You reach over and out of curiosity press the button. You hear three gentle chimes, and then there is a puff of air coming from behind that lifts you up and carries you softly up the stairs. The staircase is long, always curving around and around, so that it feel like you're always at the edge of becoming dizzy. The soft yet surprisingly strong wind carries you up, up, whooshing and ever curving to follow the stairs, past the occasional small window in the outer wall. Despite there being no obvious lights, candles, or torches along the walls; the staircase is lit with a gentle suffusing glow that comes from everywhere. Before you can really start to wonder about where the light is coming from, the breeze comes to the top of the stairs and sets you down quietly on the landing at the top.

There is another door before you set in a stone wall. The door is large and sturdy with metal bands for extra reinforcement. You get the idea that if the door were to be shut and locked, nothing would be able to get through.

There is a sculpted doorknocker in the middle of the door about head height. The doorknocker is formed to look like the head of a humanoid creature, some sort of friendly goblin or faery, with the large metal knocker-ring held in its mouth.

You reach up and grasp the knocker ring tentatively, tapping it gently against the metal rest below the head. The head opens its eyes, looks at you with a sparkle of recognition, and then manages to say "Welcome, friend!" around the ring held tightly in its mouth.

The door creaks open before you, enticing you into the room beyond. You step inside to see where you are.

The room is circular, with a series of large leaded-glass windows all around the perimeter. The windows each have latches on them so that you can open them. The ceiling above you is domed and appears to be made of an amazing framework of leaded glass as well. It looks like a beautiful stained glass flower blooming above your head.

There is a comfortable-looking wooden chair off to one side, and an adjustable stand for holding books. It looks like you could use it to read while sitting in the chair, or raise it so it could hold a book while you are standing, or lowered to hold a book while you are sitting on the floor. There is a massive, ancient looking book on the stand, lying there closed and waiting to be examined.

There is also a series of freestanding candleholders around the room, placed at regular intervals along the edge of the wall. The stands are wrought iron but don't look like they'd be hard to move around if you wanted to place them somewhere specific. There are large white candles already mounted on each of these stands.

Apart from that, the room looks pretty empty. You go to one of the windows and peer through to see what is outside.

The view is spectacular. You are quite high up, so high that you get a gorgeous view of the landscape. Looking one way, you can see mountains topped with snowy caps off in the distance, thick forests stretching a long way. In another direction you can see a large body of water, light dancing on the waves in ever-shifting sparkles. You can also see human habitation off in the distant horizons; perhaps these are towns, or even a city. There is so much to see from this vantage.

You can open a window if you like, and lean out over the strong railing to feel the sweet breezes that slip around the tower. If you open a few windows, you can get a wonderful cross breeze through the tower room.

As you are moving around the room, looking out the different windows, you discover there is a small storage closet, more of a cubbyhole, in the room as well. When you open the small door you find all sorts of interesting things tucked away in there. You find what looks like an elaborate antique telescope, a device for measuring the positions of stars, and many other things carefully tucked away. There is even a wooden chest in here with all sorts of nice surprises just waiting to be discovered.

Take your time examining the contents of this storage closet, and exploring the tower room some more. It is yours, a safe place, where you can retreat for quiet meditation, study, or just to be alone. You can also invite others to come here with you if you like. But since this space is yours, only those you invite in will be allowed in. The guardian of the tower door will not allow unwelcome visitors to enter no matter who or what they are.

When you are done exploring the tower room and its contents, be sure to put things back in their places and tidy up. When you are ready to leave, thank the door guardian and the stairs will take you down again.

The cavern in the depths

This is your astral temple. It is your space and yours alone. Anything you need or desire can be found here, and everything is yours in its most perfect form. It is just a matter of looking around for it, or calling out for it and it will be there for you.

Moving around your temple space, you discover a hidden door in the north that opens into a rough stone staircase that curves down into the earth. The stairway is dark, lit only by occasional lanterns mounted on the rough-hewn walls. The steps are wide and dry, and there are wooden handrails on both sides of the stairs leading down.

You notice a button on the wall just above the handrail by one of the top steps. On this button there is a symbol: an arrow pointing down. Curious, you press the button to see what it does.

You hear three faint chimes like tiny silver bells. A gentle gust of air comes from behind you, and before you know it the wind has picked you up in its embrace and is carrying you down the stairs.

You feel yourself going down, down, ever down, deep into the earth. The stairway is a tunnel, ancient, sturdy, and strangely comforting as it takes you down ever deeper into the earth.

Finally the gust of wind slows down and settles you gently at the bottom of the stairs, in a small open space. Before you is a huge iron door mounted securely in the stone wall.

On the door you notice a sculpted doorknocker. It is shaped like a humanoid head, perhaps some friendly goblin or faery. The little metal head is holding a large metal ring securely in its mouth.

You reach up and grasp the ring, lift it gently, and then use it to knock on the iron door.

The little metal face opens its eyes to look at you. You can see that it smiles, its lips curling up at the edges around the ring it is holding in its mouth. It manages to say, "Welcome, friend!" and winks at you. The door swings open for you, its massive weight moving silently on well-oiled hinges.

You step through the door and feel as though you have stepped into a cathedral. The room behind the door is a massive natural cavern. Stone has melted and flowed over the centuries, worked by patient drops of water, into fantastic structures. The ceiling soars above your head, and the floor is smooth and dry, with a few pools of clear dark water around the edges. You can hear water running gently somewhere, and if you explore a bit you'll find it bubbling and gurgling in a little waterfall and down into a pool, where it seeps away through an underground stream.

The cavern, despite being deep underground, is lit by strategically placed candles and lanterns. There are numerous nooks and crannies for you to explore, places to sit in contemplation, and even comfortable spots to lie down and have a nap here if you choose.

At one spot along the edge of the cavern, you discover a small hole in the wall, perhaps a hand span across. You can feel air blowing gently from this hole into the room. Investigating it more closely, you find the hole opens into some sort of narrow airshaft which goes down as well as up. And most interesting, you discover that if you listen carefully you can hear voices coming from somewhere deep below you, even farther down in the earth.

You realize that these must be the voices of deep-earth dwellers, gnomes and dwarves and dragons who rarely if ever venture to the world above. They are children of the soil and rocks, swimmers in magma and deep hidden lakes. If you show them proper respect and friendship, they will return the favour and will be your friends. In this special place you will always find there is at least one friendly voice you can talk with.

This is a sacred place, a special place, a place where you are safe and secure. Explore the cavern some more; discover some of the wonders that await you. This is your special place, your vault in the depths where you can come any time you wish.

When you feel ready to leave, tidy up the cavern a bit if you moved things around, then go back to the door and close it quietly behind you. Be sure to thank the guardian of the door. At the bottom of the stairs you will find there is a button you can press to take you back up the stairs, or if you prefer you can climb the stairs back up to ground level.

The library

This is your astral temple. It is your space and yours alone. Anything you need or desire can be found here, and everything is yours in its most perfect form. It is just a matter of looking around for it, or calling out for it and it will be there for you.

Moving around your temple space, you discover a hidden door in the northeast that opens into a large room filled with shelves, books, and comfy chairs to sit in. As you step into the room you see shelf after shelf of books, scrolls, and boxes of papers. Most things are clearly labeled but some are not. This is a treasure-trove of occult information just waiting for you to explore.

There are lamps and candles placed in convenient spots where their soft golden light illuminates the area without any harshness. You find your eyes slide easily from one book to another, from books to scrolls, onto boxes of papers. You can easily spot important details that you might need to know, like specific titles, or where to find things on topics you might be curious about. These things are all meant to be read, meant to be used. Nothing here is so fragile it can't be taken off a shelf and read.

This is a place where you can come to search for hidden information, to seek out things you need to know. Let your intuition guide you to the perfect source of information. You will always find just what you are looking for easily at hand.

Take your time to explore, to sit and relax in a chair and read if you like. This is your private library. Everything is here just for you. You can come to this room and explore everything here any time you want.

When you are done in the library, be sure to express your thanks as you leave the room to go back into your main ritual space. Whisper "thank you" as you leave, and know that nothing can ever be truly hidden from you.

The Portal in the Temple

This is your astral temple. It is your space and yours alone. Anything you need or desire can be found here, and everything is yours in its most perfect form. It is just a matter of looking around for it, or calling out for it and it will be there for you.

In the north west of your ritual space you notice a curtain on the wall. You draw the curtain back and discover a large dark-glass mirror mounted on the wall, the bottom of the mirror resting on the floor. The mirror is so large you can easily see your own reflection in it, as well as a large part of the space behind you.

The frame around the mirror is intricately engraved. As you examine it more closely, you realize that it is covered in magickal symbols and runes that appear to twine along in an elaborate knotwork pattern. The symbols make you think of the words "distance" and "motion" and "travel." There is also a symbol that makes you think of the word "bring" or "come."

The surface of the mirror is exceedingly smooth too. As you lean towards it to look more closely, you notice that your breath causes the surface of the mirror to ripple gently. The surface of the mirror appears to be almost a liquid, or perhaps a membrane like a soap film or a bubble. The mirror looks solid, and as you step back it looks just like a mirror of dark glass. But you know it is much more than that.

The mirror is a portal, a magick mirror that opens into other places, other times. It is a shortcut to take you where you want or need to go. All you need to do is ask it to show you a place or a time, and you can watch the scene from your side or step through and explore if you like.

When you go through the mirror portal, you can always come back with a mere thought. All you will need to do is think about coming back to your temple space and it will happen. The mirror is linked to you as it is a part of you.

Freeform destination

Move closer to the magickal mirror, the mystical portal, in your temple space. Stretch your hands out to the frame around the huge mirror and feel the energy pulsing through this magickal gateway. The surface of the mirror is dark, with a swirling mist undulating and flowing. Take a deep breath, and then ask the portal to show you someplace that you need to see now, someplace you can go to through the portal if you wish.

No matter where the destination is, you will be perfectly safe, perfectly protected. You can come back in an instant with a simple thought. The magickal portal is charged with protecting you as well as enabling you to travel through space and time. Only you can go through this portal, although you can allow others to come through as well if you wish. You can see through this portal to observe other places but they cannot see back through the mirror unless you specifically permit it.

Look into the portal, watch as the mist clears and the scene sharpens, becomes more solid. Notice the details that start to appear: is it bright or dark there? Is it inside or outside? What objects do you see, what furnishings or architecture? What living things can you see: are there plants, animals, people? Allow the scene to become clearer and more vivid as you watch. And if you wish, you can step into the scene and explore. You can move around inside this place and communicate with the people, with the animals and plants, with the objects you find there. They might speak to you with words or they might provide impressions or feelings that you can sense. But you will find that you can indeed communicate with everything that you find through your mystical portal.

Take some time to observe, to ask questions, to explore in perfect safety. When you are ready just think about it and you will automatically come back to your temple space. The portal will bring you back and close down so that it is sealed from this destination.

Visiting a specific time and place

Move closer to the magickal mirror, the mystical portal, in your temple space. Stretch your hands out to the frame around the huge mirror and feel the energy pulsing through this magickal gateway. The surface of the mirror is dark, with a swirling mist undulating and flowing. Take a deep breath, and then ask the portal to show you a specific place that you want to see now, someplace you can go to through the portal if you wish. The place you want to see, and perhaps explore, can be anywhere at all. It can be any point in history, whether in the past, the present, or the future. It can be in the physical realm or a spiritual realm. You can travel to a place to observe living breathing people and what they are doing, or you can go to places where mythical or fictional people and events are occurring. You are only limited by what you can imagine as a possible destination.

No matter where the destination is, you will be perfectly safe, perfectly protected. You can come back in an instant with a simple thought. The magickal portal is charged with protecting you as well as enabling you to travel through space and time. Only you can go through this portal, although you can allow others to come through as well if you wish. You can see through this portal to observe other places but they cannot see back through the mirror unless you specifically permit it.

Look into the portal, watch as the mist clears and the scene sharpens, becomes more solid. Notice the details that start to appear: is it bright or dark there? Is it inside or outside? What objects do you see, what furnishings or architecture? What living things can you see: are there plants, animals, people? Allow the scene to become clearer and more vivid as you watch. And if you wish, you can step into the scene and explore. You can move around inside this place and communicate with the people, with the animals and plants, with the objects you find there. They might speak to you with words or they might provide impressions or feelings that you can sense. But you will find that you can indeed communicate with everything that you find through your mystical portal.

Take some time to observe, to ask questions, to explore in perfect safety. When you are ready just think about it and you will automatically come back to your temple space. The portal will bring you back and close down so that it is sealed from this destination.

Visiting a specific person
Move closer to the magickal mirror, the mystical portal, in your temple space. Stretch your hands out to the frame around the huge mirror and feel the energy pulsing through this magickal gateway. The surface of the mirror is dark, with a swirling mist undulating and flowing. Take a deep breath, and then ask the portal to show you a specific person who you want to see now,

a person whom you can go to through the portal to visit if you wish. The person you want to see, and perhaps communicate with, can be anywhere at all. They can be in the past, the present, or the future. They can be in the physical realm or a spiritual realm. They can be real people or mythical or fictional people. You are only limited by what you can imagine as a possible destination.

No matter who you wish to observe or contact, you will be perfectly safe, perfectly protected. You can come back in an instant or end the contact with a simple thought. The magickal portal is charged with protecting you as well as enabling you to travel through space and time. Only you can go through this portal, although you can allow others to come through as well if you wish. You can see through this portal to observe other people but they cannot see back through the mirror unless you specifically permit it.

Look into the portal, watch as the mist clears and the scene sharpens, becomes more solid. Notice the details that start to appear: is it bright or dark there? Is it inside or outside? What objects do you see, what furnishings or architecture? What living things can you see: are there plants, animals, other people? Allow the scene to become clearer and more vivid as you watch. And if you wish, you can step into the scene and explore. You can move around inside this place and communicate with the people, with the animals and plants, with the objects you find there. They might speak to you with words or they might provide impressions or feelings that you can sense. But you will find that you can indeed communicate with everything that you find through your mystical portal.

Take some time to observe, to ask questions, to explore in perfect safety. When you are ready just think about it and you will automatically come back to your temple space. The portal will bring you back and close down so that it is sealed from this destination.

Visiting the World Tree

Move closer to the magickal mirror, the mystical portal, in your temple space. Stretch your hands out to the frame around the huge mirror and feel the energy pulsing through this magickal gateway. The surface of the mirror is dark, with a swirling mist undulating and flowing. Take a deep breath, and then ask the portal to show you the Great Tree, the axis of the world, the massive ancient tree whose branches reach up into the spiritual planes, whose trunk is in the physical realm, and whose roots reach down into the lower worlds. The Great Tree is in a timeless place, a place that is in all places yet hidden from all. The Great Tree is older than time and will outlive us all.

No matter where the destination is, you will be perfectly safe, perfectly protected. You can come back in an instant with a simple thought. The magickal portal is charged with protecting you as well as enabling you to travel through space and time. Only you can go through this portal, although you can allow others to come through as well if you wish. You can see through this portal to observe other places but they cannot see back through the mirror unless you specifically permit it.

Look into the portal, watch as the mist clears and the scene sharpens, becomes more solid. Notice the details that start to appear: is it bright or dark there? Is it inside or outside? What objects do you see there, what landscape? What living things can you see: are there plants, animals, people? Allow the scene to become clearer and more vivid as you watch. And if you wish, you can step into the scene and explore. You can move around inside this place and communicate with the people, with the animals and plants, with the objects you find there. They might speak to you with words or they might provide impressions or feelings that you can sense. But you will find that you can indeed communicate with everything that you find through your mystical portal.

Take some time to observe, to ask questions, to explore in perfect safety. Explore the place where the Great Tree is now, the landscape around the tree, and look for the things that the Tree has to teach you. The Tree is like the beanstalk in the story Jack and the Beanstalk. It is so massive, so ancient and gnarled, so huge, you can climb up the tree into the heavens, or can go inside its hollow center and climb down into the world below. Explore, ask questions, listen and observe. When you are ready just think about it and you will automatically come back to your temple space. The portal will bring you back and close down so that it is sealed from this destination.

Visiting the Holy Well

Move closer to the magickal mirror, the mystical portal, in your temple space. Stretch your hands out to the frame around the huge mirror and feel the energy pulsing through this magickal gateway. The surface of the mirror is dark, with a swirling mist undulating and flowing. Take a deep breath, and then ask the portal to show you a holy well. The mist in the mirror swirls, then dissolves to reveal a landscape with a holy well quite nearby. Watch as the scene gets clearer, the details more defined.

Take note of details about where this holy well is located. Is it outside or inside? What is the landscape like around it? Is it nighttime, daytime, dawn, or dusk? What is the weather like, what season does it look like? Are there plants around? Is it tended or wild? What is the ground like; is it rocky, sandy, rich soil? Are there any animals around, any birds, or insects, mammals? Are there any people nearby?

Take your time to explore the well and area around it. Seek answers to questions you might have, or use the time to rest in quiet contemplation and merely listen. The holy well has magickal powers in its water. It can be used to heal, to transform, to enlighten. Do what you feel is natural and respectful. Be sure to thank the holy well, the holy waters, for their blessings.

Feel free to spend as much time as you like to explore and commune with the energies and spirits here. When you are ready to leave, thank the well and anything else you met here, and then return back through your portal. When you are finished the portal will seal itself again and wait for the next time you need it.

Visiting the Faeries

Move closer to the magickal mirror, the mystical portal, in your temple space. Stretch your hands out to the frame around the huge mirror and feel the energy pulsing through this magickal gateway. The surface of the mirror is dark, with a swirling mist undulating and flowing. Take a deep breath, and then ask the portal to show you someplace where there are faeries. The mist in the mirror swirls, then dissolves to reveal a landscape. Watch as the scene gets clearer, the details more defined. It might be a forest glade, a field, a garden, deep in a cave, or by a body of water. It might be high up, or deep down. Observe the landscape carefully, noting the details. What is the weather like? What time of day or night is is? Is there much vegetation, or is plant life sparse? Is this a place you have visited before? Is this place familiar or new to you?

Take some time to observe the scene through your magick mirror, paying attention to the details and anything that draws your attention. If you wish you may step through the mirror into this place, knowing you can come back safely merely by thinking about it. If you prefer, you can stay safely in your sacred space and merely observe the scene through the mirror instead of stepping through. Nothing can come through the mirror to your sacred space unless you specifically invite it through.

Take as much time as you want to explore. You may talk with anything
or anyone you wish in this place. Be sure to treat the place respectfully,
realizing you are a visitor to their space. When you are done thank the
inhabitants of the place, and the place itself, before you return back through
your magick mirror. When you are finished the portal will seal itself again
and wait for the next time you need it.

Visiting the Beloved Dead

Move closer to the magickal mirror, the mystical portal, in your temple
space. Stretch your hands out to the frame around the huge mirror and feel
the energy pulsing through this magickal gateway. The surface of the mirror
is dark, with a swirling mist undulating and flowing. Take a deep breath, and
then ask the portal to show you a person who has died who you would like
to see and possibly talk with. The mist in the mirror swirls, then dissolves to
reveal a scene. Watch as the image gets clearer, the details more defined. It
might be inside a room, or perhaps outside somewhere. Observe the scene
carefully, noting the details. What time of day or night is is? Are there any
objects, any furniture, plants, or other items there? Is this a place you have
visited before? Is this place familiar or new to you?

You should see someone is there, perhaps more than one person. You
should be able to recognize the person you seek even though they might
have a different appearance here in the spirit realm. They will probably
appear as a healthy person, perhaps younger than you remember them. Do
not be surprised if they look a bit different from how you remember them
when you saw them last.

Take some time to observe the scene through your magick mirror, paying
attention to the details and anything that draws your attention. If you wish
you may step through the mirror into this place, knowing you can come
back safely merely by thinking about it. If you prefer, you can stay safely in
your sacred space and merely observe the scene through the mirror instead
of stepping through. Nothing can come through the mirror to your sacred
space unless you specifically invite it through. You can speak to the people
you see in the mirror if you wish, and you can hear them as well even if you
do not step through the mirror into the scene the mirror shows you.

Take as much time as you want to explore. You may talk with anything
or anyone you wish in this place. Be sure to treat the place respectfully,
realizing you are a visitor to their space. When you are done thank the
inhabitants of the place, and the place itself, before you return back through

your magick mirror. When you are finished the portal will seal itself again and wait for the next time you need it.

Devotional Work

There are other good reasons for seeking out contact with others in our astral work. In our mundane lives, building relationships with others involves a lot of give and take. If we only contact our friends to ask them to do favors for us, they tend to quickly tire of us and will start to avoid us or will deny our requests. They say that to gain a friend we must be a friend. Carrying this idea into spiritual relationships with nonphysical entities allows us to build solid friendships, mentoring relationships, or working agreements.

Spirit guides

Your astral temple is your space, your home and safe refuge outside the boundaries of normal time and space. Your ideas, wishes, and desires can be brought into manifestation here. Take the time to make this space your own. Make it comfortable, unique, a reflection of who you really are. Make it a place where you would be happy to invite your spiritual friends and family.

As we advance through magickal work we often discover we have spiritual friends or mentors, sometimes particular animals that draw us. A spirit guide can take on many forms: it might be a beloved ancestor who watches over you, the spirit of an unrelated deceased person who has taken an interest in you, or even a nonhuman spirit such as an angel or mythical creature like a unicorn or dragon. If your particular spirit guide takes an animal form it may be something familiar such as a cat or dog. Perhaps it's a wild animal like a bear, a wolf, a large wild cat. Others find that birds, reptiles, fish, or even insects are drawn to them. Whatever the form your spirit guide takes, whether you are comfortable and familiar with them or just strangely drawn to them, we can meet and befriend them here on the astral. These spirit guides are usually quite willing to come to us in the astral or in dreams, and are merely waiting for us to notice their presence.

We can encourage these friendships in the astral temple by showing reverence to them. Take a deep breath, relax, and think about how you would show honour to your spirit guide.

Perhaps you would like to build a shrine, an altar in one part of your temple devoted to your guide. Perhaps you want this to be more central and want to add some decoration, some ritual items, to your main altar that identify your connection with your guide. Focus on the form you feel your guide might take, and imagine how you would do them honor in your temple. Summon forth the things you need from the astral mists to create your special shrine if that is what you choose. Experiment with movements, gestures, words or songs if you are creating a more active way to show your respect for your guide.

As you work to show reverence for your spirit guide, new ideas will come to you about ways to further honor your guide. Perhaps it's a new image, or a song, a melody, a rhythm or movement. Perhaps it's a word or phrase, or even a whole poem or prayer. Maybe you'll be inspired to dance, or to prepare specific items such as food for your guide. Whatever it is, you will remember these things after you return to the mundane world. These new ideas are important, and will be easy to remember.

Take some time now to do what you are inspired to do. Show reverence to your spirit guide, and know that even though you might not see it now, or even feel its presence now, it knows what you are doing and will reveal itself when you and it are both ready.

Take as much time as you need to locate, identify, contact, and communicate with your guide. Time here will expand or contract so that you will have as much time as you need. An hour of astral time can pass while a second of clock-time flows by. Take all the time you need.

When you are done spending time with your guide, thank them with reverence as you part. You will feel their presence with you, or at least nearby, any time you send out a mental call. They can come to your aid, silently and invisibly, should you need it.

Communing with deity

Your astral temple is your space, your home and safe refuge outside the boundaries of normal time and space. Your ideas, wishes, and desires can be brought into manifestation here. Take the time to make this space your own. Make it comfortable, unique, a reflection of who you really are. Make it a place where you would be happy to invite your spiritual friends and family. Make it a place where you feel you could invite a god or goddess.

The Divine is around us, with us, and within us all the time whether we realize it or not. In this holy place, a space that is between the worlds and outside normal time, we are able to encounter the Divine in ways that are often difficult in other circumstances. This is your place, where you can set up the right conditions that make it easier for particular deities to manifest if you want to call Them. It is also a perfect place for you to discover if there are specific deities who have things to teach you or who wish to make contact with you. They are frequently as interested in us as we are in Them. When we are in magickal places such as here all manner of things can happen.

Take a deep breath, hold it for a moment, and then let it out. Breathe in again, drawing in mystical energy, and as you breathe out you find you are breathing out tension and impurities. Breathe in again, drawing in mysical energy, and feel it coursing through your body. You are recharging your spiritual batteries with each breath you take. You are breathing out anything that might hold you back, and problems and tensions dissolve away.

Feel the pulse of energies around you in this holy place, and open your senses up to the Divine presence that wishes to speak with you. You are safe here, protected in your astral fortress, and only the energies and beings you invite can come to you here. If there is a particular god or goddess you wish to speak with, call Their name now. If you are not sure which deity you need to speak with, do not worry – the right one will be here for you. Open your senses up and stretch them out, listening and waiting for the Divine to show Its presence. Be still and listen. Be still and feel. Observe and attend. They are here. They are here.

As you listen carefully, as you sense and feel for Their presence, each breath you take will fill you with energy to make it easier to sense Them, to make Their presence stronger to you. When you are ready, speak with Them if you wish, but be sure to listen to what They have to tell you. It might come through words, or feelings, or sensations of some sort. Perhaps They will plant a message in your mind that won't show up right away, but will leap into your consciousness at the right moment later on. Show the Divine honor and respect, show Them love, and They will impart Their wisdom and gifts to you.

Time here will expand or contract so that you will have as much time as you need. A hour of astral time can pass while a second of clock-time flows by. Take all the time you need.

When you are done spending time with the Divine, thank Them with reverence as you part. You will feel Their presence with you, or at least nearby, any time you send out a mental call. Each time you contact Them in the future, whether here or in your mundane awareness, it will be easier, and you will find your ability to perceive Them becomes much stronger.

Expanding Awareness

We're going to do a special ritual now to expand your awareness, stretching your senses to touch the infinite. Our bodies are vessels for our spirits and our spirits can expand and grow outside the boundaries of our mundane awareness. Take a deep breath, hold for a moment, and then release that breath and relax more deeply. Breathe in, pause, and breathe out, pause. Breathe in and feel your body relaxing more deeply, breathe out and feel all tensions and stresses fading away.

Breathe in and relax, and notice we are surrounded by a mist that grows thicker and thicker until we can see nothing else around us. It is a gentle, comforting mist that heals and eases our tensions. Breathe in and feel at peace, breathe out and feel the tensions draining away from your body.

The mist starts to clear and you can see your own body just below you, in the mudane world exactly as you left it. You can see how your body is positioned, see how you are dressed, and notice the things around you as you float gently just above your body. Breathe in an relax, breathe out and feel even more tension draining away. Breathe in and relax, and breathe out again.

You feel yourself slowly expanding upwards, your body below looking smaller and smaller, the room getting smaller too. You move out from where you were and can look down now where you know your body is. You're outside now, looking down where your body is resting safely and securely, protected from all harm. As you look around yourself you can see the immediate neighborhood where your body is located. You can see other buildings perhaps, maybe plants or roads or whatever is around you. As you relax and expand even more, you find you are slowly drifting upwards.

As you drift up, you can see even more now. The place where you body is resting is getting smaller and smaller, looking farther and farther away. You can see much more of the countryside now, much more of the area where your body is resting. The buildings and plants and animals and cars and people are looking smaller and smaller, farther and farther away. You breathe in and feel relaxed, breathe out and feel all tension draining away. You are perfectly safe, at ease, at peace. You can see more and more as you expand even more, moving up, and up, the land looking smaller, the waters spreading out as you see more and more of the Earth. You're expanding now into space, breathing in and relaxing, breathing out and feeling the tension drain away.

You relax even more, and find you are expanding even more. You can see the moon now, slowly turning and spinning on its way around the Earth. You can see little lights, sunlight reflecting off satellites that zip around the Earth. You relax and expand more, the Earth and the Moon growing smaller now, other planets becoming visible and getting smaller as well. The sun looks tiny now, a little sphere of light and heat with little marbles around it, going around and around in their endless dance.

You breathe in and relax, breathe out and feel tensions draining away. You expand even more, expanding so our solar system shrinks, and nearby star systems become more visible. You expand even more, expanding and expanding, relaxing and at peace, as you see the stars like sprinkles of jewels, sparkling lights that sweep across the vastness of space. You are so vast now that the stars are part of you, as you relax and breathe in and expand some more.

You expand, and expand, and relax some more. The whole galaxy is shrinking, other galaxies glowing gems of your body. You relax and expand, feel at peace, and feel love. The love grows, the life pulse of uncounted galaxies, an infinite number of solar systems, coursing through your body in gentle waves. You breathe in slowly, relaxing and feeling love and comfort, peace and healing. All is one with your body. You are one with the universe, and one with the Divine. Breathe in and relax, feel at peace, feel the love. Relax and breathe. Breathe and feel love.

Breathe and know that time is an illusion. You can sense infinity here. Boundless space and endless possibilities. You are one with all this, with the Divine, with space, with love. Breathe in and feel. Breathe out and relax even more.

Take all the time you need to feel and know this love, this peace. Breathe and feel at peace. Time here will expand or contract so that you will have as much time as you need. A hour of astral time can pass while a second of clock-time flows by. Take all the time you need.

Breathe in and relax, and notice that you are starting to condense again, shrinking down. As you breathe in you relax and feel your body shrinking again, the universe growing larger, the stars becoming larger and clearer. As you breathe in you relax, as you breathe out you relax even more and feel the shrinking.

You shrink down even more, the galaxies grown large, the star systems growing large, as you shrink and condense even more. You shrink down. You can see our solar system again. You condense even more and can see the moon, the Earth. You condense, the Earth getting larger, expanding in your awareness, as you see it grow larger and larger. Breathe in and relax, and feel your body condensing as you see the ground, the water, the place on Earth where your physical body is resting coming into view. Breathe and relax, at peace and content, as you shrink and slow down, the place where your body is coming closer, getting larger. You come down closer, getting more condensed, more solid, until you are again floating near your body. You can see the place where your body is resting quite clearly now. You can see how your body is dressed; note how you are positioned. You condense and strengthen even more now, and find you are slipping back into a mist, the mist surrounding you. The mist grows more solid, more comforting, as you know you are back to your normal size. You are back in your physical body.

Recommended Resources

The following list of books and websites are highly recommended because they provide excellent material or because they are historically significant or have been influential in the development of modern Wicca and Paganism. Keep in mind that no single book or author will have everything right. A well-rounded education involves drawing from many sources and learning to recognize when authors are stating their own opinions and not hard facts.

General Reference

Buckland, Raymond "The Witch Book: The Encyclopedia of Witchcraft, Wicca, and Neo-Paganism," (Detroit MI: Visible Ink Press, 2002.)

Drury, Nevill "The Dictionary of the Esoteric," (London UK: Watkins, 2002.)

Greer, John Michael "The New Encyclopedia of the Occult," (St. Paul MN: Llewellyn, 2003.)

Guiley, Rosemary Ellen "Harper's Encyclopedia of Mystical & Paranormal Experience," (New York NY: Harper's, 1991.)

Guiley, Rosemary Ellen "The Encyclopedia of Witches & Witchcraft, Second Edition," (New York NY: CheckMark Books, 1999.)

Jordan, Michael "Witches: An Encyclopedia of Paganism and Magic," (London UK: Kyle Cathie Ltd., 1996.)

Rabinovitch, Shelley & Lewis, James (eds.) "The Encyclopedia of Modern Witchcraft and Neo-Paganism," (New York NY: Citadel Press, 2002.)

Riland, George "The New Steinerbooks Dictionary of the Paranormal," (New York NY: Warner Books, 1980.)

Mystery Religions

Angus, S. "The Mystery-Religions," (New York NY: Dover, 1975.)

Burkert, Walter "Greek Religion," (Cambridge MA: Harvard University Press, 2000.)

Daraul, Arkon "Secret Societies: A History," (New York NY: MJF Books, 1989.)

David-Neel, Alexandra "Magic and Mystery in Tibet," (New York NY: Dover, 1971.)

Farrar, Janet & Bone, Gavin "Progressive Witchcraft: Spirituality, Mysteries & Training in Modern Wicca," (Franklin Lakes NJ: New Page Books, 2004.)

Grimassi, Raven "The Wiccan Mysteries: Ancient Origins & Teachings," (St. Paul MN: Llewellyn, 1997.)

Harrison, Jane Ellen "Prolegomena To the Study of Greek Religion," (Princeton NJ: Princeton University Press, 1991 edition but originally published in 1903.)

Meyer, Marvin W. (ed.) "The Ancient Mysteries: A Sourcebook of Sacred Texts," (Philadelphia PA: University of Pennsylvania Press, 1999.)

Mysticism

Harvey, Andrew "The Direct Path: Creating a Journey to the Divine Using the World's Mystical Traditions," (New York NY: Broadway Books, 2000.)

Hedsel, Mark "The Zelator: A Modern Initiate Explores the Ancient Mysteries," (London UK: Century Books Ltd., 1998.)

Horgan, John "Rational Mysticism: Spirituality Meets Science in the Search for Enlightenment," (New York NY: Mariner Books, 2003.)

James, William "The Varieties of Religious Experience," (New York NY: Touchstone, 1997.)

Johnson, Robert A. "Ecstasy," (San Francisco CA: HarperSanFrancisco, 1987.)

LeShan, Lawrence "The Medium, the Mystic, and the Physicist," (New York NY: Viking Press, 1974.)

Nema, "The Way of Mystery: Magick, Mysticism & Self-Transcendence," (St. Paul MN: Llewellyn, 2003.)

Sinetar, Marsha "Ordinary People As Monks And Mystics," (New York NY: Paulist Press, 1986.)

Teasdale, Wayne "The Mystic Heart," (Novato CA: New World Library, 2001.)

Underhill, Evelyn "Practical Mysticism," (Columbus OH: Ariel Press, 1942.)

Underhill, Evelyn "Mysticism," (Oxford UK: Oneworld Publications, 2001.)

Wiccan Basics

Buckland, Raymond "Buckland's Complete Book of Witchcraft," (St. Paul MN: Llewellyn, 1986.)

Buckland, Raymond "The Tree: The Complete Book of Saxon Witchcraft," (New York NY: Weiser, 1974.)

Cunningham, Scott "Wicca: A Guide for the Solitary Practitioner," (St. Paul MN: Llewellyn, 1990.)

Curott, Phyllis "Witch Crafting," (New York NY: Broadway Books, 2001.)

Farrar, Janet & Farrar, Stewart "A Witches Bible," (Blaine WA: Phoenix Publishing, 1996.)

Fisher, Amber Laine "Philosophy of Wicca," (Toronto Canada: ECW Press, 2002.)

Grimassi, Raven "Spirit of the Witch," (St. Paul MN: Llewellyn, 2003.)

Shanddaramon, "Self-Initiation for the Solitary Witch," (Franklin Lakes NJ: New Page Books, 2004.)

Starhawk "The Spiral Dance," (San Francisco CA: Harper & Row, 1979.)

Valiente, Doreen "Witchcraft for Tomorrow," (Blaine WA: Phoenix Publishing, 1978.)

Intermediate To Advanced Wicca

Berg, Wendy & Harris, Mike "Polarity Magic," (St. Paul MN: Llewellyn, 2003.)

Cat, Grey "Deepening Witchcraft," (Toronto Canada: ECW Press, 2002.)

Harrow, Judy "Spiritual Mentoring," (Toronto Canada: ECW Press, 2002.)

Lipp, Deborah "The Elements of Ritual," (St. Paul MN: Llewellyn, 2003.)

Rauls, Venecia "The Second Circle: Tools for the Advancing Pagan," (New York NY: Citadel Press, 2004.)

Reed, Ellen Cannon "The Heart of Wicca," (York Beach ME: Weiser, 2000.)

Sylvan, Dianne "The Circle Within," (St. Paul MN: Llewellyn, 2003.)

Telesco, Patricia "Advanced Wicca," (New York NY: Citadel Press, 2000.)

Magickal Basics

Bardon, Franz "Initiation Into Hermetics," (Wuppertal Germany: Ruggeberg-Verlag, 1993.)

Bardon, Franz "The Practice of Magickal Evocation," (Wuppertal Germany: Ruggeberg-Verlag, 1991.)

Bonewits, Isaac "Real Magic," (York Beach ME: Weiser, 1990.)

Crowley, Aleister "Magick In Theory and Practice," (New York NY: Dover, 1976.)

Duquette, Lon Milo "The Magick of Thelema," (Boston MA: Weiser, 1993.)

Fortune, Dion "Sane Occultism & Practical Occultism In Daily Life," (Bath UK: Aquarian Press, 1987.)

Fortune, Dion "Esoteric Orders and Their Work," (York Beach ME: Weiser, 2000.)

Fortune, Dion "The Training & Work of an Initiate," (York Beach ME: Weiser, 2000.)

Fortune, Dion "Aspects of Occultism," (York Beach ME: Weiser, 2000.)

Fortune, Dion & Knight, Gareth "An Introduction to Ritual Magic," (Loughborough UK: Thoth Publications, 1997.)

King, Francis & Skinner, Stephen "Techniques of High Magic," (New York NY: Warner Destiny Books, 1976.)

Kraig, Donald Michael "Modern Magick," (St. Paul MN: Llewellyn, 1988.)

Murphy-Hiscock, Arin "Power Spellcraft for Life," (Avon MA: Provenance Press, 2005.)

Nema, "Maat Magick," (York Beach ME: Weiser, 1995.)

Regardie, Israel "Foundations of Practical Magic," (Guildford UK: Aquarian Press, 1982.)

Watson, Nancy B. "Practical Solitary Magic," (York Beach ME: Weiser, 1996.)

Zell-Ravenheart, Oberon "Grimoire for the Apprentice Wizard," (Franklin Lakes NJ: New Page Books, 2004.)

Wiccan, Pagan, And Magickal History

Betz, Hans Dieter (ed.) "The Greek Magickal Papyri in Translation: Second Edition," (Chicago IL: University of Chicago Press, 1996.)

Bonewits, Isaac "Witchcraft: A Concise Guide," (USA: Earth Religions Press, 2001.)

Bonewits, Isaac "Bonewits's Essential Guide to Witchcraft and Wicca," (New York NY: Citadel Press, 2006.)

Coughlin, John J. "The Wiccan Rede: A Historical Journey," on the web at http://www.waningmoon.com/ethics/rede.shtml

Council of American Witches "The Principles of Wiccan Belief," on the web at http://www.religioustolerance.org/wic_stat1.htm

Crowther, Patricia "High Priestess: The Life & Times of Patricia Crowther," (Blaine WA: Phoenix Publishing, 1998.)

Davies, Morganna & Lynch, Aradia "Keepers of the Flame: Interviews with Elders of Traditional Witchcraft in America," (Providence RI: Olympian Press, 2001.)

Davis, Morgan – GeraldGardner.com website, found on the internet at http://www.geraldgardner.com

Gardner, Gerald "Witchcraft Today," (New York NY: Citadel Press, 2004.)

Gardner, Gerald "The Meaning of Witchcraft," (New York NY: Citadel Press, 2004.)

Graf, Fritz "Magic in the Ancient World," (Cambridge MA: Harvard University Press, 2002.)

Griffyn, Sally "Wiccan Wisdomkeepers," (York Beach ME: Weiser, 2002.)

Heselton, Philip "Gerald Gardner and the Cauldron of Inspiration," (Milverton UK: Capall Bann Publishing, 2003.)

Heselton, Philip "Wiccan Roots: Gerald Gardner and the Modern Witchcraft Revival," (Milverton UK: Capall Bann Publishing, 2000.)

Hutton, Ronald "The Triumph of the Moon," (Oxford UK: Oxford University Press, 1999.)

Hutton, Ronald "Witches, Druids and King Arthur," (Oxford UK: Oxford University Press, 2003.)

Jones, Prudence & Pennick, Nigel "A History of Pagan Europe," (New York NY: Barnes & Noble, 1995.)

Kelly, Aidan A. "Crafting the Art of Magic, Book 1: A History of Modern Witchcraft 1939-1964," (St. Paul MN: Llewellyn, 1991.)

Lewis, James R. (ed.) "Magickal Religion and Modern Witchcraft," (Albany NY: State University of New York Press, 1996.)

Thomas, Shea "Origins of the Rede Poem," on the web originally at http://www.draknetfree.com/sheathomas/poem.html but also available in a partial archive at http://web.archive.org/web/20031218001055/www.draknetfree.com/sheathomas/index.html

Vale, V. & Sulak, J. "Modern Pagans: An Investigation of Contemporary Paganism," (San Francisco CA: RE/Search Publications, 2001.)

Valiente, Doreen "The Rebirth of Witchcraft," (Custer WA: Phoenix Publishing, 1989.)

Wilson, Colin "The Occult," (New York NY: Vintage Books, 1973.)

Wilson, Colin "Mysteries," (Toronto Canada: Granada, 1983.)

Wilson, Colin "Beyond the Occult," (London UK: Corgi Books, 1989.)

Witt, R. E. "Isis in the Ancient World," (Baltimore MD: Johns Hopkins University Press, 1971.)

Trance And Altered States Of Consciousness

Amoda "Moving Into Ecstasy," (London UK: Thorsons, 2001.)

Ash, Mel "Shaving the Inside of Your Skull: Crazy Wisdom for Discovering Who You Really Are," (New York NY: G. P. Putnam's Sons, 1996.)

Crabtree, Adam "Trance Zero," (Toronto Canada: Somerville House Publishing, 1997.)

Endredy, James "Earthwalks for Body and Spirit," (Rochester VT: Bear & Co., 2002.)

Heller, Steven & Steele, Terry "Monsters and Magickal Sticks: There's No Such Thing As Hypnosis," (Tempe AZ: New Falcon Publications, 1987.)

Huxley, Aldous "The Doors of Perception," (New York NY: Harper & Row, 1954.)

Hyatt, Christopher S. "Undoing Yourself with Energized Meditation and Other Devices," (Tempe AZ: New Falcon Publications, 2002.)

Lawrence, D.J. (ed.) "The Best of Konton Magazine," (Tokyo: Konton Publishing, 2005. http://www.chaosmagic.com)

Mishlove, Jeffrey "The Roots of Consciousness," (New York NY: Marlowe & Co., 1993.)

Guided Meditations And Pathworking

Ashcroft-Nowicki, Dolores "The Initiate's Book of Pathworkings," (York Beach ME: Weiser, 1999.)

Galenorn, Yasmine "Magickal Meditations," (Toronto Canada: The Crossing Press, 2003.)

Houston, Jean & Masters, Robert "Mind Games: The Guide to Inner Space," (Wheaton IL: Theosophical Publishing, 1998.)

Houston, Jean "The Search for the Beloved," (Los Angeles CA: Jeremy P. Tarcher, 1987.)

Houston, Jean "The Hero and the Goddess," (New York NY: Ballantine Books, 1992.)

Kaplan-Williams, Strephon "The Jungian-Senoi Dreamwork Manual," (Novato CA: Journey Press, 1988.)

LeShan, Lawrence "How To Meditate," (New York NY: Bantam, 1975.)

Mariechild, Diane "The Inner Dance," (Freedom CA: The Crossing Press, 1987.)

Stewart, R. J. "Advanced Magickal Arts," (Shaftesbury UK: Element Books, 1988.)

Stewart, R. J. "Earth Light," (Shaftesbury UK: Element Books, 1992.)

Stewart, R. J. "Power Within The Land," (Shaftesbury UK: Element Books, 1992.)

Stewart, R. J. "The Living World of Faery," (Lake Toxaway NC: Mercury Publishing, 1999.)

Stewart, R. J. "The Underworld Initiation," (Guildford UK: Aquarian Press, 1985.)

Warren-Clarke, Ly & Matthews, Kathryn "The Way of Merlyn: The Male Path in Wicca," (Dorset UK: Prism Press, 1990.)

Wilson, Paul "The Calm Technique," (New York NY: Barnes & Noble, 1999.)

Devotions And Worship

De Grandis, Francesca "Goddess Initiation," (San Francisco CA: HarperSanFrancisco, 2001.)

Freeman, Mara "Kindling the Celtic Spirit," (San Francisco CA: HarperSanFrancisco, 2001.)

Gillotte, Galen "Book of Hours: Prayers to the Goddess," (St. Paul MN: Llewellyn, 2001.)

Gillotte, Galen "Book of Hours: Prayers to the God," (St. Paul MN: Llewellyn, 2002.)

Harrow, Judy (ed.) "Devoted To You: Honoring Deity in Wiccan Practice," (New York NY: Citadel Press, 2003.)

Houston, Jean "The Passion of Isis and Osiris," (New York NY: Ballantine/ Wellspring, 1995.)

Kondratiev, Alexei "The Apple Branch: A Path to Celtic Ritual," (New York NY: Citadel Press, 2003.)

Laurie, Erynn Rowan "A Circle of Stones: Journeys & Meditations for Modern Celts," (Chicago IL: Eschaton Productions Inc., 1995.)

Masters, Robert "The Goddess Sekhmet: Psycho-spiritual Exercises of the Fifth Way," (St. Paul MN: Llewellyn, 1991.)

Matthews, Caitlin & Matthews, John "The Western Way," (London UK: Arkana/ Penguin, 1994.)

Newcomb, Jason Augustus "21st Century Mage: Bring the Divine Down to Earth," (York Beach ME: Weiser, 2002.)

Reed, Ellen Cannon "Circle of Isis: Ancient Egyptian Magic for Modern Witches," (Franklin Lakes NJ: New Page Books, 2002.)

Rhea, Lady Maeve "Summoning Forth Wiccan Gods and Goddesses," (New York NY: Citadel Press, 1999.)
Starhawk "The Twelve Wild Swans," (San Francisco CA: HarperSanFrancisco, 2001.)

Group Work And Community

Bonewits, Isaac "Advanced Bonewits Cult Danger Evaluation Frame," found on his website at http://www.neopagan.net/ABCDEF.html.
Bonewits, Isaac "Rites of Worship: A Neopagan Approach," (USA: Earth Religions Press, 2003.)
Campanelli, Pauline & Campanelli, Dan "Circles, Groves & Sanctuaries: Sacred Spaces of Today's Pagans," (St. Paul MN: Llewellyn, 1992.)
Harrow, Judy "Wicca Covens," (Secaucus NJ: Citadel Press, 1999.)
Haugk, Kenneth C. "Antagonists in the Church: How to Identify and Deal with Destructive Conflict," (Minneapolis MN: Augsburg Publishing, 1988.)
Horowitz, Claudia "The Spiritual Activist," (New York NY: Penguin Putnam, 2002.)
K, Amber "Covencraft: Witchcraft for Three or More," (St. Paul MN: Llewellyn, 1998.)
K, Amber "Ritual Craft," (St. Paul MN: Llewellyn, 2006.)
McCoy, Edain "Inside a Witches' Coven," (St. Paul MN: Llewellyn, 1997.)
Peck, M. Scott "The Different Drum: Community Making and Peace," (New York NY: Touchstone/ Simon & Schuster, 1987.)
Pike, Sarah M. "Earthly Bodies, Magickal Selves: Contemporary Pagans and the Search for Community," (Los Angeles CA: University of California Press, 2001.)
Plant, Judith (ed.) "Healing the Wounds," (Toronto Canada: Between the Lines, 1989.)
Shaffer, Carolyn R. & Anundsen, Kristin "Creating Community Anywhere," (New York NY: Tarcher/Putnam, 1993.)
Starhawk "Dreaming the Dark," (Boston MA: Beacon Press, 1988.)
Starhawk "Truth or Dare," (San Francisco CA: Harper & Row, 1990.)
Walker, Wren & Jung, Fritz — the Witchvox website, found on the internet at http://www.witchvox.com, is the best Pagan networking resource bar none.

Endnotes

[1] The idea "all gods are one God, all goddesses are one Goddess," likely came to Wicca from Theosophy, but most likely through the work of Dion Fortune. Gerald Gardner listed Fortune's work in the bibliography of his book "The Meaning of Witchcraft." The idea itself is much older, however, and is present in Lucius Apuleius' novel, "The Golden Ass," where Isis describes Herself as being a goddess known by many people under various names, including Hecate, Persephone, Artemis, etc. Apuleius lived around 123 to 170 C.E. The concept of all gods being One is also expressed in Neoplatonism as monistic-polytheism, and in various Hindu teachings such as those regarding the One Unknowable Ultimate Deity, Brahman.

[2] Gerald Gardner was very clear that he believed Wicca was the religion of British witchcraft. It is therefore questionable whether Wiccans who say they are not witches, and do not practice magick, are really Wiccan.

[3] Dion Fortune's "The Training & Work of an Initiate," Weiser: 2000. See page 62 and following.

[4] Page 44, lines 335 to 345, editor Hans Dieter Betz's "The Greek Magickal Papyri In Translation," University of Chicago Press: 1992.

[5] Frater U.˙.D.˙.s article "Models of Magic" is available on the internet at http://www.sacred-texts.com/bos/bos065.htm

[6] See http://www.chocolate.org/ and http://www.sciencenews.org/pages/sn_arch/10_12_96/food.htm for descriptions of the psychoactive components of chocolate.

[7] See "RE:Search #12 – Modern Primitives" for many first-hand accounts of the psychological and spiritual effects of sexual and nonsexual fetish practices.

[8] Sources for this timeline include:

"The Encyclopedia of Witches & Witchcraft," by Rosemary Ellen Guiley;

"The Encyclopedia of Modern Witchcraft and Neo-Paganism," edited by Shelley Rabinovitch and James Lewis;

"Witches: An Encyclopedia of Paganism and Magic," by Michael Jordan;

"The Witch Book: The Encyclopedia of Witchcraft, Wicca, and Neo-paganism," by Raymond Buckland;

244 - The Wiccan Mystic

"Witchcraft: A Concise Guide," by Isaac Bonewits.

[9] See the entry on *Sanders, Alex,* in Rosemary Ellen Guiley's "The Encyclopedia of Witches & Witchcraft." Sanders' acquisition of the Gardnerian Book of Shadows is also discussed towards the end of chapter 4 in Patricia Crowther's book "High Priestess." Doreen Valiente also adds a lot to clear up the issue in chapter 10 of her book, "The Rebirth of Witchcraft." There is still some debate over whether Sanders was ever properly initiated into the Gardnerian tradition as even a first-degree Witch.

[10] From an essay by John J. Coughlin available at http://www.waningmoon.com/ethics/rede4.shtml and http://www.waningmoon.com/ethics/rede3.shtml

[11] For a first-hand account of this event, see pages 71 - 72 of Isaac Bonewits' "Witchcraft: A Concise Guide."

[12] "The Principles of Wiccan Belief" is published in a number of places in print and on the internet. http://www.religioustolerance.org/wic_stat1.htm is one place where it is available on the web.

[13] Evidence suggests that "The Rede of the Wiccae" could have been in private circulation possibly as early as 1968 — which was after Doreen Valiente's 1964 speech where the eight-word phrasing of the Wiccan Rede statement first appears. Since "The Rede of the Wiccae" includes the eight-word phrasing, it is unlikely that in its current form it predates Valiente's 1964 speech. Therefore, claims that Adriana Porter, Lady Gwen's grandmother, provided "The Rede of the Wiccae" in its current form are highly doubtful — she died in 1946, almost two decades before the eight-word phrasing of the Wiccan Rede statement appeared. If "The Rede of the Wiccae" was in circulation prior to 1964 then the eight-word phrasing of the Rede statement would have certainly been in evidence prior to Valiente's speech, but it's not. See the archived copy of Shea Thomas' "Origins of the Rede Poem" at http://web.archive.org/web/20031218001055/www.draknetfree.com/sheathomas/index.html and John J. Coughlin's "The Wiccan Rede: A Historical Journey" at http://www.waningmoon.com/ethics/rede.shtml for a discussion of the poem and the Wiccan Rede statement's history.

Index

About the Author

Ben Gruagach is an eclectic Wiccan practitioner who has been active in this spiritual path for over twenty years. He has worked with a number of different Wiccan groups in both Canada and the United States. His most recent group is the Willow Moon coven, an egalitarian eclectic Wiccan coven based in Eden Prairie, Minnesota. Ben lives with his spouse, two sons, and a rather demanding feline.

Ben has had articles published regularly in *Circle Magazine* as well as a number of online periodicals such as the *MysticWicks.com Magazine*, the *ecauldron.com* newsletter, and the *Northumberland Mystical Gatherings* newsletter. He has also been an active participant in online Pagan forums since the pre-internet days of PODSNet, and has essays appearing at *Witchvox.com*, *Sacred-Texts.com*, and on his own website, *WitchGrotto.com*.

To contact the author please visit

http://www.witchgrotto.com